The Wildflowers of Ireland

A FIELD GUIDE

Zoë Devlin

The Collins Press

Zoë Devlin has asserted her moral right to be identified as the author of this work
in accordance with the Copyright and Related Rights Act 2000.

A CIP record for this book is available from the British Library.

ISBN: 978-1-84889-202-6

Design and typesetting by Fairways Design
Typeset in Baskerville
Printed in Poland by Białostockie Zakłady Graficzne SA

The National Biodiversity Data Centre collates and manages information on
the distribution of Ireland's plants. Please submit records of the plants that you
observe, however common, to help improve our knowledge of the Irish flora:
http://records.biodiversityireland.ie

Bloody Crane's-bill
(Crane's-bill Fam.)

Great Mullein
(Figwort Fam.)

Spring Gentian
(Gentian Fam.)

Heather
(Heather Fam.)

Yellow Iris
(Iris Fam.)

Born in Dublin, ZOË DEVLIN has been interested in wildflowers and the environment since childhood. After retirement, she fulfilled an ambition to bring together her twin interests of botany and photography. By developing her own website, www.wildflowersofireland.net, Zoë has created a forum for others interested in seeking out, identifying and sharing wildflowers in Ireland. Her first book, *Wildflowers of Ireland: A Personal Record*, was published in 2011.

www.wildflowersofireland.net
Follow Zoë on Facebook at: facebook.com/zoe.
devlin.33?fref=ts

PYRAMIDAL ORCHID (P. 192)

CONTENTS

This book is dedicated to two rare, lovable and unique species, Nik and Petra, most cherished members of the Devlin family, who have always, with great patience, interest and love, encouraged my obsession.

I would like to acknowledge the following persons for the help which I received from them in preparing this book:

Paul Green, for his immense botanical knowledge and endless encouragement. Also great help came from (in alphabetical order) Dave Denby, Petra Radford Devlin, Úna Fitzpatrick, Howard and Peg Frost, Jimmy Goodwin, Matthew Jebb, Trudy Lomax, Glen McArdle, Jackie O'Connell, Michael O'Donnell, Colette O'Flynn, Paula O'Meara, Sharon Parr, Ulli Peiller, Brendan Sayers, Noeleen Smyth, Stephen Ward, Nicholas Williams and all at The Collins Press. And last, but by no means least, the best 'roadie' in the business, Pete.

NETTLE-LEAVED BELLFLOWER (P. 229)

INTRODUCTION

Ireland has a most diverse and interesting collection of native wildflowers. They number about 815 and are joined by many introduced species which have, over time, established themselves in the wild. It also possesses a wide variety of habitats from coastal sites to raised bogs and from limestone to woodland – both deciduous and coniferous. Urban areas offer opportunities for finding new species – not just in public parks or on canal banks but on waste ground, gardens, walls and even in pavement cracks.

In this book, more than **530** species, mainly native but also introduced, are described and illustrated. Particular emphasis is given to special features of a species to help narrow down the search for a name for that species. Flower parts are described and illustrated on p. 2, flower arrangements and leaf shapes are illustrated on p. 3–4.

Initially plants have been grouped together by colour with **six** colour categories:

White ~ Yellow ~ Pink ~ Red-orange ~ Blue-purple ~ Green-brown

- Colour grouping is intended to be a *general* help towards finding your species. If you can't find your species in one colour segment, try looking for it in under another colour as many species come in a variety of subtly-differing shades and one person's purple could be another's pink. Within each colour segment, species are categorised, *initially* by number of petals, *subsequently* by general shape of flower-head.
- Grouping is intended to be *intuitive*, i.e. species are grouped under headings which describe what those species *seem to be*, not what they scientifically are.

For example:

- Wood Anemone is categorised as a 'White 6-Petalled' flower. It looks like one but the 6 white parts are, in fact, **sepals.**

- Fuchsia is categorised as a 'Red 4-Petalled' flower – however, the red parts are the **sepals**, and the **petals** are violet.

- Meadow Saffron is categorised as a '6-Petalled' flower. However, it has 3 **petals** and 3 **sepals** but this is not apparent to a beginner.

- White Clover is categorised as a White Round Cluster (peaflowers) because it is a collection of **small** Peaflowers which **is held in** a round head or cluster.

1

PARTS OF A FLOWERING PLANT

PETALS are leaf-like parts, usually coloured. Normally arranged in a **corolla** or whorl, their role is to make the flower attractive to pollinating insects. Some flowers have no petals at all – see Common Nettle (p. 267).

SEPALS are also leaf-like parts, most often green. Usually arranged in a **calyx** (plural: calyces) or cup around the **corolla**, their role is to protect the flower-bud. The term **tepal** is used when sepals and petals are similar and not differentiated – see Meadow Saffron (p. 173).

STAMENS are pollen-bearing male organs of the flower, situated inside the flower. Each consists of an **anther** (top) and a **filament** (stalk).

The **STIGMA** is the receptive surface of the flower's female organ which receives pollen from the stamens. Situated at the centre of the flower, it is supported by a **style** or stalk which connects it to the **ovary**.

FLOWERS are the reproductive organs of flowering plants and can be found with or without stalks, in leaf axils, in flower-heads, in clusters or solitarily. After successful pollination, they produce fruit and seeds.

LEAVES – usually green – are organs which are necessary for photosynthesis, water storage and the continued life of the plant. They are usually composed of a **petiole** or leaf-stalk, a **lamina** or leaf-blade and **stipules** or small, leaf-like structures either side of the petiole. Leaves are arranged in a variety of ways, optimising their ability to collect light, and come in many shapes and sizes (see p. 4).

The **STEM** is the main ascending or procumbent stalk of a flowering plant. Usually divided into **nodes** and **internodes**, it supports the flowers and leaves, also conducting fluids between the roots and the other parts of the plant.

The **ROOT** anchors the plant to the ground, obtaining nutrients and fluids from the soil. (See also definition of a **stolon** and a **rhizome** in the Glossary).

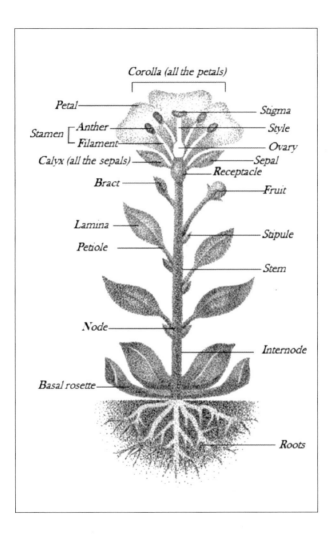

Corolla (all the petals)

Petal

Stamen {
Anther
Filament

Calyx (all the sepals)

Bract

Lamina

Petiole

Node

Basal rosette

Stigma

Style

Ovary

Sepal

Receptacle

Fruit

Stipule

Stem

Internode

Roots

FORMS OF FLOWERS AND LEAVES

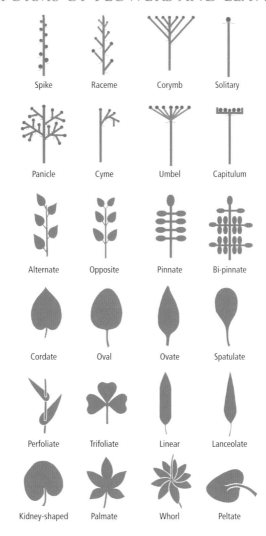

Spike

Raceme

Corymb

Solitary

Panicle

Cyme

Umbel

Capitulum

Alternate

Opposite

Pinnate

Bi-pinnate

Cordate

Oval

Ovate

Spatulate

Perfoliate

Trifoliate

Linear

Lanceolate

Kidney-shaped

Palmate

Whorl

Peltate

PLANT CLASSIFICATION

To learn how plants are classified, one needs to understand the family tree.

A **Family** contains one genus or several related genera, e.g. Violaceae.

> **Common Dog-violet/ *Viola riviniana* –
> member of the Violaceae/Violet family**

A **Genus** contains a single species or several related species.
This name is normally written in *italics*, e.g. *Viola*.

> **Marsh Violet/ *Viola palustris* – *Viola* being
> the genus part of the name.**

A **Species** is a unit of like individuals. This name is always
written in *italics*, e.g. *tricolor* and the species name can refer to a
description of the flower or type of habitat in which it is found.

> **Wild Pansy/ *Viola tricolor* – *tricolor*
> meaning 'three-coloured'.**

A **Subspecies** is a major division of a species. The name
follows the word 'subspecies' (or ssp.) and is in *italics*, e.g. ssp.
curtisii.

> **Sand Pansy/ *Viola tricolor* ssp. *curtisii* –
> *Viola tricolor* being the species and 'ssp.
> *curtisii* ' meaning the subspecies (after
> botanist Charles Curtis).**

USEFUL TERMINOLOGY

Annual	Starts out as a seed ~ Completes its life cycle in one single year ~ Flowers ~ Produces seeds ~ Dies.
Biennial	Germinates in year 1 ~ Grows a small clump or rosette of leaves ~ Lays down food reserves for year 2 ~ Flowers in year 2 ~ Produces seeds ~ Dies.
Perennial	Flowers year after year ~ The top usually dies off in autumn ~ The rootstock overwinters.
Shrubs	Plants with woody stems which flower year after year from maturity.
Native	Plants thought to have arrived by natural means *before* 1500 AD.
Introduced	Plants brought in intentionally or accidentally *since* 1500 AD.
Invasive aliens	Introduced plants which threaten native species.

'Invasive Aliens' are the 39 species of flora listed by the
National Biodiversity Data Centre that are considered to be
a problem or potential problem in Ireland.

Abbreviations and symbols explained:

Ht.	**Height** given is the *upper* limit of any plant – often not attained.
Fls.	**Flower** measurements are *across* unless otherwise stated.
Lvs.	**Leaves** are named as in diagrams on p. 4.
Hab.	**Habitats** and areas in Ireland where the species may be found.
Fam.	**Family** as a natural group with certain features in common.
Ssp.	**Subspecies** is a subdivision of a species with genetic differences or conspicuous characteristics.
Agg.	**Aggregated** species or group of very closely related species.
Var.	**Variety** is a subdivision or a species or subspecies with only one or few differences.
AKA	Also known as …
Note:	Images and illustrations in this book are *not to scale.* Sizes given for flowers are *averages*.

Distribution symbols:

✿✿✿	Widespread throughout Ireland
✿✿	Common within specific habitat
✿	Uncommon or rare species
⊞	Species either legally protected or worthy of protection in any part of Ireland, NI or RoI.
⊛	Invasive alien species
🏃	Garden escape
⚠	Poisonous species
☺	Added point of interest
▶	See also ...

IRELAND'S HABITATS

Ireland has many habitats and while some plants may thrive in a variety of these, others may be confined to only one. Climatic conditions – rain, wind, heat or cold – also affect the ability of certain species to tolerate a particular habitat. Being an island country, our coasts offer a wide variety of places in which to look for plants and Ireland has other interesting wet areas inland, such as bogs, lakes and rivers. There is an abundance of grass and heathland, with deciduous and coniferous woodlands. Urban sites, old walls, ruins and waste ground can often produce interesting finds too. The following is just a brief idea of what may be found in particular areas.

Woodland: *Deciduous woodland* – best examples include those found in Counties Waterford, Wicklow and Offaly – particularly in early spring before the leaves start to cast shade. ▶Lesser Celandine, Wood Anemone, Wood-sorrel, Bluebells, Ramsons, Bugle, Wood Speedwell. At the borders of the woods ▶Primroses and Early-purple Orchids. *Coniferous woodland* – supports a small number of species which grow on acid soil. ▶Common Cow-wheat, Foxglove, Winter-cress.

Wetlands: *Marshes* (wet but not peaty) *and bogs* (wet, peaty, acid). ▶ Marsh-orchids, Ragged-robin, Bog Asphodel, Bog Pimpernel. Carnivorous species grown *in nutrient-poor soil* ▶Sundews, Common and Pale Butterwort. *In fens* (peaty but rich in minerals and calcium) ▶ Bogbean, Marsh-marigolds, Marsh Cinquefoil. *Rivers, canals, lakes and ponds.* ▶ Yellow Loosestrife, Water-pepper, Water-crowfoots.

Grassland: a mainly man-made habit, previously cleared and grazed. ▶ Oxeye Daisy, Yellow-rattle, Cuckooflower, Meadow Buttercup, Common Spotted-orchid.

Limestone: Principally the central plain, County Sligo and the Burren, where 70 per cent of our wildflower species may be found. ▶Grass-of-Parnassus, Saxifrages, Common Twayblade, Mountain Everlasting. *Turloughs* – lakes of limestone areas which can fill up in heavy rainfall and dry out a few days later, mainly in Counties Clare, Mayo and Galway. ▶ Marsh Pennywort, Silverweed, Water Mint and Lesser Spearwort.

Coastal: *Saltmarshes* ▶ Sea Aster, Sea-lavender and other salt-tolerant species. *Beaches, shingle, cliffs, sand-dunes* ▶ Thrift, Rock Samphire, Sea-holly, Common Centaury, Autumn Ladies-tresses, Sea-spurreys, Sea Bindweed, Bee Orchid.

Hedgerows: Very variable, supporting wide variety of wildflowers. ▶ Dog-rose, Meadowsweet, Purple-loosestrife, Greater and Lesser Stitchwort, Cow Parsley.

Heathland: Can occur on both limestone and upland, acid soils. ▶Heather, Cross-leaved Heath, Bell Heather, Gorse, Bilberry, Bog-rosemary, Tormentil.

Walls, urban and waste ground: ▶ Navelwort, Ivy-leaved Toadflax, Wild Teasel, Rosebay Willowherb, Colt's-foot, Knotgrass, Common Poppy.

Equal-leaved Knotgrass
Polygonum arenastrum
Glúineach ghainimh

Ht. Prostrate. **Fls.** 1.5mm, 5-lobed, white, tinged-pink with green interiors; *lobes fused 1/3 of length;* in clusters in leaf axils on sprawling stems.

Lvs. Oval, hairless, *all leaves on main & side branches the same size*.

Hab. Bare, sandy, coastal ground, on pathways, tracks & shingle. Native annual, scattered fairly commonly throughout Ireland.

Fam. Knotweed/Polygonaceae.

☺ Nut-like fruits are enclosed by withering flower.

☺ The size of leaves helps to identify this from other species.

✿✿✿ Jun–Nov.

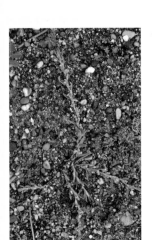

Ray's Knotgrass
Polygonum oxyspermum
Glúineach ghlé

Ht. Prostrate. **Fls.** 3mm, green-white, pink-edged, 5-lobed; in clusters of 2–6 in leaf axils on sprawling, ridged stems.

Lvs. Alternate, oval, leathery, grey-green; margins slightly downturned.

Hab. Undisturbed, sandy beaches, shingle at extreme high-tide level. Occasional coastal native annual.

Fam. Knotweed/Polygonaceae.

☺ Nut-like fruits protrude beyond the withering flower, unlike Knotgrass or Equal-leaved Knotgrass.

☺ Occasionally spreads to 1m long.

✿ Aug–Sep.

Knotgrass
Polygonum aviculare
Glúineach bheag

Ht. Prostrate to 50cm. **Fls.** 2mm,
5 overlapping lobes or tepals,
white-edged with green centres,
sometimes pink-tinged; *lobes fused
for ¼ of length*; in small clusters at
leaf axils, wrapped in an ochrea
– a paper-like sheath – on finely
ridged stems.

Lvs. Alternate, oval, leathery,
untoothed; *stem leaves larger than
leaves on side branches.*

Hab. Waste places, arable fields,
roadsides, seashores. Widespread
native annual.

Fam. Knotweed/Polygonaceae.

☺ Nut-like fruits are enclosed by
withering flower.

✿✿✿ Jun–Oct.

Mind-your-own-business
Soleirolia soleirolii
Lus na ndeor

Ht. Prostrate. **Fls.** Absolutely
tiny, 1–2mm at most, white to pale
pink, like a little starburst; in leaf
axils, both male & female on same
plant; on red, thread-like stems.

Lvs. Evergreen, alternate, 5mm,
shiny above, matt below, rounded,
untoothed, with white hairs; on
slender, wiry stems, rooting at
nodes.

Hab. Mat-forming on
walls, paths, cracks in
paving, damp, shaded
areas. Introduced
perennial, common in S,
SE & NE.

Fam. Nettle/Urticaceae.

✿✿ April–Aug.

Enchanter's-nightshade
Circaea lutetiana
Fuinseagach

Ht. 60cm. **Fls.** 4–8mm, 2 deeply-notched petals, 2 stamens which are longer than petals & 2 sepals, resembling wings; in tall, loose racemes, flowers often tinged with pink; on slender, leggy, branching, stems.

Lvs. Paired, oval, lower heart-shaped.

Hab. Shaded woodlands & hedgerows. Widespread native perennial.

Fam. Willowherb/Onagraceae.

☺ Drooping fruit is club-shaped & covered with hooked bristles.

✿✿✿ May–Aug.

Chilean-iris
Libertia formosa
Murúch shneachta

Ht. 60cm. **Fls.** 30mm, 3 creamy-white petals; in stiff spikes on erect, dark stems.

Lvs. Dark-green, sword-shaped in abundant tufts arising from rhizomes; leaves remain throughout the year.

Hab. A garden escape, this plant has established itself on dry, sandy soil & waste ground. Introduced perennial, infrequently found, mainly in E & SW coastal areas.

Fam. Iris/Iridaceae.

☺ Chilean-iris is one of 39 species listed by National Biodiversity Data Centre, considered a problem or potential problem in Ireland.

✿ Apr–Aug. 🏃 🌀

Arrowhead
Sagittaria sagittifolia
Rinn saighde

Ht. 80cm. **Fls.** 20mm, 3-petalled,
bright white; in whorls of 3–5 on erect
spikes.

Lvs. Upper leaves deeply-veined,
arrow-shaped & held well clear of water
on long stalks; floating leaves are ovate &
submerged leaves are grass-like.

Hab. Margins of still or very
slow-moving fresh water. Native
perennial, very infrequent except for
some Midlands sites.

Fam. Water-plantain/Alismataceae.

☺ Upper whorls consist of male
flowers with many stamens, lower
whorls consist of female flowers.

☺ All petals have a purple spot at
base.

✿ Jul–Aug.

Water-plantain
Alisma plantago-aquatica
Corrchopóg

Ht. 1m. **Fls.** 10mm with
3 white, rounded petals
(often tinged pink-lilac),
hint of yellow towards
centre of flower, in tiers of
whorled branches.

Lvs. Oval, parallel-veined &
long-stalked.

Hab. Margins of canals, ponds &
shallow, wet places. Widespread native
perennial.

Fam. Water-plantain/Alismataceae.

☺This plant is best seen in afternoon
sunshine when flowers open up,
showing 6 yellow stamens.

▶ Lesser Water-plantain (p. 144)

✿✿✿ Jun–Aug.

Woodruff
Galium odoratum | Lus moileas

Ht. 25cm. **Fls.** 3–5mm, *star-shaped*, in loose heads on upright, square stems.

Lvs. Lanceolate in whorls of 6–8.

Hab. Shady, damp woodland. Widespread native perennial, mainly in N & E.

Fam. Bedstraw/Rubiaceae.

☺ AKA Sweet Woodruff – has a faint scent of hay.

✿✿ May–Jun.

Northern Bedstraw
Galium boreale | Rú crua

Ht. 50cm. **Fls.** 4mm, in abundant clusters on robust, upright stems.

Lvs. 3-veined, blunt, leathery, dark-green, in whorls of 4 up stiff stem.

Hab. Damp soil & rocky ground. Native perennial, locally common in Clare, Galway & NE.

Fam. Bedstraw/Rubiaceae.

☺ Round fruits with hooked bristles. ✿✿ Jun–Aug.

Limestone Bedstraw
Galium sterneri | Rú beag

Ht. 20cm. **Fls.** 3mm, creamy-white or greenish, in *domed* clusters.

Lvs. Narrowly oblong, bristle-tipped with *backward-pointing margin bristles.*

Hab. Limestone grassland, never acid soil. Scarce, native perennial; mainly the Burren & County Galway.

Fam. Bedstraw/Rubiaceae.

✿ Jun–Jul.

Heath Bedstraw
Galium saxatile | Luibh na bhfear gonta

Ht. 30cm. **Fls.** 2–4mm, in loose racemes on spreading, weak stems.

Lvs. Blunt-tipped, lanceolate in whorls of 4–6; margins with *forward-pointing* bristles.

Hab. Unimproved grassland, acid heaths. Common native perennial, but less in Midlands.

Fam. Bedstraw/Rubiaceae.

☺ Fruits *smooth & round without* hooks.

✿✿✿ Jun–Aug.

*Members of the **Bedstraw** family are recognised by the arrangement of their leaves in whorls. Sepals are minute or absent. Fruits are nutlets.*
▶ *Lady's Bedstraw (p. 89)*

Cleavers
Galium aparine | Garbhlus

Ht. Scrambling to 1m. **Fls.** 2mm, in clusters on stalks arising from leaf axils; on sprawling, square, rough stems.

Lvs. Narrow with *backward-pointing* bristles; in whorls of 6–8.

Hab. Hedgerows, disturbed ground. Widespread, native annual.

Fam. Bedstraw/Rubiaceae.

☺ Entire plant & seeds are covered in tiny hooks aiding spread of plant.

✿✿✿ May–Sep.

Common Marsh-bedstraw
Galium palustre | Rú corraigh

Ht. 50cm. **Fls.** 3–4mm, in open clusters on delicate stems.

Lvs. *Stalkless*, narrow in whorls of 4–6; 4-edged stem; tip *blunt*.

Hab. Ditches, marshes, damp meadows. Widespread, native perennial. Similar to Cleavers.

Fam. Bedstraw/Rubiaceae.

✿✿✿ Jun–Aug.

Hairy Bitter-cress
Cardamine hirsuta | Searbh-bhiolar giobach

Ht. 30cm. **Fls.** 2–3mm, with **4** stamens; borne in loose clusters on hairless stems.

Lvs. Basal rosette of pinnate leaves; few stem leaves.

Hab. Damp, disturbed ground. Widespread, native annual.

Fam. Cabbage/Brassicaceae.

☺ Seedpods reach above flowers.

☺ Shorter, straighter stems than Wavy Bitter-cress.

☺Persistent garden weed.

✿✿✿ Jan–Dec.

Wavy Bitter-cress
Cardamine flexuosa | Searbh-bhiolar casta

Ht. 50cm **Fls.** 3–4mm, **6** stamens; loose clusters on hairy, grooved, wavy stems.

Lvs. Pinnately divided with ovate, rounded lobes; 4–10 stem leaves.

Hab. Bare, damp ground. Widespread, native perennial or biennial.

Fam. Cabbage/Brassicaceae.

☺ Stamen count helps identification.

✿✿✿ Mar–Sep.

Garlic Mustard
Alliaria petiolata | Bóchoinneal

Ht. 1m. **Fls.** 3–6mm, 4-petalled, in elongated racemes on hairy, stiff slender stems.

Lvs. Light green, glossy, heart-shaped, toothed.

Hab. Roadsides, hedges, wood margins. Native biennial found in E half of Ireland.

Fam. Cabbage/Brassicaceae.

☺ Crushed leaves/roots smell of garlic.

☺ Seeds in long, thin pods. ✿✿✿ Apr–Jun.

Shepherd's-purse
Capsella bursa-pastoris
Lus an sparáin

Ht. 35cm. **Fls.** 2–3mm, in terminal clusters on erect, stiff, branching stems.

Lvs. Lanceolate & lobed, in basal rosette; toothed leaves clasp stem.

Hab. Tracks, wasteground, bare & cultivated ground. Widespread, very common native annual.

Fam. Cabbage/ Brassicaceae.

☺ Distinctive seedpods are green, notched, flat & heart-shaped.

☺ Could be confused with Thale Cress (p. 16) but latter has long, thin seedpods.

✿✿✿ Jan–Dec.

> Members of the **Cabbage** family have distinctive, regular flowers with 4 sepals & 4 petals which alternate with the sepals. The fruit is usually a pod.

Smith's Pepperwort
Lepidium heterophyllum
Piobar an duine bhoicht

Ht. 40cm. **Fls.** 2–3mm with 4 widely-separated petals, in crowded clusters on erect hairy stems.

Lvs. Grey-green, lower oval & withering, arrow-shaped; upper clasping stem.

Hab. Dry waste-ground, below hedgerows. NE, E, SE mainly. Also S Munster. Native perennial.

Fam. Cabbage/ Brassicaceae.

☺ Distinctive oblong seedpods with flattened wing & projecting style at top.

✿✿ May–Aug.

Common Whitlowgrass
Erophila verna | Bosán anagair

Ht. 15cm. **Fls.** 3–6mm, 4 deeply-cleft petals in loose racemes on long stalks from base.

Lvs. Narrow, slightly toothed in basal rosette; seeds in oval flattened pods.

Hab. Dry banks, dunes & bare gravelly places. Uncommon native annual.

Fam. Cabbage/ Brassicaceae.

✿ Mar–May.

Thale Cress
Arabidopsis thaliana | Tailís

Ht. 30cm. **Fls.** 3–4mm, in branched racemes on spindly stems.

Lvs. Basal rosette of oval leaves, withers quickly; few alternate stem leaves; bears seeds in slightly curved pods.

Hab. Bare, waste ground, sandy soil. Native annual, widespread except for Connacht.

Fam. Cabbage/Brassicaceae.

✿✿ Apr–Oct.

Hoary Cress
Lepidium draba | Piobracas liath

Ht. 60cm. **Fls.** 5–6mm, in crowded, flat-topped clusters on erect stems.

Lvs. Lanceolate, somewhat grey, slightly toothed, clasping stem; plant covered in fine down.

Hab. Disturbed ground, field margins, in large patches. Introduced perennial, mainly recorded in E & part S Leinster.

Fam. Cabbage/Brassicaceae.

✿ May–Jun.

Water-cress
Nasturtium officinale
Biolar

Ht. 50cm. **Fls.** 4–6mm, 4-petalled, in dense racemes on hollow stems; petals almost twice as long as sepals.

Lvs. Pinnate with rounded lobes, remaining green throughout winter.

Hab. Shallow streams, ditches, ponds & marshes. Widespread, common native perennial.

Fam. Cabbage/Brassicaceae.

☺ Seeds are borne in 2 distinct rows in narrow, cylindrical pods.

☺ Although this plant is edible, before eating take care it is growing in clean conditions & not where parasites might lie.

▶ Fool's-water-cress (p. 62)

✿✿✿ May–Oct.

Narrow-fruited Water-cress
Nasturtium microphyllum
Biolar mion

Ht. 40cm. **Fls.** 4–6mm, 4-petalled; in crowded, terminal clusters on erect stems.

Lvs. Pinnately divided, shiny green but tending to turn purple in autumn, lasting throughout winter.

Hab. Ditches & streams, tolerant of more acid conditions than Water-cress. Locally frequent but not as commonly found as Water-cress. Native perennial.

Fam. Cabbage/Brassicaceae.

☺ Seedpods are longer than those of Water-cress, only containing one row of seeds. Those of Water-cress bear double row of seeds.

✿✿ May–Oct.

Hairy Rock-cress
Arabis hirsuta
Gas caillí giobach

Ht. 60cm. **Fls.** 3–5mm, 4-petalled, in dense clusters on erect, stiff stems.

Lvs. Slightly toothed ovate leaves in a basal rosette & numerous, erect, semi-clasping, untoothed stem leaves.

Hab. Limestone, chalky grassland, sand dunes & walls. Mainly in W half of Ireland. Native biennial.

Fam. Cabbage/ Brassicaceae.

☺ Stems & leaves are *extremely* hairy.

✿✿ Jun–Aug.

Field Penny-cress
Thlaspi arvense
Praiseach fhia

Ht. 60cm. **Fls.** 4–6mm, 4-petalled, in racemes on erect stems, each white flower with *yellow* anthers.

Lvs. No basal rosette but narrow, arrow-shaped leaves clasp the stem, lower leaves being oblong, stalked & toothed, upper leaves sessile.

Hab. Arable soil, fields & fertile ground. Found mainly in Munster, NE Ulster & E Leinster. Introduced annual.

Fam. Cabbage/ Brassicaceae.

☺ This plant emits a most unpleasant smell when it is crushed.

✿✿ May–Sep.

Sea-kale
Crambe maritima
Praiseach thrá

Ht. 70cm. **Fls.** 6–14mm, 4-petalled, in large, flat-topped clusters on stiff, waxy stems; some flowers have a creamy-yellow hue.

Lvs. Broad, hairless, succulent, grey-green, with wavy margins, sometimes purple-tinged.

Hab. Shingle beaches, stony banks & sandy shores, above tide-line. Rare, native perennial species found on S & SE coasts mainly, also on Aran Islands.

Fam. Cabbage/Brassicaceae.

☺ This plant is like a very large, squat cabbage & the leaves are not unlike the curly-kale eaten at Halloween.

☺ In Aug & Sep, pea-shaped pods are formed, each containing 1, occasionally 2, seeds.

✿ Jun–Aug. ✚

Common Scurvygrass
Cochlearia officinalis
Biolar trá

Ht. 50cm. **Fls.** 8–10mm, 4 white –
rarely lilac – petals, 2–3 times as long as
sepals; in crowded clusters on hairless,
ascending stems.

Lvs. Hairless, fleshy, basal rosette of
kidney or heart-shaped leaves tapering
into long stalks; upper leaves oblong,
coarsely toothed, stalkless, clasping
stem.

Hab. Saltmarshes, coastal cliffs,
sea walls. Locally frequent native
biennial or perennial.

Fam. Cabbage/Brassicaceae.

☺ Fruits 3–6mm, rounded,
longer than stalk.

✿✿✿ Apr–Sep.

Danish Scurvygrass
Cochlearia danica
Carrán creige

Ht. 20cm but frequently
prostrate. **Fls.** 4–6mm,
4 white, *often pale mauve*,
petals, well spaced; 4 sepals
visible between petals; on
hairless, mat-forming stems.

Lvs. Basal leaves long-stalked,
cordate, shallowly lobed,
sometimes tinged purple; stem
leaves lobed, stalked, lowest
ivy-shaped with 3–7 lobes; all
fleshy & shiny.

Hab. Sandy, shingly coastal
areas. Native annual, common in
coastal regions.

Fam. Cabbage/Brassicaceae.

☺ 6mm long fruits are ovoid.

✿✿ Jan–Aug.

English Scurvygrass
Cochlearia anglica
Carrán muirisce

Ht. 35cm. **Fls.** 10–14mm, white, in crowded racemes on stiff stems.

Lvs. Oblong, long-stalked basal leaves, upper leaves clasp stem.

Hab. Estuaries, muddy seashores, saltmarshes & coastal mudflats. Uncommon native biennial or perennial, mainly found on S & SW coasts.

Fam. Cabbage/Brassicaceae.

☺ Fruits are 10–15mm, elliptical & flattened.

☺ English & Common Scurvygrass frequently hybridise, making identification extremely difficult.

✿✿ Apr–Jun.

Wild Radish
Raphanus raphanistrum ssp. *raphanistrum*
Meacan raidigh

Ht. 60cm. **Fls.** 25–30mm, white, occasionally yellow, with deep lilac veins, petals twice as long as mauve sepals, in loose heads on erect, hairy stems.

Lvs. Pinnately-lobed, lower more than upper; entire plant rough & hairy.

Hab. Weed of cultivation favouring arable or waste ground. Introduced annual or biennial, locally common in S half of Ireland.

Fam. Cabbage/Brassicaceae.

☺ Seeds are in beaded pods.

▶ Sea Radish (p. 87)

✿✿ May–Sep.

Lesser Swine-cress
Lepidium didymum
Cladhthach mhín

Ht. Prostrate, occasionally to 5cm.
Fls. 1mm, 4 petals, often absent, smaller than sepals; in racemes on creeping, spreading, stems.
Lvs. Light green, alternate, finely-divided, pinnate; narrow segments, feathery lobes.
Hab. Waste ground, disturbed areas, arable. Annual or biennial, probably introduced, common in S half & NE of Ireland.
Fam. Cabbage/Brassicaceae.

☺ Fruit notched above & below.

✿✿ Jun–Oct.

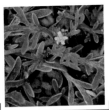

Swine-cress
Lepidium coronopus
Cladhthach

Ht. Prostrate. **Fls.** 2–3mm, white with 6 stamens; stalkless, in dense racemes on stem tips & in axils of branches; on spreading, branching stems.
Lvs. Light green, deeply pinnate, coarsely toothed leaflets.
Hab. Waste ground, disturbed areas, arable. Annual or biennial, probably introduced. Occasional, mainly in coastal areas.
Fam. Cabbage/Brassicaceae.

☺ Fruit kidney-shaped, pointed above with raised ridges.

✿ May–Sep.

22

Traveller's-joy
Clematis vitalba
Gabhrán

Ht. Climbs to 15m. **Fls.** 15–20mm, 4 greenish-white, petal-like sepals with numerous prominent stamens; in clusters on rambling stems.

Lvs. Opposite, pinnate in 5 leaflets.

Hab. Roadsides, hedgerows. Introduced perennial, common in southern half.

Fam. Buttercup/Ranunculaceae.

☺ Bears silvery plumes of seeds, hence its other name – Old Man's Beard.

☺ Seeds can remain viable in the ground for years after dispersal.

☺ Classed as 'Potentially Invasive'.

✿✿ Jul–Aug.

Sea Mouse-ear
Cerastium diffusum
Cluas luchóige mhara

Ht. 25cm at most but usually prostrate. **Fls.** 3–6mm, 4 petals, sepals, stamens & styles; sepals stickily-hairy; hairs do not project beyond sepal-tip; sepals longer than petals; entire plant is glandular hairy.

Lvs. Green, opposite, ovate; all bracts totally green without pale or transparent margins.

Hab. Sand-dunes, gravelly ground, particularly near sea. Native annual, commonly found in coastal areas.

Fam. Pink/Caryophyllaceae.

☺ Petals are cleft to no more than ¼ of their length.

▶ Common & Sticky Mouse-ears (p. 28).

✿✿ Apr–Jul.

White Ramping-fumitory
Fumaria capreolata ssp. *babingtonii*
Camán searraigh bán

Ht. Sprawling to 80cm **Fls.** 10–12mm long, creamy-white with purple tips; tubular, two-lipped with 2 outer petals, 2 narrow inner petals; in long spike of up to 20 flowers.

Lvs. Alternate, pinnate; flat, oblong lobes.

Hab. Hedge banks, disturbed land & coastal sites. Infrequent introduced annual.

Fam. Poppy/Papaveraceae.

▶ Yellow Corydalis (p. 139) & Common Ramping-fumitory (p. 181).

✿ May–Sep.

Holly
Ilex aquifolium | Cuileann

Ht. 10m. **Fls.** 6–10mm, slightly pink-tinged, in clusters on upright stems.

Lvs. Evergreen, glossy, stiff & leathery with spiny margins.

Hab. Woodland & country lanes. Widespread native tree.

Fam. Holly/Aquifoliaceae.

☺ Best known for bright scarlet berries. ☺ Not related to Sea-holly (p. 235). ✿✿✿ May–Jul.

Wild Privet
Ligustrum vulgare | Pribhéad

Ht. 10m. **Fls.** 4–6mm, creamy-white, strongly-scented in dense spikes on upright branches.

Lvs. Semi-evergreen, lanceolate, leathery & opposite.

Hab. Hedgerows, sea-cliffs, dunes, usually on limestone. Considered in some parts to be a native shrub, other parts introduced. Widespread.

Fam. Ash/Oleaceae.

☺ Bears poisonous, black, shiny berries. ✿✿✿ May–Jun. ⚠

Pond Water-crowfoot
Ranunculus peltatus
Néal uisce scéithe

Ht. Floating. **Fls.** 15–30mm, 5-petalled, white, with golden circle at centre surrounding matching stamens.

Lvs. Floating leaves rounded, lobed; submerged leaves short & thread-like.

Hab. Rivers, lakes, ponds & ditches. Native annual or perennial, found more across N half of Ireland than S.

Fam. Buttercup/ Ranunculaceae.

☺ Nectaries are pear-shaped.

✿✿ May–Aug.

Common Water-crowfoot
Ranunculus aquatilis
Néal uisce coiteann

Ht. Floating. **Fls.** 10–18mm, 5 white petals becoming yellow at centre of flower; on upright stems.

Lvs. Deeply-lobed floating leaves & finely-divided, thread-like submerged leaves (see below).

Hab. Still & slow-flowing water, shallow ponds, small lakes. Native perennial, uncommon & scattered, mainly in NE, E & SE.

Fam. Buttercup/ Ranunculaceae.

☺ Nectaries are circular.

✿ Apr–Aug.

Ivy-leaved Crowfoot
Ranunculus hederaceus
Néal uisce eidhneach

Ht. Creeping. **Fls.** 4–8mm, 5 narrow petals, 5 sepals.

Lvs. Numerous kidney-shaped leaves with 5 shallow lobes, dark splotches at centres; *no finely divided* leaves.

Hab. Shallow ditches, muddy, bare wet places. Native annual or perennial, widespread except for centre of Ireland.

Fam. Buttercup/Ranunculaceae.

✿✿ Apr–Aug.

Round-leaved Crowfoot
Ranunculus omiophyllus
Néal uisce cruinn

Ht. Floating. **Fls.** 8–16mm, 5 well-separated petals, twice as long as sepals; greeny-white towards centre of flower, surrounding golden stamens.

Lvs. Fleshy, shallowly divided, lobes narrowest at base; *no finely divided leaves.*

Hab. Wet, acidic, nutrient-poor soil. Native annual or perennial, common in E Leinster & Munster.

Fam. Buttercup/Ranunculaceae.

✿✿ May–Aug.

Brackish Water-crowfoot
Ranunculus baudotii | Néal uisce sáile

Ht. Floating. **Fls.** 12–18mm, 5-petalled, white with yellow centre; sepals usually blue-tipped.

Lvs. Floating leaves deeply lobed, submerged leaves thread-like & do not collapse out of water.

Hab. Brackish, coastal pools. Scarce native annual or perennial.

Fam. Buttercup/Ranunculaceae.

☺ Nectaries are crescent-shaped.

✿ Apr–Aug.

Thread-leaved Water-crowfoot
Ranunculus trichophyllus
Néal uisce ribeach

Ht. Floating or growing low on mud. **Fls.** 6–10mm, white with 5 well-spaced petals with yellow at centre of flower.

Lvs. No floating leaves, but submerged, finely divided thread-like leaves which fan out, branching repeatedly.

Hab. Brackish water, ponds, damp ditches. Native annual/perennial, not very common, infrequently found in W.

Fam. Buttercup/Ranunculaceae.

☺ Nectaries are crescent-shaped.

✿✿ May–Jun.

Crowfoots & Water-crowfoots are mainly aquatic. Two types of leaves can be present: floating, lobed, palmate leaves & submerged, finely divided leaves. Nectaries are very small, pouch-like structures on petals which secrete nectar collected by insects.

Stream Water-crowfoot
Ranunculus penicillatus
Néal uisce bréige

Ht. Floating. **Fls.** 15–25mm, 5 white petals becoming golden at centre of flower; on upright stems.

Lvs. Submerged leaves long, thread-like; floating leaves lobed.

Hab. In fast-flowing rivers & streams. Native annual or perennial, local in S & NE.

Fam. Buttercup/Ranunculaceae. ✿✿ May–Jun.

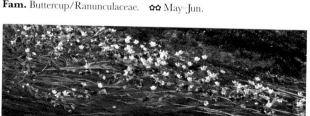

Common Mouse-ear
Cerastium fontanum | Cluas luchóige choiteann

Ht. 30cm. **Fls.** 5–10mm, 5 deeply-cleft petals, sepals of equal length; in loose clusters on hairy, ascending stems.

Lvs. Grey-green, lanceolate, opposite pairs.

Hab. Roadsides, laneways & disturbed ground. Widespread, native *perennial*.

Fam. Pink/Caryophyllaceae.

☺ Densely covered with whitish *non-glandular* hairs.

▶ Sea Mouse-ear (p. 23). ✿✿✿ Apr–Oct.

Sticky Mouse-ear
Cerastium glomeratum

Cluas luchóige ghreamaitheach

Ht. 40cm. **Fls.** 10–15mm with 5 cleft petals, very short flower-stalks, in *compact* clusters; sepals (5) are extremely hairy right up to the tip; on erect stems.

Lvs. Yellow-green, pointed-ovate, in opposite pairs.

Hab. Arable ground, roadsides, sand-dunes & walls. Widespread, native *annual* – sometimes overwintering.

Fam. Pink/Caryophyllaceae.

☺ Extremely sticky & *glandular* hairy.

✿✿✿ Mar–Oct.

Common Chickweed
Stellaria media | Fliodh

Ht. 30cm. **Fls.** 5–8mm with 5 deeply-notched petals, 3–8 red-violet stamens; on spreading, much-branched stems; *single* line of hairs along stem.

Lvs. Fresh green, ovate, opposite.

Hab. Waste ground, gardens, walls & pavements. Widespread, native annual.

Fam. Pink/Caryophyllaceae.

✿✿✿ Jan–Dec.

Greater Stitchwort

Stellaria holostea | Tursarraing mhór

Ht. 50cm. **Fls.** 15–20mm, snow-white, in clusters of 7–11 on *rough-edged*, square stems; petals divided halfway, sepals half petal length; on straggling stems.

Lvs. *Greyish*, rough, narrow, unstalked.

Hab. Roadsides, laneways but *not on acid soil*. Widespread except in Connacht. Native perennial.

Fam. Pink/Caryophyllaceae.

☺ Tends to scramble over other plants.

✿✿✿ Mar–Jun.

Lesser Stitchwort

Stellaria graminea | Tursarraing bheag

Stitchworts, Mouse-ears & Chickweeds have such deeply divided petals that there appears to be twice the number.

Ht. 50cm. **Fls.** 5–15mm with 5 deeply cleft petals only slightly longer than sepals; stamens often grey-violet; in loose cymes on *smooth-edged* stems.

Lvs. *Green*, long, narrow, smooth, pointed.

Hab. Meadows, hedgerows, acid soil, heaths & grassland. Widespread, native perennial.

Fam. Pink/Caryophyllaceae.

✿✿✿ May–Aug.

Bog Stitchwort

Stellaria alsine | Tursarraing mhóna

Ht. 25cm. **Fls.** 5–6mm, 5 widely-separated, deeply-divided, pointed petals; sepals much longer than petals; on smooth, weak, angled stems.

Lvs. Ovate, unstalked, blue-green.

Hab. Bogs, ditches, streams, damp places. Widespread native perennial.

Fam. Pink/Caryophyllaceae.

✿✿✿ May–Jun.

Sea Sandwort
Honckenya peploides
Gaineamhlus mara

Ht. Prostrate. **Fls.** 6–8mm, 5 white well-separated petals, 5 yellow-green sepals, longer than petals.

Lvs. Distinctive, yellowish-green, pointed leaves in opposite pairs closely behind each other up creeping stems.

Hab. Gravelly seashores & beaches. Native perennial, widespread in coastal locations.

Fam. Pink/Caryophyllaceae.

☺ Very fleshy, maritime plant which has deep root system.

☺ Seeds are yellow-green & globular.

✿✿ May–Aug.

> *Sandworts* are small, slender plants with flowering stems which are repeatedly forked or branched. Stem junctions are swollen.

Thyme-leaved Sandwort
Arenaria serpyllifolia
Gaineamhlus tíme

Ht. 15cm. **Fls.** 5–6mm, starry, with 5 unnotched, pointed petals, shorter than 5 pointed sepals; yellow anthers; in clusters on slender, wiry stems.

Lvs. Grey-green, untoothed, opposite, oval to lanceolate & without stalks.

Hab. Dry places & bare walls. Native annual, widespread.

Fam. Pink/Caryophyllaceae.

☺ Could be confused with Common Chickweed (p. 28) but *unnotched petals & unstalked leaves* help identification.

✿✿✿ May–Sep.

Spring Sandwort
Minuartia verna
Gaineamhlus earraigh

Ht. Low, cushion-forming. **Fls.** 7–9mm, 5 shining, white, unnotched, oval petals & 5 shorter, green sepals, 3 styles & 10 red-purple anthers; on creeping, fleshy stems.

Lvs. Dark green, rigid, 3-veined, narrow, needle-like, in whorls on slender stems.

Hab. Native perennial, abundant only on limestone of the Burren & Aran Is & NE coast of Ireland.

Fam. Pink/Caryophyllaceae.

☺ Similar to Knotted Pearlwort (p. 34) but has *only 3 styles*.

✿ May–Sep. ✛

Three-nerved Sandwort
Moehringia trinervia
Gaineamhlus féitheach

Ht. Straggling to 40cm. **Fls.** 5–6mm with 5 undivided petals; sepals, which have white margins, are longer than petals; on long stalks.

Lvs. Ovate, slightly downy, with 3–5 distinctive veins on each leaf; stems hairy all around.

Hab. Undisturbed woodlands & rich soils. Uncommon, native annual, scattered mainly in SE.

Fam. Pink/Caryophyllaceae.

✿ Apr–Jul.

English Stonecrop
Sedum anglicum
Póiríní seangán

Ht. 5cm. **Fls.** 12mm, star-shaped, petals white above, pink below, in small cymes on creeping, mat-forming, fleshy stems.

Lvs. Evergreen, hairless, alternate, egg-shaped, fleshy, *clasping* stem at base.

Hab. Dry banks, stone walls, shingle. Native perennial, common in coastal locations, especially Munster & Connacht.

Fam. Stonecrop/Crassulaceae.

☺ Flowers larger than White Stonecrop.

☺ Leaves tend to be reddish.

▶ Biting Stonecrop (p. 102)

✿✿ Jun–Sep.

White Stonecrop
Sedum album
Grafán bán na gcloch

Ht. 15cm. **Fls.** 6–9mm, white, star-shaped, in flat-topped clusters on hairless, succulent stems.

Lvs. Evergreen, fleshy, hairless, shiny, green, egg-shaped, alternate, *not clasping* stem at base.

Hab. Mat-forming on rocky ground, old walls, graveyards. Commonly found, introduced perennial.

Fam. Stonecrop/Crassulaceae.

☺ Leaves can also be red-tinged.

☺ Potentially invasive species.

✿✿ Jun–Sep. ❂

Round-leaved Sundew
Drosera rotundifolia
Drúchtín móna

Ht. 25cm. **Fls.** 5–10mm, in one-sided, drooping, spikes, on stem arising from *centre* of rosette; sometimes not opening unless in full sunshine, often not at all.

Lvs. Round, red, with long stalks, fanning out in basal rosette.

Hab. Wet, boggy heaths, peaty, acid soil & mountainsides. Locally common, native perennial.

Fam. Sundew/Droseraceae.

☺ Leaves have hairs with a little drop of 'dew' at the end of each hair; 'dew' is in fact a 'glue'. Insects get stuck on it, leaf rolls over, trapping them.

☺ As this plant is often self-pollinating, sometimes the flowers do not open at all.

✿✿ Jun–Aug.

Sundews are insectivorous plants which grow on soils deficient in nitrogen or other minerals. In order to survive, they obtain their nutrients by trapping insects on their sticky leaves; by use of enzymes, they then digest these creatures.

Oblong-leaved Sundew
Drosera intermedia
Cailís Mhuire

Ht. 20cm. **Fls.** 8–10mm, in spike on stem arising from *side* of leaf rosette.

Lvs. Long, narrow, tapering abruptly to long stalk, reddish, in basal rosette.

Hab. Wet heaths, moors, on sphagnum & peat. Native perennial found mainly in Kerry, Galway, Mayo & Donegal.

Fam. Sundew/Droseraceae

☺ Not as commonly found as Round-leaved Sundew.

✿ Jun–Aug.

Knotted Pearlwort
Sagina nodosa | Mongán glúineach

Ht. 12cm. **Fls.** 10mm, starry petals, *twice* as long as sepals; on tufted stems.

Lvs. Small, lanceolate in tufts at intervals on delicate, upright stems.

Hab. Heaths, damp dunes, coastal, mountains, on acid & lime soil. Native perennial, more common in W.

Fam. Pink/Caryophyllaceae.

☺ Similar to Spring Sandwort (p. 31) but has *5 styles*.

▶ Procumbent Pearlwort & Sea Pearlwort (p. 262). ✿✿✿ Jul–Oct.

Corn Spurrey
Spergula arvensis | Corrán lín

Ht. 30cm. **Fls.** 4–7mm, 5 petals, 5 sepals of equal length, 5 styles; in forked cymes on straggly, stickily hairy stems.

Lvs. Narrow, blunt-tipped leaves in whorls along stems.

Hab. Arable ground, tilled fields, sandy soil. Introduced annual, widespread apart from Midlands.

Fam. Pink/Caryophyllaceae.

▶ Greater, Lesser & Rock Sea-spurrey & Sand Spurrey (pp. 154 & 155). ✿✿✿ May–Sep.

Sea Campion
Silene uniflora | Coireán mara

Ht. 20cm. **Fls.** 20–25mm, 5 snow-white, overlapping, deeply-notched petals; sepal-tube inflated, forming bladder with reddish markings; in loose clusters on fleshy, mat-forming stems.

Lvs. Grey-green, oval.

Hab. Sea cliffs, shingle beaches. Native perennial, rare in mountains, common in coastal locations.

Fam. Pink/Caryophyllaceae. ✿✿✿ May–Aug.

Bladder Campion
Silene vulgaris
Coireán na gcuach

Ht. 80cm. **Fls.** 16–18mm with 5 deeply-divided petals, not overlapping; 3 styles; calyx is a *very* inflated bladder with network of pink veins; in drooping cymes on erect, *usually* hairless, stems.

Lvs. Grey-green, pointed-ovate, sometimes having hairy margins, in opposite pairs.

Hab. Chalky, well-drained soil, coastal areas. Native perennial, common in areas other than NW.

Fam. Pink/Caryophyllaceae.

☺ Flowers larger than Sea Campion.

☺ Scent of cloves at night-time attracts moths.

▶ Red Campion (p. 156)

✿✿ Jun–Aug.

White Campion
Silene latifolia
Coireán bán

Ht. 1m. **Fls.** 25–30mm with 5 deeply-forked white petals, 5 styles; calyx tube glandular-hairy, veined; in branched clusters on erect, hairy stems.

Lvs. Ovate-lanceolate, opposite & stickily hairy; lower stalked, upper unstalked.

Hab. Cultivated ground, roadsides, calcareous soil. Introduced perennial, locally common in Leinster & Munster.

Fam. Pink/Caryophyllaceae.

☺ Flowers dioecious: females larger with calyces 20-veined, males smaller with calyces 10-veined.

✿✿ May–Oct.

Brookweed
Samolus valerandi
Falcaire uisce

Ht. 25cm. **Fls.** 2–3mm, petals joined halfway; in racemes on erect stems.

Lvs. Pale green, hairless, spoon-shaped, short-stalked in basal rosette; stalkless, alternate on stems.

Hab. Damp, calcareous & saltwater soils, muddy lakeshores. Native perennial, found in NW, W, SW & coastal locations throughout.

Fam. Primrose/Primulaceae.

☺ Fruits are spherical capsules.

✿✿ Jun–Aug.

Black Nightshade
Solanum nigrum
Fuath dubh

Ht. 60cm. **Fls.** 7–10mm, white reflexed petals, bright yellow anthers in a cone; in loose, nodding clusters on purple-black stems.

Lvs. Alternate, oval, pointed, untoothed or slightly toothed, wavy margins.

Hab. Disturbed soil, shingle, scrub, hedges, gardens. Introduced annual, occasional in SE.

Fam. Nightshade/Solanaceae.

☺ Fruit is a glossy, spherical berry – green at first ripening to black. Consumption not advised.

▶ Bittersweet (p. 228).

✿ Jul–Sep. ⚠

Round-leaved Wintergreen
Pyrola rotundifolia ssp. *maritima*
Glasluibh chruinn

Ht. 30cm. **Fls.** 8–12mm, pure white, with curved, spreading petals; style 4–6mm, anthers orange-yellow; in racemes on upright stems.

Lvs. Dark, shiny, evergreen, rounded, with veins ending in tiny point at leaf margins; in basal rosette.

Hab. Calcareous dune slacks. Rare, protected native perennial, found in County Wexford.

Fam. Heather/ Ericaceae.

☺ Style hangs downward initially, subsequently curving forward to receive pollen from anthers above.

✿ May–Aug. ⊞

Springbeauty
Claytonia perfoliata
Plúirín earraigh

Ht. 30cm. **Fls.** 5–8mm, 5 scarcely-notched petals, in loose clusters on erect, hairless stems.

Lvs. Basal leaves long-stalked; stem leaves fused across stem.

Hab. Dunes, wasteland, disturbed sandy ground. Uncommon, introduced annual.

Fam. Blinks/Montiaceae.

☺ Good example of a perfoliate leaf.

✿ Apr–Jul. 🏃

Rue-leaved Saxifrage
Saxifraga tridactylites | Mórán balla

Ht. 15cm. **Fls.** 4–6mm, in sparse clusters or solitary on stickily-hairy, often reddish stems.

Lvs. Reddish, untoothed, pinnately divided into 3 or 5 lobes.

Hab. Old walls, bare stony places, dry calcareous ground. Common native annual.

Fam. Saxifrage/Saxifragaceae.

☺ Red tinge is often due to drought condition of soil. ✿✿ Mar–May.

St Patrick's Cabbage
Saxifraga spathularis | Cabáiste an mhadra rua

Ht. 30cm. **Fls.** 6–9mm, each petal with 1–3 yellow spots at base, many red spots above; in loose panicle on erect leafless stems.

Lvs. Hairless, *spoon-shaped*, sharply-toothed, in *compact* basal rosette, stems long, flattened.

Hab. Damp, rainy, rocky places. Native perennial, locally common in W. Connacht, W. Cork, Kerry, Donegal.

Fam. Saxifrage/Saxifragaceae.

☺ Like Kidney Saxifrage but leaves in that species are rounded or kidney shaped.

✿ Jun–Aug. ✚

Kidney Saxifrage
Saxifraga hirsuta | Mórán giobach

Ht. 30cm. **Fls.** 7–8mm, each petal with yellow blotch near base, usually red spots above; on erect stems.

Lvs. Densely hairy, *round to kidney-shaped*, blunt teeth; leaf stalks not flattened; basal rosette *not* compact.

Hab. Damp, rocky places. Uncommon native perennial, mainly Kerry & W. Cork.

Fam. Saxifrage/Saxifragaceae.

✿ May–Jul.

Mossy Saxifrage
Saxifraga hypnoides
Mórán caonaigh

Ht. 20cm. **Fls.**
10–15mm, slightly
overlapping, green-veined
petals; *nodding* buds; in
clusters on erect, *hairless* stems.

Lvs. Rosettes of leaves with 3–5 narrow,
pointed lobes.

Hab. Mat-forming on rock ledges, screes,
grassy damp ground. Native perennial found
locally in County Sligo & the Burren, also
Comeragh Mountains, County Waterford.

Fam. Saxifrage/Saxifragaceae.

☺ Numerous non-flowering shoots give
moss-like appearance.
☺ *Has long runners, unlike* Irish Saxifrage.

✿ May–July.

Irish Saxifrage
Saxifraga rosacea ssp. *rosacea*
Mórán gaelach

Ht. 10cm. **Fls.** 12–18mm,
petals pure white except
towards centre; *no* nodding buds; in
few-flowered clusters on erect, *hairy*
stems.

Lvs. Wedge-shaped, with 3–7
pointed lobes; long glandular &
non-glandular hairs; in compacted
cushions *without* non-flowering
runners; bright red during flowering
season.

Hab. Shallow depressions in
limestone, damp rocky places.
Rare, native perennial found in the
Burren, occasionally in N Kerry.

Fam. Saxifrage/Saxifragaceae.

✿ May–Jul.

Fairy Flax
Linum catharticum
Lus na mban sí

Ht. 25cm. **Fls.** 4–6mm, with veined petals, in loose, forked clusters, nodding in bud, on slender, hairless stems.

Lvs. Opposite, narrow, with 1 vein.

Hab. Wet & dry grassland, calcareous soil, sand dunes. Widespread native annual.

Fam. Flax/Linaceae.

☺ Easily overlooked species due to small size.

☺ AKA Purging Flax.

▶ Pale Flax (p. 220)

✿✿✿ May–Sep.

Wood-sorrel
Oxalis acetosella
Seamsóg

Ht. 10cm. **Fls.** 10–15mm, lilac-veined petals, bell-shaped flower with golden centre, solitary on slender stem directly from root.

Lvs. Long-stalked, trifoliate, each lobe notched or heart-shaped, folding at night; creeping plant.

Hab. Old, undisturbed woodland, moss-covered walls. Widespread, native perennial.

Fam. Wood-sorrel/ Oxalidaceae.

☺ Underside of leaves is often purplish.

✿✿✿ Apr–Jun.

Grass-of-Parnassus
Parnassia palustris
Fionnscoth

Ht. 30cm. **Fls.**
15–20mm, saucer-shaped
with greenish-veined,
white petals, 5 sepals,
5 little semicircles of
fringed stamens tipped
with nectar-bearing
glands, alternating with
5 stamens with anthers;
at centre of flower is a
4-lobed stigma; on erect,
unbranched stems.

Lvs. Untoothed, heart-
shaped, long-stalked,
mostly basal; single stem
leaf clasps unbranched
stem.

Hab. Damp, limestone
soil, grassland & moors.
Native perennial found
mainly in NW, W,
Midlands & Counties
Kildare & Carlow.

Fam. Grass-of-
Parnassus/Parnassiaceae

☺ Bees & pollinating
insects are attracted
to the plant by a mild
honey-like scent.
☺ Recommended
viewing through
hand lens.

✿✿ Jun–Sep.

Meadowsweet
Filipendula ulmaria
Airgead luachra

Ht. 1.2m. **Fls.** 5–8mm, creamy white, with numerous stamens, in large panicles on tall, erect, reddish stems.

Lvs. Dark-green, toothed oval leaflets with smaller toothed leaflets between; terminal leaflet 3–5 lobed.

Hab. Damp waysides, meadows, marshes & woodland. Widespread native perennial.

Fam. Rose/Rosaceae.

☺ Flowers are heavily scented with an aroma of almonds.

▶ Dropwort (p. 50)

✿✿✿ Jun–Sep.

Field Pansy
Viola arvensis
Lus croí

Ht. 15cm. **Fls.** 10–15mm, 5 irregular petals; upper 2 are slightly overlapping & erect; 2 are spread laterally & 1 is a spreading lower lip; creamy-white, frequently with golden-orange flush on lower petal, occasionally purple tinged; dark lines run into throat which is fringed in inverted 'V' created by 2 lateral petals; sepals at least as long as petals; on erect, spreading stems.

Lvs. Narrow, toothed, with stipules.

Hab. Arable, cultivated ground. Native annual, occasional in NE, E & S.

Fam. Violet/Violaceae.

☺ AKA Corn Pansy.

▶ Sand Pansy (p.104) & Wild Pansy (p. 225).

✿✿ Apr–Oct.

Bogbean
Menyanthes trifoliata
Báchrán

Ht. 15cm. **Fls.** 15mm, star-shaped, pinkish-white, fringed all over with curly white hairs; dark pink in bud; in terminal racemes on hairless, spongy stems.

Lvs. Hairless, trifoliate, held above water's surface.

Hab. Creeping on rhizomes through shallow water, fens, bogs, canals. Native perennial, widespread throughout most of Ireland.

Fam. Bogbean/Menyanthaceae.

☺ Long-styled & short-styled forms ensure pollination in same manner as Cowslips (p. 98) & Primroses (p. 99).

☺ AKA Bearnán lachan.

✿✿✿ Mar–Jun.

Meadow-foam
Limnanthes douglasii
Cúr léana

Ht. 10cm. **Fls.** 20–30mm, 5 slightly-lobed, curved petals, outer half of petals white; large yellow centre to flower; supported by 5 pale green sepals.

Lvs. Pale green, pinnate.

Hab. Carpets dry, waste ground. Introduced annual, occasional in SE & N.

Fam. Meadow-foam/Limnanthaceae.

☺ AKA Poached-egg plant

✿ May–Jul. 🏃

Blackthorn
Prunus spinosa
Draighean

Ht. To 4m. **Fls.** 10–15mm, white, numerous, prominent stamens with orange anthers; in short, dense spikes, appearing before leaves, on blackish bark.

Lvs. Toothed, elliptical-lanceolate, hairy on midrib below.

Hab. Hedgerows, scrub, in dense thickets. Widespread native shrub.

Fam. Rose/Rosaceae.

☺ Fruit is a blue-black 'sloe' or round, fleshy berry with a single stone.

☺ Twigs have many thorn-like spurs.

✿✿✿ Mar–May.

Rowan
Sorbus aucuparia
Caorthann

Ht. 20m. **Fls.** 8–12mm, creamy-white, in wide, flat-topped clusters.

Lvs. Pinnate, up to 9 pairs of toothed, oblong leaflets, downy below when immature.

Hab. Glens, mountainsides, by streams & rocky places, rarely on limestone. Widespread through most of Ireland. Native tree.

Fam. Rose/Rosaceae.

☺ Fruit is a red berry.

☺ AKA Mountain Ash.

✿✿✿ May–Jun.

Wild Strawberry
Fragaria vesca
Sú talún fiáin

Ht. 30cm. **Fls.** 15–20mm; round petals only occasionally overlap; calyx of 5 pointed sepals showing through slightly; in loose cymes of around 6 on slender, downy, erect, branched stems.

Lvs. Trifoliate, pleated & toothed; *appressed* or flattened hairs below; terminal tooth of end leaflet *longer* than those adjacent.

Hab. Hedgerows, woodlands & sunny banks. Widespread native perennial.

Fam. Rose/Rosaceae.

☺ Fruits are very tiny, sweet, succulent strawberries.

☺ *Long* rooting stolons.

✿✿✿ Apr–Jul.

Barren Strawberry
Potentilla sterilis
Sú talún bréige

Ht. 15cm. **Fls.** 10–15mm, petals *widely separated*, calyx clearly visible; on downy stems.

Lvs. Blueish-green, trifoliate, toothed; terminal tooth of end leaflet *shorter* than adjacent teeth; hairs on underside *not* flattened.

Hab. Open, dry woodland, grassy banks. Widespread, native perennial.

Fam. Rose/Rosaceae.

☺ Fruits are dry, inedible strawberries.

☺ Has *short* rooting stolons.

✿✿✿ Mar–May.

Hawthorn
Crataegus monogyna
Sceach gheal

Ht. 6m. **Fls.** 12mm, occasionally blushed pink; 1 style, numerous stamens; in flat-topped clusters on branching stems.

Lvs. Shiny, dark-green, deeply lobed.

Hab. Hedgerows, scrub, more often dry soils. Widespread native shrub.

Fam. Rose/Rosaceae.

☺ Fruit is a mealy, edible, red berry.

☺ Unpleasantly scented.

✿✿✿ May–Jun.

Dewberry
Rubus caesius
Eithreog

For more information on the **Rose** family, see p. 160.

Ht. Sprawling to 80cm. **Fls.** 20–25mm, always white; raggy petals, numerous stamens, star-shaped calyx.

Lvs. Trifoliate, toothed, wrinkled, on biennial stems with weak prickles.

Hab. Dry grassland, scrub, calcareous soil. Native perennial, common in diagonal band from Mayo to Wexford.

Fam. Rose/Rosaceae.

☺ Fruit could be confused with Bramble (p. 160) but Dewberry has fewer, larger drupes & these are covered with a bluish, waxy bloom.

✿✿ Jun–Aug.

Burnet Rose
Rosa spinosissima
Briúlán

Ht. 50cm. **Fls.** 30–50mm,
white, cream or pink heart-
shaped petals; on stems bearing
numerous *straight* thorns.

Lvs. Hairless, pinnate, 7–11
oval, toothed leaflets.

Hab. Frequent coastal shrub,
on limestone, calcareous
grassland, heaths & dunes.
Native perennial.

Fam. Rose/Rosaceae.

☺ Fruits are purplish-black,
spherical hips.

▶ Dog-rose (p. 161).

✿✿ May–Jul.

Field-rose
Rosa arvensis
Rós léana

Ht. 1m. **Fls.** 3–5cm, 5 petals, golden styles
united to form column at least as long as
stamens; on trailing, purplish stems with
sparse, narrow, arched prickles.

Lvs. Hairless, pinnate, 5–7 oval leaflets.

Hab. Scrubby hedgerows, woodland.
Native perennial, frequent
towards E half of Ireland.

Fam. Rose/Rosaceae.

☺ Sepals are hairless, usually
falling before fruit ripens into
red, oblong hip.

☺ Could be confused with
Dog-rose (p. 161), which can
also bear white flowers but
styles *not* projecting in that
shrub.

✿✿ Jun–Aug.

Strawberry-tree
Arbutus unedo
Caithne

Ht. 10m. **Fls.** 8mm long, creamy white tinged-green, urn-shaped with 5 teeth, 10 stamens; in drooping panicles on thin, red-brown branches with peeling bark.

Lvs. Short-stalked, evergreen, shiny dark green above, paler below; elliptical, toothed, pointed at both ends.

Hab. Oak woods, rocky ground. One of the Lusitanian species (see p. 51), this shrub is native only in Counties Sligo, Kerry & Cork.

Fam. Heather/Ericaceae.

☺ Fruit – or 'strawberry' – is a bland, mealy, 20mm spherical berry, yellow initially ripening to reddish orange, covered in rough warts.

✿ Sep–Dec. ✚

Prickly Heath
Gaultheria mucronata
Fraoch deilgneach

Ht. 1.2m. **Fls.** 5–6mm, pearly-white, urn-shaped; corollas constricted at mouth; sepals & petioles white; in clusters on bushy, evergreen stems.

Lvs. Small, alternate, ovate, dark green, sharply pointed.

Hab. Heaths, moors, acid soils. Spreads by suckering; this is an introduced shrub, occasionally found in Donegal, Connemara & NE.

Fam. Heather/Ericaceae.

☺ This plant bears its fruit in a white to purple capsule.

☺ Now considered to be *potentially invasive*, Prickly Heath is currently listed as a problematic species that needs to be monitored for range expansion & potential impact.

✿ May–Jun. 🏃 🔞

Hedge Bindweed
Calystegia sepium
Ialus fáil

Ht. 3m. **Fls.** 30–50mm, pure white, 5-lobed, funnel-shaped; 2 epicalyx bracts, which *do not overlap*, surround the sepals; on twisting, twining, slender stems.

Lvs. Alternate, heart or arrow-shaped.

Hab. Hedgerows, riversides & woodland edges, climbing over other plants for support. Widespread, native perennial.

Fam. Bindweed/ Convolvulaceae.

☺ These flowers stay open overnight on bright moonlit nights attracting hawkmoths to their nectar.

▶ Sea Bindweed & Field Bindweed (p. 172).

✿✿✿ Jun–Sep.

Large Bindweed
Calystegia silvatica
Ialus mór

Ht. 4m. **Fls.** 60–70mm, white, funnel-shaped; 2 epicalyx bracts, which *overlap*, surround & conceal sepals; on strong, twining stems.

Lvs. Long, arrow-shaped.

Hab. Disturbed ground, roadside verges, twining across other plants. Introduced perennial, far less common than Hedge Bindweed.

Fam. Bindweed/Convolvulaceae

☺ Distinctions between Hedge & Large Bindweed are seen on examination of the 2 bracts which are located *inside the sepals*; also the flowers of the latter are considerably larger than those of the former.

✿✿✿ Jun–Sep.

Dropwort
Filipendula vulgaris
Lus braonach

Ht. 60cm. **Fls.** 10–20mm, 6-petalled, creamy white above, flushed red below with numerous stamens; unscented; in terminal, flat-topped clusters.

Lvs. Lower leaves in rosette; numerous, dark-green, pinnate; also alternate on stem, with 8–20 pairs of leaflets & tiny leaflets between each of main leaves.

Hab. Calcareous meadows, rocky, limestone heaths. Rare native perennial only found in the Burren & SW Galway.

Fam. Rose/Rosaceae.

☺ Differs from Meadowsweet in having larger flowers, fewer in cluster.

✿ May–Aug. ✚

White Water-lily
Nymphaea alba
Bacán bán

Ht. Aquatic plant. **Fls.** 15–20cm, with over 20 oval-shaped petals, numerous golden stamens, 4–6 large, greenish sepals.

Lvs. Leaves almost circular, lobed, waxy, rain forming droplets on upper surfaces.

Hab. Forming large patches in still or slow-moving water. Scattered, native perennial.

Fam. Water-lily/Nymphaeaceae.

▶ Yellow Water-lily (p. 107).

✿✿ Jun–Aug.

Mountain Avens
Dryas octopetala
Leaithín

Ht. 6cm. **Fls.** 20–40mm, 8 or more snow-white petals, circle of numerous golden stamens; solitary, on dark green or red stems.

Lvs. Glossy, dark-green like miniature oak-leaves with silvery undersides.

Hab. Forms dense mats on limestone ledges, cliffs. Native perennial mainly found in the Burren & parts of Sligo.

Fam. Rose/Rosaceae.

☺ Fruits are heads of achenes with long, twisted, feathery, silvery styles.

☺ One of the Lusitanian flora, a group of plants thought to have come to Ireland from the Mediterranean while Ireland was still physically joined to Britain & continental Europe.

✿ May–Aug. ⊞

Wood Anemone
Anemone nemorosa
Lus na gaoithe

Ht. 30cm. **Fls.** 20–40mm, 6–12 hairless sepals resembling petals, usually white with hint of lilac beneath; numerous yellow stamens; solitary, nodding, on long, thin stalks.

Lvs. Long-stalked basal leaves with deeply-lobed divisions; upper leaves similar but short-stalked.

Hab. Carpet-forming in deciduous woods & by streams. Rare on heather moorland. Native perennial, found in most of Ireland.

Fam. Buttercup/Ranunculaceae.

☺ Flowers early in woodland before the trees are fully leafed.

✿✿ Mar–May.

Summer Snowflake
Leucojum aestivum
Plúirín samhraidh

Ht. 60cm. **Fls.** 15–20mm long, snow-white, each petal with green patch near tip; bell-shaped flowers in umbels of 2–5 flowers emerge from spathe; carried on hollow, winged stem.

Lvs. Bright green, strap-shaped, same length as flowering stems.

Hab. Shady part of damp riverside meadows, wet woods. Scarce, native perennial.

Fam. Onion/Alliaceae.

☺ AKA Loddon Lily.

✿ Apr–Jun.

Kerry Lily
Simethis mattiazzii
Lile Fhíonáin

Ht. 25cm. **Fls.** 20mm,
6 glistening, silvery-white
petals, purple-grey beneath;
6 fuzzy, woolly, filaments
topped with golden anthers;
3–7 flowers in loose panicles
on slender, erect stems.

Lvs. All basal, narrow,
grass-like, often curled, up to
30cm long.

Hab. Grows from bulbous
rootstock on windswept,
coastal slopes in a few
locations in County Kerry.
Rare, native perennial.

Fam. Asphodel/
Xanthorrhoeaceae.

☺ This is a rare &
legally-protected
plant species.

✿ May–Jul. ✚

Three-cornered Garlic
Allium triquetrum
Glaschreamh

Ht. 30cm. **Fls.** 20mm long, bell-like, white with narrow, green line down centre of tepals; in drooping one-sided umbel of 3–15 flowers, on 3-sided stem.

Lvs. 2–3, floppy, linear, grey-green, flat or markedly angled.

Hab. Bulb which is found in large clumps on roadsides, hedgerows, shady places. Introduced perennial, found in some E & S regions.

Fam. Onion/Alliaceae.

☺ Also known as Three-cornered Leek.
☺ Smells strongly of garlic when disturbed.

✿✿ Mar–Jun. 🏃

Ramsons
Allium ursinum
Creamh

Ht. 35cm. **Fls.** 15–20mm, star-shaped, 6 tepals spread widely, in globular heads emerging from papery spathes; on 3-angled stem.

Lvs. Broad, ovate to elliptical, all basal, up to 25cm long.

Hab. Carpet-forming in damp woodlands, calcareous soils. Bulbous, native perennial, fairly commonly found but not in Connacht.

Fam. Onion/Alliaceae.

☺ Smells strongly of garlic when disturbed.
☺ Often grows alongside Bluebells & Lesser Celandines.
☺ Fruits are in 3-part capsules borne on umbel rays.

✿✿ Apr–May.

White Clover
Trifolium repens
Seamair bhán

Ht. 30cm. **Fls.** Small, creamy-white or palest pink peaflowers, in tightly-packed, dense, rounded 2cm heads; on long, hairless, creeping stalks.

Lvs. Trifoliate with finely-toothed, oval leaflets often with white 'V' mark & translucent lateral veins.

Hab. Grassy places, meadows, hedgerows. Widespread native perennial.

Fam. Pea/Fabaceae.

☺ Flowers are scented.

☺ White Clover spreads on creeping, rooting stems unlike Alsike Clover (p. 176).

▶ Strawberry Clover (p. 177). ✿✿✿ May–Oct.

Cow Parsley
Anthriscus sylvestris
Peirsil bhó

Ht. 1.2m.
Fls. White, 5-petalled, in long-stalked terminal umbels; umbels have 8–12 rays, without bracts; on unspotted, stout, hollow, grooved stems.

Lvs. Bright green, ferny, large, triangular, 2–3 times pinnate.

Hab. Roadsides, hedgerows, shady places, woodland margins. Widespread native perennial.

Fam. Carrot/Apiaceae.

☺ Fruits are black & elongated.

▶ Fool's Parsley (p. 57).

✿✿✿ Apr–Jun.

Hemlock Water-dropwort
Oenanthe crocata
Dáthabha bán

Ht. 1.5m. **Fls.** 2mm, white, 5-petalled in large, domed umbels, 15–35 rays; umbels sometimes have bracts; on stout, hollow, grooved stems.

Lvs. Triangular, tri-pinnate, with tapering, toothed lobes.

Hab. Damp meadows, near lakes, rivers, ditches. Native perennial, common except for centre of Ireland.

Fam. Carrot/Apiaceae.

☺ Cylindrical, long styles.
☺ Highly poisonous plant.

✿✿ Jun–Aug. ⚠

Pignut
Conopodium majus
Cúlarán

Ht. 50cm. **Fls.** Tiny, white in umbels 3–6cm, on smooth hollow stems.

Lvs. Hairless, feathery, 2–3 pinnate, finely divided; upper narrow, clasping the stems, lower basal leaves, elliptical to lanceolate, withering.

Hab. Shady woodland, mainly acid soil. Widespread native perennial.

Fam. Carrot/Apiaceae.

☺ Fruit narrow, ovoid, with erect styles.

✿✿✿ Apr–Jun.

Parsley Water-dropwort
Oenanthe lachenalii
Dáthabha peirsile

Ht. 1m. **Fls.** Small, white, in terminal, slender-rayed 2–6cm umbels, 6–15 flower-heads in each umbel; on slender, almost solid, ridged stems.

Lvs. Sparse, thin, bi-pinnate, upper leaves narrower than lower.

Hab. Brackish marshes, damp meadows, mostly coastal. Infrequently found native perennial.

Fam. Carrot/Apiaceae.

☺ Ovoid, ribbed, without swollen corky bases.

✿✿ Jun–Sep.

Fool's Parsley
Aethusa cynapium
Peirsil amaide

Members of the **Carrot** family usually bear flowers in compound umbels. Look for leaf shape, bracts, & shape of ripe fruit

Ht. 50cm. **Fls.** 2–3mm, 5-petalled, in 2–3cm umbels; 3–5 *drooping* bracts below umbel; on slender, ribbed stems.

Lvs. Bi-pinnate or tri-pinnate, flat, triangular; emit an unpleasant smell when crushed.

Hab. Arable, waste ground. Introduced annual found mainly in Leinster & Munster.

Fam. Carrot/Apiaceae.

☺ Fruits are ovoid & ridged.
☺ Highly poisonous plant.

▶ Cow Parsley (p. 55).

✿✿ Jun–Aug. ⚠

Ground-elder
Aegopodium podagraria
Lus an easpaig

Ht. 1m. **Fls.** 2–3mm, creamy-white, 5 notched, even-sized petals in compact, domed umbels; umbels are without bracts & have 10–20 rays; on erect, hollow, grooved stems.

Lvs. Bright-green, toothed, roughly triangular, twice trifoliate with oval leaflets.

Hab. Spreading on underground rhizomes, forms large patches on damp & disturbed ground, along lanes & shady woodland. Widespread introduced perennial.

Fam. Carrot/Apiaceae.

☺ Fruit ovoid, hairless with narrow ridges.

✿✿✿ May–Aug.

Burnet-saxifrage
Pimpinella saxifraga
Ainís fhiáin

Ht. 80cm. **Fls.** 2mm, white, in umbels with 6–20 rays, usually without bracts; petals with long, *inwardly-curved* point; on erect, rough, downy, slightly-ridged stems.

Lvs. Basal leaves oval, toothed, pinnate, 3–7 pairs; stem leaves bi-pinnate, divided into long, narrow segments.

Hab. Sandy, dry, grazed grassland, calcareous ground. Native perennial, common generally in Munster & Leinster.

Fam. Carrot/Apiaceae.

☺ Fruit oval, slightly ridged.

✿✿✿ Jun–Sep.

Wild Carrot
Daucus carota
Mealbhacán

Ht. 1m. **Fls.** 2–3mm, creamy-white, tinged pink before opening, in broad, flat umbels; outer florets larger than inner, central flower of umbel sometimes red; *distinctive bracts* surrounding umbel are 3-lobed, showy, curving upwards when in fruit; on branched, solid, erect, ridged stems.

Lvs. Feathery, hairy, finely cut, bi- or tri-pinnately divided with narrow leaflets.

Hab. Hedgerows, country lanes, coastal grassland. Widespread native perennial.

Fam. Carrot/ Apiaceae.

☺ Fruits oval with spiny ridges in cup-shaped umbel.

✿✿✿ Jun–Sep.

59

Lesser Marshwort
Apium inundatum
Smaileog bháite

Ht. Creeping. **Fls.** Small, 5-petalled, in stalked, 2–4 ray umbels, 1–2cm wide, in leaf axils, on slender stems.

Lvs. Lower leaves pinnate, narrow, thread-like; upper leaves are pinnate with broader 3-lobed segments.

Hab. Wet, bare, muddy places, ditches, shallow water. Native perennial, local throughout.

Fam. Carrot/Apiaceae.

☺ Often submerged, stems root at nodes.

✿✿ Jun–Jul.

Wild Celery
Apium graveolens
Smaileog

Ht. 1m. **Fls.** Tiny, 0.5mm, greenish-white, in terminal, short-stalked or unstalked umbels of 6–10 unequal rays; no bracts or bracteoles; on stout, erect, hairless, grooved, hollow stems.

Lvs. Shiny, lower pinnate or bi-pinnate, upper trifoliate; leaflets diamond-shaped, coarsely lobed.

Hab. Mainly coastal, brackish ground, saltmarshes. Uncommon native biennial.

Fam. Carrot/Apiaceae.

☺ Smells strongly of celery.

✿ Jun–Aug.

Hogweed
Heracleum sphondylium
Feabhrán

Ht. 1.5m. **Fls.** Creamy-white, with notched, unequal petals, in large umbels up to 20cm across on hollow ridged stems.

Lvs. Toothed, pinnately lobed with inflated leaf base, leaflets are toothed, downy below.

Hab. Grassland, roadsides, meadows. Widespread native biennial or perennial.

Fam. Carrot/Apiaceae.

☺ Fruits are elliptical, flattened, hairless.

✿✿✿ May–Aug.

Giant Hogweed
Heracleum mantegazzianum
Feabhrán capaill

Ht. 3m. **Fls.** 10mm, creamy-white, in large 50cm umbels on stout, ridged, purple-blotched stems.

Lvs. Long, pinnately divided, with sharply pointed leaflets.

Hab. Woodlands, meadows, roadsides, riverbanks. Uncommon, introduced biennial or perennial.

Fam. Carrot/Apiaceae.

☺ Fruits are flattened, narrowly oval.
☺ Phototoxic plant; causes severe blistering of skin if in contact.
☺ Classed as Invasive.

✿✿ Jun–Jul.

Hemlock
Conium maculatum
Moing mhear

Ht. 2m. **Fls.** 2mm, creamy-white, in short-stalked umbels of 10–20 rays, on much-branched, smooth, hollow, *purple-blotched* stems.

Lvs. Large, long-stalked, triangular in outline, up to 4 times divided into fine, feathery leaflets.

Hab. Hedgerows, riverbanks, damp ground. Widespread, long-established, introduced perennial, more common in S.

Fam. Carrot/Apiaceae.

☺ Fruits almost spherical with wavy ridges.

☺ Highly poisonous, strong-smelling plant.

✿✿✿ Jun–Jul. ⚠

Fool's-water-cress
Apium nodiflorum
Gunna uisce

Ht. 20cm. **Fls.** Tiny, white, in open, short-stalked, 3–12 spoked umbels in leaf axils; on ascending, lightly ridged, hollow stems.

Lvs. Bright green, pinnate, toothed, with 4–6 pairs of oval to lanceolate leaflets.

Hab. Rivers, ditches, damp places & streams. Widespread, native perennial.

Fam. Carrot/Apiaceae.

☺ Toothed leaves help to differentiate from Water-cress (p. 17).

✿✿✿ Jul–Aug.

Sanicle
Sanicula europaea
Bodán coille

Ht. 60cm. **Fls.**
Tiny, whitish-
pink, 5-petalled,
5 protruding
stamens, in small umbels on dark
stems.

Lvs. Basal are long-stalked with
5–7 toothed lobes, upper are
smaller with short stalks.

Hab. Deciduous woodland,
wooded river banks.
Widespread native perennial.

Fam. Carrot/Apiaceae.

☺ Fruits oval with hooked
bristles.

✿✿✿ May–Aug.

Guelder-rose
Viburnum opulus
Caor chon

Ht. 4m. **Fls.**
Creamy-white
in flat, umbel-like heads; outer flowers
in a circle of 5-petalled flowers, each
15–20mm across with neither stamens
nor pistils; inner flowers 4–7mm, in a
disc; on grey, hairless stems.

Lvs. Opposite, palmate with 3–5
toothed lobes.

Hab. Hedgerows, thickets & scrub.
Widespread native shrub.

Fam. Honeysuckle/Caprifoliaceae.

☺ Fruits are red berries in
clusters.
☺ Flowers are beautifully
fragrant.

✿✿✿ May–Jul.

Elder
Sambucus nigra
Trom

Ht. 6m. **Fls.** 5–6mm, 5-lobed, creamy-white, in dense, flat-topped corymbs; on deeply-furrowed, corky stems.

Lvs. Pinnate, divided into 5–9 oval, stalked leaflets.

Hab. Hedgerows, thickets, waste places & scrub. Widespread native shrub.

Fam. Honeysuckle/Caprifoliaceae.

☺ Fruits are dark purple berries in wide, flat clusters.

☺ Flowers are heavily scented.

✿✿✿ Jun–Jul.

Dwarf Elder
Sambucus ebulus
Tromán

Ht. 1.5cm. **Fls.** 3–5mm, white, sometimes tinged pink, 5-petalled; anthers purple; in dense umbels, 6–10cm across; on stout, erect, grooved stems.

Lvs. Pinnate, oblong-lanceolate, in 7–13 sharply-toothed leaflets; oval stipules at base of leaves.

Hab. Roadsides, hedgerows. Introduced shrub, scattered throughout.

Fam. Honeysuckle/ Caprifoliaceae.

☺ Strong, unpleasant-smelling leaves.

☺ Flowers pleasantly scented.

✿✿ Jun–Aug.

Branched Bur-reed
Sparganium erectum
Rísheisc

Ht. 1m. **Fls.** 15mm, green-white,
flower-heads at *lower* part of stem
contain *female flowers*; style-tips are
white & protrude from spherical
head; *upper flower-heads contain male*,
green-brown flowers, each with more
than 3 stamens; in clusters, more
male heads than females, on *branched*,
upright, hairless stems.

Lvs. Strap-shaped, erect,
3-sided.

Hab. Ditches, marshy
places, still or slow-flowing
fresh water. Widespread
native perennial.

Fam. Bulrush/Typhaceae.

✿✿✿ Jun–Aug.

Gypsywort
Lycopus europaeus
Feorán corraigh

Ht. 90cm. **Fls.**
3–5mm, white, 4-lobed
with tiny purple spots &
2 protruding stamens; calyx
with spine-like teeth; in dense whorls
around square stems at axils of
upper leaves.

Lvs. Opposite, ovate to lanceolate,
coarsely-toothed, shortly-stalked,
veined.

Hab. Damp ground by fresh water,
ditches, ponds. Scattered, local
native perennial.

Fam. Dead-nettle/Lamiaceae.

☺ Unlike many of its family, this
plant has no aroma.

✿✿ Jul–Sep.

Two-spined Acaena
Acaena ovalifolia
Spíochnó

Ht. 15cm. **Fls.** Extremely tiny, greenish-white without petals but 4 sepals; in compact, spherical heads on upright stems.

Lvs. Toothed, glossy green, pinnately divided with 3–4 pairs of leaflets.

Hab. Disturbed & coastal ground, woodland paths. Uncommon introduced perennial.

Fam. Rose/Rosaceae.

☺ Spreads itself by means of red, spiny seeds which grip onto animals' fur.

☺ Classed as 'Potentially Invasive'.

✿ Jun–Sep. 🚫

Pirri-pirri-bur
Acaena novae-zelandiae
Lus na holla

Ht. 20cm. **Fls.** Tiny, white, in round heads, solitary on erect stalks rising from creeping stems.

Lvs. Glossy green, toothed, pinnate, 3–4 pairs & 1 terminal leaflet.

Hab. Dry, sandy soil, heathland. Introduced perennial, not widespread.

Fam. Rose/Rosaceae.

☺ Fruit in barbed, red, spiny, round heads.

☺ Classed as 'Potentially Invasive'.

✿ Jun–Jul. 🚫

Pipewort
Eriocaulon aquaticum
Píbín uisce

Ht. Aquatic plant to 60cm. **Fls.** Tightly-packed, domed, whitish, button-like heads, 10–15mm, on slender, erect, angled stems.

Lvs. Narrow, flattened, fine-pointed, at base of stem.

Hab. Shallow, peaty, bog-pools & lakes. Native perennial, only found in Donegal, Connemara & Kerry.

Fam. Pipewort/Eriocaulaceae.

☺ A monoecious plant, this species bears male flowers in the centre of the head surrounded by female flowers.

✿ Jul–Sep.

Bilbao Fleabane
Conyza floribunda
Lus garbh na ndreancaidí

Ht. 1m. **Fls.** 4–19mm flower-heads, creamy-white disc florets in loose panicles; on much-branched, hairy, robust & stiff stems.

Lvs. Alternate, lanceolate, sparsely-toothed; basal rosette of ovate-lanceolate, shallowly-toothed leaves.

Hab. Waste ground, pavements, roadsides. Introduced annual found mainly in SE.

Fam. Daisy/Asteraceae.

☺ AKA Hispid Fleabane.

✿✿ Jul–Oct.

Mexican Fleabane
Erigeron karvinskianus
Nóinín balla

Ht. 50cm. **Fls.** 13–16mm flower-heads, with yellow disc florets at centre surrounded by narrow, spreading ray florets, white or deep pink above, pink below; on slender, spindly, much-branched, leafy stems.

Lvs. Lower ovate, toothed, upper linear & toothless.

Hab. Old walls, cliffs, dry rocky places. Introduced perennial found infrequently in E & S of Ireland.

Fam. Daisy/Asteraceae.

☺ Widely naturalised garden escape.

✿ May–Sep. 🏃

> **Ray** florets are flat, outer, strap-like flowers that surround the central disc in a composite flower, as in the white parts of a **Daisy**.
>
> **Disc** florets are inner flowers in a composite flower, as in the yellow parts of a **Daisy**.

Scentless Mayweed
Tripleurospermum inodorum
Meá drua

Ht. 75cm. **Fls.** 20–40mm flower-heads, with yellow disc florets at centre, white ray florets; solitary on long-stalked, straggly, branching stems; *not aromatic*.

Lvs. Alternate, feathery, much divided.

Hab. Disturbed, arable & cultivated ground. Native perennial, common in S, E & NE.

Fam. Daisy/Asteraceae.

☺ Receptacle at centre of flower-head is *domed & solid.*

✿✿✿ Apr–Oct.

Sea Mayweed
Tripleurospermum maritimum
Lus Bealtaine

Ht. 60cm. **Fls.** 20–40mm flower-heads, with yellow disc florets at centre surrounded by spreading, white ray florets; *no scales between disc florets;* on branched stems.

Lvs. Fleshy, alternate, pinnately cut into many divisions.

Hab. Coastal shingle & sand, old walls, cliffs, dry soils. Native perennial, widespread in coastal locations.

Fam. Daisy/Asteraceae.

☺ Receptacle at centre of flower-head is *domed & solid.*

☺ Ray florets *can also be reflexed.*

✿✿✿ Apr–Oct.

Scented Mayweed
Matricaria chamomilla
Fíogadán cumhra

Ht. 60cm. **Fls.** 20–30mm flower-heads, with yellow disc florets at centre, white ray florets which *turn back soon after opening;* flowers on long-stalked stems.

Lvs. Alternate, feathery, divided.

Hab. Disturbed, arable & waste ground. Occasional introduced annual, found in a few locations in E, S & Shannon estuary.

Fam. Daisy/Asteraceae.

☺ Receptacle at centre of flower-head is *conical & hollow.*

☺ Entire plant is aromatic.

✿ Jun–Sep.

Daisy
Bellis perennis
Nóinín

Ht. 10cm. **Fls.** 15–25mm flower-heads, with yellow disc florets at centre surrounded by white, spreading, ray florets; solitary on erect, slender, leafless stem.

Lvs. Bright green, stalked, spoon-shaped, in extremely *low-growing* basal rosettes.

Hab. Lawns, short grasslands, roadsides. Widespread native perennial.

Fam. Daisy/Asteraceae.

☺ Ray florets can often be tinged with crimson.

✿✿✿ Feb–Oct.

Feverfew
Tanacetum parthenium
Lus deartán

Ht. 50cm. **Fls.** 10–12mm flower-heads, yellow disc florets & few broad, white ray florets, in loose, flat-topped clusters, on stiff, erect stems.

Lvs. Light green, alternate, oblong, pinnately lobed; lower leaves stalked, upper unstalked.

Hab. Grassy places, roadsides, cultivated places. Introduced perennial, more common in Ulster & Leinster, occasional elsewhere.

Fam. Daisy/Asteraceae.

☺ Feverfew is strongly aromatic

✿✿ Jun–Sep. 🏃

Oxeye Daisy
Leucanthemum vulgare
Nóinín mór

Ht. 60cm. **Fls.** 30–50mm
flower-heads, with yellow disc florets
at centre surrounded by white,
spreading, ray florets; no scales
between disc florets; on branched or
unbranched, ridged stems.

Lvs. Dark green, toothed; basal leaves
spoon-shaped, stalked; stem leaves are
pinnately lobed, stalkless & oblong.

Hab. Patch-forming on grass verges,
meadows, embankments, disturbed sites.
Widespread native perennial.

Fam. Daisy/Asteraceae.

☺ Overlapping involucral bracts with
dark purplish edges are at rear of
flower-head.

☺ AKA Dog Daisy

✿✿✿ May–Sep.

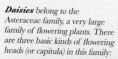

Daisies belong to the
Asteraceae family, a very large
family of flowering plants. There
are three basic kinds of flowering
heads (or capitula) in this family:

* *Radiate* – daisy-like, with
  disc florets in the middle &
  ray florets surrounding.

* *Discoid* – thistle-like, with
  disc or tubular florets only.

* *Ligulate* – dandelion-like,
  with ray florets only.

White Dead-nettle
Lamium album
Teanga mhín

Ht. 40cm. **Fls.** 25–30mm long,
2-lipped, hood-like upper lip very hairy,
lower lip toothed, sometimes streaked
green; in whorls in axis of upper leaves,
on square stems.

Lvs. Paired, coarsely toothed, oval to
heart-shape, lower leaves stalked, upper
short-stalked.

Hab. Roadsides, rivers & disturbed
ground. Common in NE & SE only.
Introduced perennial.

Fam. Dead-nettle/Lamiaceae

☺ Hairs on this plant are *non-stinging*

☺ Plant is faintly scented.

▶ Red & Cut-leaved Dead-nettle
(p. 186).

✿✿ Jan–Dec.

Small Nettle
Urtica urens
Neantóg bheag

Ht. 50cm. **Fls.** Tiny, creamy-white,
pendulous catkins in a short spike.

Lvs. Bright green, oval, sharp-
tipped, deeply-toothed, lower leaves
shorter than their stalks.

Hab. Arable, disturbed ground.
Introduced annual, scattered
throughout.

Fam. Nettle/Urticaceae.

☺ Male & female flowers are borne
on the same plant unlike those of
Common Nettle (p. 267) where
flowers are found on separate-sex
plants.

✿✿ Jun–Sep.

Yarrow
Achillea millefolium
Athair thalún

Ht. 50cm. **Fls.** 4–6mm yellowish-cream disc florets with white ray florets, often tinged deep pink; in dense, 6–10cm flat-topped umbel-like clusters; on erect, downy, furrowed stems.

Lvs. Dark green, feathery, finely cut into numerous pinnate divisions, basal & alternate.

Hab. Grassy places, hedgerows, meadows. Widespread native perennial

Fam. Daisy/Asteraceae.

☺ Entire plant is aromatic

✿✿✿ Jun–Nov.

Sneezewort
Achillea ptarmica
Lus corráin

Ht. 60cm. **Fls.** 12–20mm flower-heads of greenish-white disc florets with oval, white ray florets; in loose, few-flowered, branched clusters; on stiff, angular stems.

Lvs. Stalkless, lanceolate, undivided, finely toothed, pointed leaves.

Hab. Damp grassy places, marshes, usually acid soil. Native perennial, common in N half of Ireland, also E coast, N Kerry & County Clare.

Fam. Daisy/Asteraceae.

☺ This plant spreads on woody stolons.

✿✿ Jul–Sep.

Glassworts agg.
Salicornia agg.
Lus na gloine

Ht. 30cm. **Fls.** Minute, white tufts of *equal* size, appearing at stem junctions, in threes; cactus-like stems, succulent, erect, slender, waisted, swollen or beaded; initially green often turning red as they mature.

Lvs. Fused into stems, forming enlarged sheaths which encircle stems.

Hab. Coastal areas, on saltmarshes, intertidal mudflats. Scattered, locally abundant in coastal places. Native annuals.

Fam. Goosefoot/Amaranthaceae.

☺ Glassworts are a very difficult group of plants for an amateur to attempt to identify with only slight variations between a number of species in Ireland.

✿✿ Aug–Sep.

Perennial Glasswort
Sarcocornia perennis
Lus gloine buan

Ht. 30cm. **Fls.** Microscopic, yellow, in groups of 3, *central one larger*.

Lvs. Dark green, fused, on distinctive, slightly woody stems which become orange with age; very succulent, forming large patches on subterranean root-systems or rhizomes.

Hab. Creeping through lower muddy reaches of saltmarshes & also on firmer, sandy, mid-level parts. Extremely rare native perennial, only found on S coast of County Wexford.

Fam. Goosefoot/Amaranthaceae.

☺ This rare species is protected under the Flora Protection Order.

✿ Aug–Oct. ✚

Cherry Laurel
Prunus laurocerasus
Labhras silíní

Ht. 10m. **Fls.** 6–8mm with 5
well-separated white petals, dark-cream
centre with prominent stigma, circle of
stamens; in elongated, erect racemes; on
upright woody stems, green in first year.

Lvs. Evergreen, dark green, shiny,
leathery, oblong with small teeth.

Hab. Woodland, forming dense thickets.
Introduced shrub found commonly except
in Donegal, Sligo, Mayo.

Fam. Rose/Rosaceae.

☺ Classed as 'Potentially
Invasive', Cherry-laurel
contains cyanide.

✿✿ Apr–Jun. 🏃 ⚠ ⊘

White Comfrey
Symphytum orientale
Compar bán

Ht. 70cm. **Fls.** 10–18mm long, white,
tubular with straight corolla lobes; often
spotted with rusty marks; in coiled
clusters on erect, softly hairy, branched,
unwinged stems.

Lvs. Rough, veined, oval, pale green,
stalked, forming basal rosette in first
year; upper leaves narrow, tending to
clasp stem.

Hab. Waste ground, shady hedgerows,
open woodland. Uncommon,
introduced biennial or perennial.

Fam. Borage/Boraginaceae.

☺ AKA Soft Comfrey.

▶ Tuberous Comfrey (p. 140),
Common & Russian Comfreys (p. 242).

✿ Apr–May.

Japanese Knotweed
Fallopia japonica
Glúineach bhiorach

Ht. 2m. **Fls.** 5mm, 5 white-pink tepals, 8 stamens; in loose, branched, racemes from axis of upper leaves; on tall, erect, thicket-forming stems.

Lvs. Large (6–12cm), stalked, broad, triangular, truncated at base, hairless; on reddish, zigzagging stems.

Hab. Waste ground, riverbanks, railway embankments, roadsides. Widespread introduced perennial.

Fam. Knotweed/Polygonaceae.

☺ Classed as an 'Invasive Species'.

✿✿✿ Aug–Oct. 🏃‍♂️🌸

Russian-vine
Fallopia baldschuanica
Fíniún Rúiseach

Ht. 10m. **Fls.** 5–8mm long, 5-lobed white, tinged-greenish-pink; flowers hang on short stalks in branched, drooping clusters, 15cm long; flowers sometimes turn bright pink as fruit develops; on climbing stems which are woody below.

Lvs. Oval-triangular with heart-shaped bases, long leaf-stalk.

Hab. Casual garden discard, railway embankments. Introduced perennial, found in SE & E.

Fam. Knotweed/Polygonaceae.

☺ AKA Mile-a-minute.

✿ Jul–Oct. 🏃‍♂️

Narrow-leaved Helleborine
Cephalanthera longifolia
Cuaichín caol

Ht. 60cm. **Fls.** 12mm long, pure white, bell-shaped, with small bract; in loose spike of 3–20, each with orange spot at the base of the lip; each flower is stalked; on tall, erect stem.

Lvs. Numerous strap-shaped, dark green.

Hab. Edges of deciduous & wet marshy woods. Rare native perennial.

Fam. Orchid/ Orchidaceae.

☺ Rare, protected plant.

✿ May–Jun. ✚

*Members of the **Orchid** family (which includes **Helleborines**) have three petals & three sepals. Two identical petals are held within the flower, the third petal being the elaborate 'lip' or labellum. Sepals are to the rear of the flower, behind the petals, one on either side & one above, usually helping to form the 'hood' which protects the reproductive organs.*

O'Kelly's Spotted-orchid
Dactylorhiza fuchsii var. *okellyi*
Nuacht bhallach Uí Ceallaigh

Ht. 25cm. **Fls.** 8–12mm long, snow-white petals & sepals; lip is flat, unmarked with 3 deeply-cut lobes; in dense, tapering spike; on erect stem.

Lvs. Light green, long, narrow with shorter leaves on stem.

Hab. Calcareous grassland, limestone pavement. Rare, native perennial mainly found in the Burren.

Fam. Orchid/Orchidaceae.

☺ Flower is faintly scented.

▶ Common & Heath Spotted-orchids (p. 191)

✿ Jun–Aug.

Dense-flowered Orchid
Neotinea maculata
Magairlín glas

Ht. 20cm. **Fls.** Small, green-white, almost closed over with only lower, forked lip protruding from hood; 10–30 flowers in tightly-packed spike 2–6cm long; on stout stem.

Lvs. 2–3 narrow at base with smaller – sometimes spotted – leaves hugging the stem.

Hab. Limestone pavements, dunes & short calcareous grassland. Rare, native perennial, confined to few locations in W. half of Ireland.

Fam. Orchid/Orchidaceae.

✿ Apr–May. ✚

Autumn Lady's-tresses
Spiranthes spiralis
Cúilín Muire

Ht. 12cm. **Fls.** 5–7mm, white, fragrant, lower lip or labellum is greenish; without spur; single spiral of flowers in downy spike; lower flowers bloom first; on erect, grey-green stem.

Lvs. Basal rosette of small, blue-green leaves, withering early; few small scale-like leaves on stem.

Hab. Limestone grassland, coastal grassland, dunes & short turf. Native perennial, locally common in S & W.

Fam. Orchid/Orchidaceae.

☺ Scented flower.

✿✿ Aug–Sep. ⊞

Irish Lady's-tresses
Spiranthes romanzoffiana
Cúilín gaelach

Ht. 25cm. **Fls.** Small, green-white, tubular, open-mouthed, in 3 short, tight, close-together spirals; each flower backed by sharp-pointed, green sheath; on upright stem.

Lvs. Linear-lanceolate at base, few stem leaves.

Hab. Lake margins, wet, peaty bogs. Rare native perennial found only occasionally in W, S & N.

Fam. Orchid/Orchidaceae.

☺ An endangered species worthy of our protection.

✿ Jul–Aug. ⊞

Small White Orchid
Pseudorchis albida
Magairlín bán

Ht. 20cm. **Fls.** 2–3mm long, greenish-creamy-white; tepals forming short hood & 3-lobed, down-turned lip, centre lobe slightly longer than other two; flowers appear to be bell-shaped; with downward-curving short spur; in dense cylindrical spike on erect stem.

Lvs. Oblong-lanceolate lower leaves, unspotted; narrow, short stem leaves.

Hab. Mountain grassland, rock ledges. Rare native perennial.

Fam. Orchid/Orchidaceae.

☺ Vanilla scented.

☺ Rare protected species.

✿ Jun–Jul. ✚

Bird's-nest Orchid
Neottia nidus-avis
Magairlín neide éin

Ht. 35cm. **Fls.** 10mm long, honey-brown, 2-lobed lip; 20–80 in dense spike; sweet, sickly aroma; on pale, erect stem.

Lvs. Stem-clasping scales in place of leaves.

Hab. Deep humus in beech & oak woodland. Rare native perennial found only occasionally in W, S & N.

Fam. Orchid/Orchidaceae.

☺ This species lacks chlorophyll, obtaining its nutrition as a *saphrophyte*, feeding on dead leaves.

✿ May–Jul. ✚

Lesser Butterfly-orchid
Platanthera bifolia
Magairlín beag an fhéileacáin

Ht. 30cm. **Fls.** 10–15mm,
greenish-white with long narrow lip,
spreading 'wings', long, *slender* spur;
pollen sacs *parallel* to one another; up
to 25 on erect spike.

Lvs. Oval pair at base, few smaller
on stem.

Hab. Limestone & heathy
grassland, open woodland. Native
perennial, locally common in W &
N, occasional elsewhere.

Fam. Orchid/Orchidaceae

☺ Flowers emit sweet scent at
night attracting their primary
pollinators – evening & night-
flying moths.

✿ May–Jul. 🞣

Greater Butterfly-orchid
Platanthera chlorantha
Magairlín mór an fhéileacáin

Ht. 50cm. **Fls.** 10–20mm, greenish-
white with long narrow lip, spreading
'wings', long spur, becoming *wider* &
slightly greener towards tip; pollen
sacs *converging above in inverted V-shape*;
up to 25 on erect spike.

Lvs. Broad, ribbed, oval pair at base,
few smaller on stem.

Hab. Limestone & heathy grassland,
open woodland, cutaway bogs.
Native perennial, more common in
N half of Ireland than S.

Fam. Orchid/Orchidaceae.

☺ Flowers have a weaker scent than
those of Lesser Butterfly-orchid.

✿ May–Jul. 🞣

Large-flowered Evening-primrose
Oenothera glazioviana
Coinneal oíche mhór

Ht. 1.8m. **Fls.** 6–8cm, 4 soft, floppy, wide petals; style longer than filaments; 4 narrow, red-striped sepals twisted into yellow point, falling back as flower fades; in racemes on stems which are densely covered with tiny red, bulbous-based hairs.

Lvs. Elliptic, wavy-edged, often twisted.

Hab. Quarries, roadsides, sandy soil. Introduced biennial found mainly in SE.

Fam. Willowherb/Onagraceae.

☺ Flowers often open shortly after dusk, only lasting 2 nights.

✿✿ Jun–Sep. 🏃

Greater Celandine
Chelidonium majus
Garra bhuí

Ht. 80cm. **Fls.** 2–3cm, 4 well-separated petals, numerous stamens, 2 hairy sepals; in loose umbels of 2–6 on brittle, hairy stems which, when broken, are found to contain yellow/orange latex.

Lvs. Pale grey-green, pinnately lobed, round segments.

Hab. Garden escape, naturalised in shaded places, along old walls, hedgerows. Introduced perennial, scattered through eastern part of Ireland.

Fam. Poppy/Papaveraceae.

☺ Not related to Lesser Celandine (p. 108).

✿✿ Apr–Oct. 🏃

Yellow Horned-poppy
Glaucium flavum
Caillichín na trá

Ht. 90cm. **Fls.** 6–8cm, 4 overlapping
orange-yellow petals, numerous stamens;
2 sepals fall as soon as flower opens;
solitary on stout, grey-green, fleshy stems.

Lvs. Grey-green, fleshy, lobed, upper
clasping stem; basal leaves deeply
pinnate, rough.

Hab. Coastal shingle, beaches &
unstable sea-cliffs. Native
biennial or perennial.
Occasional on E & S coasts.

Fam. Poppy/
Papaveraceae.

☺ 30cm long, curved
capsules containing seeds explain the
'horn' in this species name.

✿ Jun–Sep.

Welsh Poppy
Meconopsis cambrica
Poipín Breatnach

Ht. 50cm. **Fls.** 4–8cm, 4
overlapping, bright yellow
petals; at centre of each flower is
circle of yellow stamens; borne
solitarily on slender, almost
hairless stems.

Lvs. Long-stalked, divided into
coarsely toothed lobes.

Hab. Mountains, damp places,
shady woods. Native perennial
in some areas, garden escape in
others; occasional in N & E.

Fam. Poppy/Papaveraceae.

☺ Seeds are borne in ribbed
capsules with slits for distribution.

✿✿ Jun–Aug.

Medium-flowered Winter-cress
Barbarea intermedia
Treabhach meánach

Ht. 80cm. **Fls.** 5–6mm, in clustered, terminal heads; on ridged, hairless erect stems.

Lvs. Shiny, dark green, *all lobed*; basal leaves have 3–5 pairs lateral lobes.

Hab. Waste ground, damp places. Introduced perennial, local in NE & SE.

Fam. Cabbage/Brassicaceae.

☺ Seeds are in long, narrow, 4-sided pods.

✿✿ Mar–Aug.

*For more information on the **Cabbage** family, see p. 15.*

Winter-cress
Barbarea vulgaris
Treabhach

Ht. 90cm. **Fls.** 7–9mm, in dense, terminal heads which elongate in fruit; on upright, hairless stems.

Lvs. Shiny, dark green; lower stem leaves pinnately lobed with end lobe large & oval; *upper leaves undivided*.

Hab. Damp places, laneways. Widespread native perennial.

Fam. Cabbage/Brassicaceae.

☺ Seeds are in long, narrow, 4-sided pods pressed closely to stems.

✿✿✿ May–Aug.

Hedge Mustard
Sisymbrium officinale
Lus an óir

Ht. 80cm. **Fls.** 3mm, 4
well-separated petals; on
stiff, erect stems, in terminal
clusters which elongate as
fruits develop.

Lvs. Lower leaves stalked,
pinnate with end lobe largest;
upper leaves narrow, unstalked.

Hab. Waste ground,
hedgerows, disturbed soil.
Widespread native annual or
biennial.

Fam. Cabbage/Brassicaceae.

☺ Fruits cylindrical, pressed
close to stem.

✿✿✿ May–Oct.

Treacle-mustard
Erysimum cheiranthoides
Coinneal leighis

Ht. 70cm. **Fls.** 6–10mm, petals longer
than sepals; in flat racemes which stretch
out as plant matures & seeds develop; on
erect, square, branching stems, covered in
short, white, appressed hairs.

Lvs. Shallowly-toothed, dark, lanceolate,
in basal rosette which dies off before
flower blooms; also upper narrow,
alternate leaves which persist.

Hab. Arable field margins, waste
ground. Introduced annual,
occasional in centre of Ireland.

Fam. Cabbage/Brassicaceae.

☺ Seeds are borne in
long-stalked, long, narrow
pods.

✿✿ Jun–Sep.

Creeping Yellow-cress
Rorippa sylvestris
Biolar buí reatha

Ht. 50cm. **Fls.** 5–6mm, deep yellow, petals *twice length* of sepals; in terminal heads on *solid* stems.

Lvs. Shiny, deeply-divided, pinnate, with lanceolate lobes.

Hab. Damp meadows, riverbanks. Scarce, native perennial.

Fam. Cabbage/Brassicaceae.

☺ Seeds are in narrow, elliptical pods.

✿ Jun–Oct.

Annual Wall-rocket
Diplotaxis muralis
Ruachán buí

Ht. 60cm. **Fls.** 10–15mm, with 4 rounded petals; arranged alternately up erect, usually hairy, stem.

Lvs. Hairless, waxy, mostly basal, pinnately lobed.

Hab. Sandy soil, waste ground. Scattered, introduced annual found mainly in E Leinster & near Shannon estuary.

Fam. Cabbage/Brassicaceae.

☺ Very strong, unpleasant smell is released when leaves are crushed.

☺ AKA Wall Rocket & Stinkweed.

☺ Seeds are in 2 rows in long, stalked, cylindrical pods.

✿ May–Sep.

Wallflower
Erysimum cheiri
Lus an bhalla

Ht. 60cm. **Fls.** 25mm, 4 broad, orange-yellow petals; in clusters which elongate as fruits develop; on stiff, erect stems, woody at the bottom of this bushy plant.

Lvs. Alternate, oblong-lanceolate; upper leaves narrower than lower.

Hab. Old walls, dry limestone rocks, embankments. Scattered, introduced perennial.

Fam. Cabbage/Brassicaceae.

☺ A garden escape with fragrant flowers.

☺ Typical flower of the Cabbage family.

✿✿ Apr–Aug. 🏃

Sea Radish
Raphanus raphanistrum ssp. *maritimus*
Meacan mara

Ht. 60cm. **Fls.** 20mm, 4 veined petals; in loose racemes on rough, hairy stems.

Lvs. Pinnate, toothed lower leaves with large terminal lobe.

Hab. Coastal shingle, sand & grassland. Native annual common except NW.

Fam. Cabbage/Brassicaceae.

☺ Seeds are in pods with up to 5 *beaded* segments.

▶ Wild Radish (p. 21).

✿✿ May–Jul.

87

Rape
Brassica napus
Ráib

Ht. 1.5m. **Fls.** 15–30mm, in long racemes, on slightly bristly, branched stems.

Lvs. Grey-green; basal leaves lobed, stem leaves clasping.

Hab. Cultivated as crop but frequently escapes into arable land, waste ground, roadsides. Introduced annual or biennial, common in S half of country.

Fam. Cabbage/Brassicaceae.

☺ Seedpods are cylindrical, with prominent slender beaks.

✿✿ Apr–Sep.

Charlock
Sinapis arvensis
Praiseach bhuí

Ht. 1.5m. **Fls.** 15–20mm, 4 unnotched yellow petals, in dense, terminal clusters; sepals often down-turned; on bristly, often dark red or purple stems.

Lvs. Lower stalked with large terminal lobe, few small upper leaves unlobed.

Hab. Arable, waste ground. Widespread annual, possibly introduced.

Fam. Cabbage/Brassicaceae.

☺ Seeds are in short cylindrical pods with *prominent* beaks.

✿✿✿ Apr–Oct.

White Mustard
Sinapis alba
Sceallagach

Ht. 1.5m. **Fls.** 15–25mm, 4 regular petals, 4 spreading sepals, 6 stamens of which 4 are long & 2 are short; in elongating raceme.

Lvs. Alternate, stalked, coarsely hairy, pinnately divided, terminal lobe large.

Hab. Arable, waste ground. Scattered, introduced annual, most common in Cork/Waterford area.

Fam. Cabbage/Brassicaceae.

☺ Distinctive seedpods are cylindrical with flattened beak & *white* hairs.

✿✿ May–Sep.

Lady's Bedstraw
Galium verum | Boladh cnis

Ht. 30cm. **Fls.** 2–3mm, 4-lobed, star-shaped, golden-yellow; in dense, branched panicles; on round stems with 4 lines of hairs.

Lvs. Narrow, hairless, dark green, with down-rolled margins, in whorls of 8–12.

Hab. Dry grassland, roadsides, banks. Widespread native perennial.

Fam. Bedstraw/Rubiaceae.

☺ Smells fragrantly of hay.

▶ Bedstraws (pp. 12 & 13).

✿✿✿ Jun–Sep.

Tormentil
Potentilla erecta
Néalfartach

Ht. 30cm. **Fls.** 7–15mm, 4 slightly notched, bright yellow petals; solitary on slender stalks, *not rooting* at nodes.

Lvs. Downy, unstalked, trifoliate, with 2 large stipules at base making the leaf seem 5-lobed; basal rosette *dies back early*.

Hab. Grassy places, meadows, bogs, heaths, woodland. Widespread, native perennial.

Fam. Rose/Rosaceae.

☺ Similar to Trailing Tormentil but that species has *rooting nodes*.

☺ Do not confuse with Creeping Cinquefoil (p. 100) & Silverweed (p. 101) which *each have 5 petals*.

✿✿✿ May–Sep.

Trailing Tormentil
Potentilla anglica
Néalfartach shraoilleach

Ht. 25cm. **Fls.** 14–18mm, 4 (sometimes 5) slightly notched petals; on long stems which *root at nodes*.

Lvs. Hairy, upper short-stalked, lower leaves longer; *basal rosette persists.*

Hab. Coastal grassland, paths. Widespread native perennial.

Fam. Rose/Rosaceae.

☺ Main difference between Tormentil & Trailing Tormentil is that the *latter roots at the nodes* on creeping stems or stolons.

☺ Flowers of Trailing Tormentil are slightly larger than those of Tormentil.

✿✿✿ June–Sep.

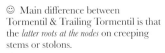

Marsh-marigold
Caltha palustris
Lus buí Bealtaine

Ht. 25cm. **Fls.** 10–50mm, 5–8 golden, spreading, petal-like sepals surrounding numerous golden stamens, with green carpels at centre; in loose, branched clusters; on erect, stout, hollow stems which rise from rhizomes.

Lvs. Hairless, mainly basal, deep green, kidney-shaped, fleshy; increasing in size after plant has flowered.

Hab. Wet woodland, ditches, stream margins, bogs, fens, marshes. Widespread, native perennial.

Fam. Buttercup/Ranunculaceae.

☺ AKA Goldilocks.

☺ Not related to Corn Marigold (p. 125).

✿✿✿ Mar–Jul. ⚠

Lesser Spearwort
Ranunculus flammula
Glasair léana bheag

Ht. 50cm. **Fls.** 7–20mm, 5 glossy petals; in very loose clusters, on furrowed, purple-tinged, hollow, branching, sprawling stem.

Lvs. Basal oval, stem-leaves spear-shaped, usually untoothed.

Hab. Damp places, lake margins, ditches, riversides. Widespread native perennial.

Fam. Buttercup/Ranunculaceae.

☺ Sometimes prostrate, the stems root at the nodes.

☺ Fruit is a cluster of achenes.

✿✿✿ Jun–Oct. ⚠

Meadow Buttercup
Ranunculus acris
Fearbán féir

Ht. 1m. **Fls.** 15–25mm, shiny, *cup-shaped*, with numerous stamens; sepals closely pressed to petals; on long, graceful, branched, *round*, unfurrowed flower stalks.

Lvs. Deeply divided, with 3–7 lobes – central lobe having no separate stalk.

Hab. Damp meadows, ditches, roadsides, woodland. Widespread native perennial.

Fam. Buttercup/Ranunculaceae.

☺ Flowers are smaller than those of Creeping Buttercup & plant is much taller.

✿✿✿ Apr–Oct. ⚠

Creeping Buttercup
Ranunculus repens
Fearbán

Ht. 50cm. **Fls.** 20–30mm, shiny, *saucer-shaped*, numerous stamens at centre; sepals pressed closely to petals; on *square* flower stalk; on creeping stems which root at nodes.

Lvs. Hairy; basal & lower stem leaves 3-lobed, central lobe stalked.

Hab. Lawns, grassy places, disturbed & cultivated land. Widespread native perennial.

Fam. Buttercup/Ranunculaceae.

☺ Leaves are good means of making identification.

☺ Usually, low-growing compared to Meadow Buttercup.

✿✿✿ May–Sep. ⚠

Bulbous Buttercup
Ranunculus bulbosus
Tuile thalún

Ht. 50cm. **Fls.** 20–30mm, 5 bright-yellow petals, sepals which *fold down fully* once flower is fully opened; on branched, ridged stems.

Lvs. Basal leaves stalked, 3-lobed; narrow-lobed upper leaves.

Hab. Dry grassland, sandhills. Native perennial, abundant in most areas.

Fam. Buttercup/Ranunculaceae.

☺ Markedly swollen, bulb-like stem-base underground.

*Members of the **Buttercup** family mainly have yellow or white, 5-petalled flowers. Leaves can be either entire or divided. Most are very poisonous.*

✿✿✿ Mar–Jul. ⚠

Celery-leaved Buttercup
Ranunculus sceleratus
Toircheas fiáin

Ht. 50cm. **Fls.** 5–10mm, pale yellow, shiny, round petals surrounding circle of stamens & green, oblong cluster of carpels; reflexed sepals as long as petals; on stout, furrowed, hollow stems.

Lvs. Yellow-green, basal are stalked, deeply 3-lobed, lobes further segmented into narrow divisions; upper leaves shiny, divided into 2–3 lobes.

Hab. Ditches, marshes, stagnant water. Native annual, scattered throughout with exception of Connacht.

Fam. Buttercup/Ranunculaceae.

☺ Fruit is a cluster of achenes.

✿✿ May–Sep. ⚠

Square-stalked St John's-wort
Hypericum tetrapterum
Beathnua fireann

Ht. 80cm. **Fls.** 20mm, pale yellow, *narrow* petals; sepals narrow, pointed *without* black dots; many stamens; in broad panicles on branched, square, *narrowly-winged*, erect stems.

Lvs. Oval with translucent dots.

Hab. Damp ditches, marshy places. Widespread native perennial.

Fam. St John's-wort/ Hypericaceae.

☺ Look for *4-winged* stem & a *translucent* network of veins on leaves.

✿✿✿ Jun–Sep.

*Members of the **St John's-wort** family have stalkless, opposite leaves, often with translucent dots & tiny dots on petals & sepal margins.*

Perforate St John's-Wort
Hypericum perforatum
Lus na Maighdine Muire

Ht. 75cm. **Fls.** 25mm, rich yellow petals with *tiny black dots* or streaks on margins, sometimes pointed; numerous stamens in 5 bundles; sepals also edged with dots; in terminal panicles on round stem with *2 opposite, ridged lines*.

Lvs. Opposite, ovate to linear, hairless, blunt with numerous translucent dots & black gland dots.

Hab. Grassy places, open woodland, road verges. Native perennial more common in E half of country.

Fam. St John's-wort/Hypericaceae.

☺ Network of veins on leaves *not translucent*.

✿✿✿ May–Sep.

Slender St John's-wort
Hypericum pulchrum
Beathnua baineann

Ht. 60cm. **Fls.** 15mm, deep yellow petals with *red spots*, dark marginal dots; reverse of petals red-veined; *sepals also dotted* on margins; prominent, long, erect stamens with orange anthers; on slender, round, reddish stems.

Lvs. Paired, hairless, oval, with translucent dots.

Hab. Heaths, mountains, mainly acid soil. Widespread native perennial.

Fam. St John's-wort/Hypericaceae.

☺ Hand lens recommended.

✿✿✿ Jul–Aug.

Trailing St John's-wort
Hypericum humifusum
Beathnua sraoilleach

Ht. Prostrate.
Fls. 8–10mm, pale yellow petals with little *black dots* along their margins; petals are 1.5 x length of sepals; sepals unequal, also with black glands; in leafy cymes on *2-ridged* stems.

Lvs. Elliptic with translucent dots; in pairs.

Hab. Bare, acid heaths, open ground. Native perennial, scattered throughout except in central Ireland.

Fam. St John's-wort/Hypericaceae.

☺ Flowers only open in *full sunshine*. Easily overlooked plant.

✿✿ Jun–Sep.

Tutsan

Hypericum androsaemum
Meas torc allta

Ht. 80cm. **Fls.** 15–25mm, 5 oval petals; stamens as long as petals, in 5 bundles; in few-flowered inflorescence on erect, 2-edged, usually red, stems.

Lvs. Oval, hairless, stalkless, often red-tinged, with *translucent dots*; in opposite pairs.

Hab. Woods, hedgerows, limestone pavement. Widespread native perennial.

Fam. St John's-wort/ Hypericaceae.

☺ 5 unequal sepals persist behind fruit which is a large, red berry, ripening black.

✿✿✿ Jun–Aug.

Yellow Pimpernel

Lysimachia nemorum
Lus Cholm Cille

Ht. Creeping to 40cm. **Fls.** 10–15mm, star-shaped, with 5 petals fused together near base; solitary on stems arising from upper leaf-axils; *pointed* sepals not overlapping; on creeping, hairless, slender stems, rooting at intervals.

Lvs. Evergreen, oval, *pointed*, opposite.

Hab. Shady places, woodland, damp mountain pastures. Native perennial common except in centre of Ireland.

Fam. Primrose/Primulaceae.

☺ Could be confused with Creeping-jenny (see opposite page).

▶ Bog Pimpernel (p. 157) & Scarlet Pimpernel (p. 200).

✿✿✿ May–Aug.

Creeping-jenny
Lysimachia nummularia | Lus an dá phingin

Ht. Creeping to 50cm. **Fls.** 15–24mm,
cup-shaped with 5 pointed lobes, 5 *broad* sepals;
on long, hairless, slender stalks arising from leaf
axils; plant rooting at intervals on stolons.

Lvs. Evergreen, smooth, round-oval, *blunt*,
short-stalked, paired all along stem; covered in
tiny, black dots.

Hab. Damp meadows, near rivers, wet
ditches, often submerged in pools. Introduced
perennial, more common in N than S.

Fam. Primrose/Primulaceae. ✿✿ Jun–Sep.

Yellow Loosestrife
Lysimachia vulgaris | Breallán léana

Ht. 1m. **Fls.** 15–20mm, with 5
pointed lobes; orange margins to
sepals; in pyramidal clusters on erect
woolly stems.

Lvs. Opposite, ovate-lanceolate in whorls
of 2–4, *often dotted black*.

Hab. Riverbanks, lakeshores, fens. Native
perennial found mainly in N & NW.

Fam. Primrose/Primulaceae.

☺ Not related to Purple-loosestrife
(p. 241).

✿✿ Jun–Aug.

Dotted Loosestrife
Lysimachia punctata | Breallán dlúth

Ht. 1.2m. **Fls.** 15–20mm, in clusters on
short stalks in axils of stem leaves.

Lvs. Opposite, downy, ovate, *never black-
dotted*, with hairy margins.

Hab. Waste ground, grassland.
Introduced perennial, occasional.

Fam. Primrose/Primulaceae.

✿ Jun–Sep. 🏃

Cowslip
Primula veris
Bainne bó bleachtáin

Ht. 25cm. **Fls.** 8–15mm, 5 joined, notched, deep yellow petals, orange markings at centre of flower; pale green bell-shaped calyx; in drooping, one-sided clusters on downy stems.

Lvs. Hairy, very wrinkled, tapering to basal rosette.

Hab. Roadsides, woodland. Native perennial, widespread across central part of Ireland, less frequent in N & S.

Fam. Primrose/Primulaceae.

✿✿✿ Apr–May.

False Oxlip
Primula x polyantha
Baisleach bréige

Ht. 20cm. **Fls.** 15–20mm, pale Primrose yellow, 5 lobed, notched petals, orange marks at centre of flower; long, pale green calyx with folds similar to Cowslips; in umbels (*not one-sided* as in Cowslips) of 8–20, on downy stems.

Lvs. Oval, crinkled, tapering into basal rosette.

Hab. Grassland, woodlands, hedgerows. Infrequent, scattered native perennial.

Fam. Primrose/Primulaceae

☺ False Oxlip is a *naturally occurring hybrid* between Cowslip & Primrose, only found where both parents occur.

✿ Mar–May.

Primrose
Primula vulgaris
Sabhaircín

Ht. 20cm. **Fls.** 20–30mm, notched, pale yellow petals, deep yellow towards centre of flower; pointed sepals joined halfway to form calyx tube; solitary on hairy, leafless stalks.

Lvs. Long, oval, crinkled, tapering quite gradually into centre of basal rosette.

Hab. Woods, grassy banks, roadsides. Widespread native perennial.

Fam. Primrose/Primulaceae.

✿✿✿ Feb–May.

*Some **Primrose & Cowslip** plants have flowers which are 'thrum-eyed', others are 'pin-eyed'. Thrum-eyed (left) short stigma, longer anthers: Pin-eyed (right) long stigma, shorter anthers. Pollen adheres to different parts of insects depending on which 'model' they visit, transferring it to other form of flower, thus ensuring cross-pollination.*

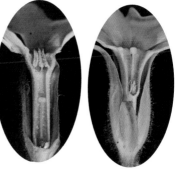

Creeping Cinquefoil
Potentilla reptans
Cúig mhéar Mhuire

Ht. 20cm. **Fls.** 15–25mm, 5 heart-shaped petals, 5 sepals & 5-pointed epicalyx; solitary on slender, creeping stems.

Lvs. Hairless, long-stalked, palmate with 5, toothed leaflets; their stalks arise from nodes at which point plant sends down roots.

Hab. Sand-dunes, grassland, hedge banks, waste or cultivated ground. Native perennial, widespread in all but extreme NE.

Fam. Rose/Rosaceae.

☺ Flowers similar to Trailing Tormentil (p. 90) & Silverweed (p. 101) but leaves are quite different.

✿✿✿ Jun–Sep.

Shrubby Cinquefoil
Potentilla fruticosa
Tor cúigmhéarach

Ht. 1m. **Fls.** 20mm, saucer-shaped; with 5 but occasionally 6, round, unnotched petals; in loose clusters on woody stems, often with flaky bark.

Lvs. Untoothed, grey-green, pinnate with 3–7 lanceolate leaflets.

Hab. Around turloughs & other rocky areas subject to flooding. Rare native shrub, found mainly in the Burren & County Galway.

Fam. Rose/Rosaceae.

☺ Plants dioecious, i.e. they are either male or female, former *bearing* stamens, latter *without* stamens.

☺ Growing around turloughs, this shrub is often submerged.

✿ May–Jun. ⊞

Silverweed
Potentilla anserina
Briosclán

Ht. Creeping to 20cm. **Fls.**
15–20mm,
5 unnotched petals, 5 sepals half
length of petals; also epicalyx;
solitary on long, erect, leafless stems
arising from axils.

Lvs. Distinctive, hairy, pinnate with
15–25 sharply-toothed alternate
leaflets, underside more silvery than
upper.

Hab. Damp places, dunes,
grassland. Widespread native
perennial.

Fam. Rose/Rosaceae.

☺ Spreads by rooting down
at nodes on creeping stolons,
thus creating new plants.

✿✿✿ May–Aug.

Wood Avens
Geum urbanum
Macall coille

Ht. 60cm. **Fls.** 8–20mm, 5 spreading
petals surrounding ring of stamens &
dense cluster of carpels; 5 sepals visible
between petals, backed by epicalyx;
solitary on downy stem, initially erect but
drooping when bud has opened.

Lvs. Hairy, toothed; basal leaves pinnate
with 3–6 pairs leaflets & large terminal
leaflet; stem leaves 3-lobed; leafy stipules
on stem.

Hab. Hedgerows, shady places.
Widespread native perennial.

Fam. Rose/Rosaceae.

☺ Fruits bur-like with little red
hooked spines.

☺ AKA Herb Bennet. ✿✿✿ May–Aug.

Biting Stonecrop
Sedum acre
Grafán na gcloch

Ht. 10cm. **Fls.** 12–15mm, bright yellow, star-shaped, with yellow anthers, in small terminal clusters on fleshy, frequently-rooting stems.

Lvs. Alternate, egg-shaped, succulent, crowded on short stems.

Hab. Spreads widely, forming mats on sand dunes & old walls. Frequent native, evergreen perennial.

Fam. Stonecrop/Crassulaceae.

☺ Leaves have a peppery taste.

▶ White & English Stonecrops (p. 32).

✿✿ May–Jul.

Procumbent Yellow-sorrel
Oxalis corniculata
Seamsóg bhuí

Ht. Prostrate. **Fls.** 6–10mm, bright yellow, usually 5 petalled, on slender, creeping, rooting stems.

Lvs. Trifoliate with 3 heart-shaped lobes, slightly larger than flowers.

Hab. Garden escape which grows abundantly over dry, bare ground; now an extremely persistent garden weed. Introduced perennial, mainly confined to SE.

Fam. Wood-sorrel/Oxalidaceae.

✿ May–Sep. 🏃

☺ *Oxalis corniculata* var. *atropurpurea*, with similar flowers but dark bronze leaves, is also found in Ireland, generally as a garden escape. Somewhat invasive, it tends to prefer a greenhouse habitat. Also known to climb.

Hoary Rock-rose
Helianthemum oelandicum ssp.
piloselloides
Grianrós liath

Ht. Prostrate to 25cm.
Fls. 10–15mm, bright yellow,
crinkly petals, slightly reflexed,
surrounding prominent bundle
of stamens; in small clusters on
creeping, pinkish stems.

Lvs. Opposite, small, very
narrow, dark green, silvery
beneath, without stipules.

Hab. Limestone, dry rocky
places. Very rare native perennial
found only in the Burren.

Fam. Rose/Rosaceae.

☺ *Helianthemum* means sunflower
and, in common with other
rock-roses, this species only opens
when the sun is shining.

✿ May–Jul. ⊞

This is one of our many rare or
very vulnerable plants, afforded a
degree of protection by law & is
most worthy of safeguarding for
future generations to enjoy.

Sand Pansy
Viola tricolor ssp. *curtisii*
Goirmín duimhche

Ht. 12cm. **Fls.** 12–25mm, 2 top petals, slightly overlapping, 2 wing-like side petals & single larger petal which extends backward into a short spur; dark lines lead insects into centre of flower over which is translucent fringe; on erect, spreading stems.

Lvs. Alternate, toothed, oval with heart-shaped base & pinnately-lobed, leaf-like stipules.

Hab. Dry grassland, coastal sandy soil. Native perennial, local to coastal districts.

Fam. Violet/Violaceae.

☺ ▶ Field Pansy (p. 42) & Wild Pansy (p. 225).

✿✿ Apr–Aug.

Monkeyflower
Mimulus guttatus
Buí an bhogaigh

Ht. 50cm. **Fls.** 25–45mm, rich yellow, 2-lipped, upper lip divided in 2, lower divided in 3; centre lobe has few small dark red spots, mostly towards mouth of flower; also has 2 bulges covered in small, upright bristles; in open terminal clusters on upright, square stems.

Lvs. Paired, oval, toothed.

Hab. Damp soil, streams, rivers, ponds, lake margins. Introduced perennial, infrequent, mainly in S.

Fam. Monkeyflower/ Phrymaceae.

☺ Species from S. America now naturalised in some areas.

✿ Jun–Sep. 🏃

Honeysuckle
Lonicera periclymenum
Féithleann

Ht. 5m. **Fls.** 20–50mm long, slender, trumpet-shaped corolla with 4-lobed upper lip, 1-lobed lower lip with protruding stamens; cream-yellow when in flower, pink in bud; in whorls on twining, woody stems.

Lvs. Opposite, oval, untoothed, grey-green.

Hab. Hedgerows, scrub, woodland. Widespread native climbing shrub.

Fam. Honeysuckle/Caprifoliaceae.

☺ Beautifully fragrant.

☺ Fruits are shining red berries.

☺ AKA Woodbine.

✿✿✿ Jun–Aug.

Henbane
Hyoscyamus niger
Gafann

Ht. 80cm. **Fls.** 20–30mm, cream-yellow, 5-lobed, trumpet-shaped with tracery of purple veins leading into dark-purple centre; in clusters on stickily hairy stems.

Lvs. Oval, pointed; lower leaves toothed, alternate upper leaves clasping stem.

Hab. Sandy, coastal sites, waste & disturbed ground. Rare, native annual or biennial, found in E & SE coastal areas.

Fam. Nightshade/Solanaceae.

☺ Strong, unpleasant & sickly smelling, the entire plant is poisonous.

✿ Jun–Aug. ⊞ ⚠

Wall Lettuce
Mycelis muralis
Leitís bhalla

Ht. 80cm. **Fls.** Flower-heads 7–10mm, comprising 5 bright-yellow ray florets; beneath flower-heads is a ring of outer spreading bracts, usually red; in open panicles on angular, leggy, branched, dark-red stems.

Lvs. Pinnate, toothed, end lobe triangular, upper leaves clasping stems have rounded, toothed lobes.

Hab. Rocks, walls, limestone pavement. Introduced biennial or perennial, scattered & found mainly in the Burren & County Galway.

Fam. Daisy/Asteraceae.

☺ Leaves tend to have a reddish tint especially towards autumn.

☺ Classed as 'Potentially Invasive'.

✿ Jun–Sep. ⬣

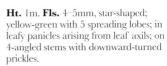

Wild Madder
Rubia peregrina
Garbhlus na Boirne

Ht. 1m. **Fls.** 4–5mm, star-shaped; yellow-green with 5 spreading lobes; in leafy panicles arising from leaf axils; on 4-angled stems with downward-turned prickles.

Lvs. *Bronze initially*, turning green; lanceolate, prickles at margins & on rear of midrib; in whorls of 4–6.

Hab. Mainly coastal, scrub, hedgerows. Native perennial found in the Burren, Limerick, Cork, Waterford & Wexford.

Fam. Bedstraw/Rubiaceae

☺ Fruits are black berries.

✿ Jun–Aug.

Yellow Water-lily
Nuphar lutea
Cabhán abhann

Ht. Aquatic. **Fls.** 6cm; 5 or 6 large sepals, overlapping, green-yellow exteriors initially, turning yellow, smaller yellow petals forming circle inside sepals; numerous stamens; on fleshy stems that rise above water's surface.

Lvs. Large heart-shaped to oval (up to 40cm across) with overlapping basal lobes carpeting water's surface; other leaves thin, translucent & submerged.

Hab. Canals, rivers, pools, lakes, slow-moving, unpolluted water. Native perennial, more frequent in N.

Fam. Water-lily/Nymphaeaceae.

☺ Fruit is shaped like brandy-bottle; smells of alcohol, attracting insects.

▶ White Water-lily (p. 50).   ✿✿ Jun–Sep.

Yellow Iris
Iris pseudacorus
Feileastram

Ht. 1m. **Fls.** 8–10cm, 3 small, erect upper petals & 3 larger, downward-curved petals, marked with oval of red-purple lines; erect buds of twisted, closely-folded petals; in clusters of 2–3 with spathe below; on thick, leafy stems.

Lvs. Bright-green, flattened, sword-shaped, with raised midrib.

Hab. Clump-forming plant found in wet places, river margins, lakes, bogs. Widespread native perennial.

Fam. Iris/Iridaceae.

☺ AKA Yellow Flag, this is Ireland's only native Iris.

✿✿✿ May–Jul.

Yellow-wort
Blackstonia perfoliata
Dréimire buí

Ht. 30cm. **Fls.** 10–15mm, 6–8 yellow petals, deeply divided sepal tube, in loose clusters on branched, erect stems.

Lvs. Distinctive, grey-green, in fused-together ovate pairs; also oval leaves at base of stem.

Hab. Bare, sandy soil, limestone grassland, dunes. Native annual, frequent in rough, wide diagonal band from Wexford to Galway.

Fam. Gentian/Gentianaceae.

☺ This leaf arrangement is termed 'perfoliate' as the stem appears to pass through the middle of a single leaf.

✿✿ Jun–Oct.

Lesser Celandine
Ficaria verna
Grán arcáin

Ht. 25cm. **Fls.** 20–30mm, 8–12 shiny, narrow, yellow petals; petals pale as they age; back of petals is brown with yellow rim; 3 sepals; solitary on long, hairless stems arising from root.

Lvs. Mostly basal, fleshy, dark-green, heart-shaped with blotches & wavy margins.

Hab. Woodland, damp grassy places, roadsides, ditches, streams, river margins. Native perennial, widespread throughout except in N Connacht.

Fam. Buttercup/Ranunculaceae.

☺ Not related to Greater Celandine (p. 82).

✿✿✿ Feb–May.

Sea Spurge
Euphorbia paralias
Bainne léana

Ht. 50cm. **Fls.** Tiny, yellowish with petal-like horned lobes & bracts, no petals or sepals; in 3–6 branched umbels on several upright stems.

Lvs. Fleshy, oval, untoothed, grey-green, often tinged red; overlapping closely along the stem; midrib *not prominent* as in Portland Spurge.

Hab. Coastal sand, dunes, shingle, beaches. Native perennial, mainly confined to E, S & SW coasts.

Fam. Spurge/ Euphorbiaceae.

☺ Fruit capsule is 3-lobed & smooth.

✿✿ Jun–Oct.

Spurges have alternate, simple leaves, and acrid latex in their stems. Inflorescence is complex – flowers having 3–5 sepals & petals – or none; stamens varying from one to many. Easiest way to tell Sun & Petty Spurge apart is by numbers of rays in the umbel. Sea & Portland Spurge differ in that the latter has less fleshy, more spreading leaves with prominent midrib at back of leaf.

Sun Spurge
Euphorbia helioscopia
Lus na bhfaithní

Ht. 40cm. **Fls.** No petals or sepals but tiny, yellow-green stamens surrounding stalked ovary; crescent-shaped glands around flowers; in flat-topped, *5-branched* umbels with whorl of bracts below; on hairless, solitary, erect stems.

Lvs. Yellow-green, oval, finely toothed.

Hab. Disturbed, cultivated ground, roadsides. Widespread annual, probably introduced.

Fam. Spurge/Euphorbiaceae.

☺ 3-lobed fruit capsule is smooth.

☺ Stems produce white latex which can cause irritation.

✿✿✿ May–Nov. ⚠

Petty Spurge
Euphorbia peplus
Gearr nimhe

Ht. 30cm. **Fls.** Tiny, yellow-green flowers which have neither petals nor sepals but oval bracts, similar to leaves, & crescent-shaped glands; in *3-branched* umbels with 3 spoon-shaped bracts at base; on hairless stems.

Lvs. Alternate, oval, untoothed, short-stalked.

Hab. Similar to Sun Spurge, also arable land & gardens. Widespread introduced annual.

Fam. Spurge/ Euphorbiaceae.

☺ 3-lobed fruit capsule has 2 keels on back of each lobe.

☺ Stems produce white latex when cut which can poison cattle or horses.

✿✿✿ Apr–Oct. ⚠

Portland Spurge
Euphorbia portlandica
Spuirse ghainimh

Ht. 40cm. **Fls.** Petals & sepals absent but has 3–6 rayed, umbel-like clusters of yellowish, *triangular* bracts & yellow, crescent-shaped glands with prominent horns; on stems – often red-tinged – branched from base & ascending or prostrate.

Lvs. Grey-green, spreading, spoon-shaped to ovate, tapering towards base, untoothed with *prominent midrib beneath*.

Hab. Sandy sea-shore, cliffs, coastal grassland. Uncommon, native perennial, local in coastal areas of S, E & NW.

Fam. Spurge/Euphorbiaceae.

☺ Fruit is a capsule with pitted seeds.

✿✿ Apr–Sep. ⚠

Irish Spurge
Euphorbia hyberna
Bainne caoin

Ht. 60cm. **Fls.** Yellow, without petals or sepals; bracts elliptical, upper have heart-shaped bases; 5 oval or kidney-shaped yellow glands; in 4–6 rayed, flat-topped umbels; on hairless, upright stems.

Lvs. Untoothed, oblong, tapering & stalkless.

Hab. Shady hedgerows, damp woodland, scrub, on acid soil. Native perennial, local to Counties Cork, Kerry & Waterford.

Fam. Spurge/Euphorbiaceae.

☺ Fruit is long, slender, 3-lobed capsule covered in warts.

✿ May–Jul. ⚠

Alexanders
Smyrnium olusatrum
Lusrán grándubh

Ht. 1.25m. **Fls.** 2–3mm with 5 yellow, even, turned-in petals, in umbels 4–6cm, with 8–12 spokes or rays, no bracts; on stout, hairless, solid stems which become hollow with age.

Lvs. Shiny, green, triangular in outline; 3 broad, oval, toothed leaves & 3-lobed terminal leaf.

Hab. Hedgerows, ditches, coastal grasslands & cliffs. Introduced biennial, widespread in E, S & SW, less in N.

Fam. Carrot/Apiaceae.

☺ Fruit is egg-shaped with slender ridges.

☺ Plant is aromatic when crushed.

☺ Leaf bases have *inflated* sheaths.

✿✿ Mar–Jun.

Wild Parsnip
Pastinaca sativa
Cuirdín bán

Ht. 1m. **Fls.** 1.5mm, yellow, 5 petals rolled inwards, in bractless umbels of 5–15 uneven rays; on upright, hollow, angled, ridged stems; hairy plant.

Lvs. Alternate, pinnate, with 5–11 toothed, oval, leaflets.

Hab. Introduced perennial, occasional, mainly in SE.

Fam. Carrot/Apiaceae.

☺ Sap causes serious blistering.

☺ Fruit is 2-parted, oval, flattened & winged.

> *Members of the Carrot family – previously known as the Umbellifers – usually bear 5-petalled flowers in compound umbels. Outer petals of outer flowers may be enlarged in some species.*

✿ Jun–Sep. ⚠

Rock Samphire
Crithmum maritimum
Craobhraic

Ht. 40cm. **Fls.** 2mm,
yellow-green, in 3–6cm
umbels with 8–30 rays;
many narrow bracts
encircle hairless, solid, ridged
stem below flower-head.

Lvs. Fleshy, greyish-green, triangular
in outline, pointed, untoothed;
membranous leaf-base sheathing stem.

Hab. Coastal, on rocks, shingle,
sea-cliffs. Native perennial, common on
most coasts.

Fam. Carrot/Apiaceae.

☺ Fruit is 2-parted, egg-shaped, ridged,
spongy.

✿✿ Jun–Oct.

Fennel
Foeniculum vulgare
Finéal

Ht. 2m. **Fls.** 2–3mm, bright yellow,
in bractless 4–8cm-wide umbels with
up to 30 rays; on stiff, erect, faintly
ridged grey-green stems, initially solid
but becoming hollow.

Lvs. Feathery, lobed into numerous
thread-like, spreading leaflets,
broadly triangular in outline.

Hab. Grassy places, coastal
locations. Introduced perennial
scattered mainly along E & S coasts.

Fam. Carrot/Apiaceae.

☺ Fruits are narrow, ridged,
2-parted, ovoid.
☺ Smells strongly of aniseed.

✿✿ Jul–Oct.🏃

Black Medick
Medicago lupulina
Dúmheidic

Ht. 30cm. **Fls.** Tiny, bright yellow peaflowers (10–50) in crowded, globe-shaped 3–8mm heads; on long, slender, hairy, spreading stems.

Lvs. Alternate, oblong to diamond-shaped, trifoliate with each leaflet *bearing tiny point at outer end of midrib*.

Hab. Grassy, well-drained places, old walls, waste ground. Native annual, widespread except for NW.

Fam. Pea/Fabaceae.

☺ Tiny point at centre of leaflet helps to differentiate from Lesser Trefoil (see opposite page) which has *no point*.

☺ Ripe seeds are in clusters of coiled, black pods which do not have spines.

✿✿✿ Apr–Oct.

*Members of the **Pea** family – formerly known as the Legumes – have irregular flowers: 5 petals are arranged as 1 upper petal or standard, 2 lateral wings & a lower lip or keel comprised of 2 fused lower petals (see Glossary). Plants in this family often have tendrils & usually have trifoliate or pinnate leaves. Seeds are formed in pods. See Trefoils, Vetches, Clovers, Mellilot, Gorse, Broom, Restharrow & Tare. Root nodules help to fix nitrogen into the soil.*

Spotted Medick
Medicago arabica
Meidic bhreac

Ht. Prostrate. **Fls.** Yellow peaflowers (1-6) in loose 5–7mm clusters; flower stalks shorter than leaf stalks, almost hairless.

Lvs. Trifoliate, toothed, heart-shaped leaflets with *1 dark spot at centre* of each leaflet; narrow stipules attached to stem at base of leaf stem.

Hab. Bare, grassy & sandy places. Introduced annual, confined mainly to coastal areas of S & SE.

Fam. Pea/Fabaceae.

☺ Fruits are spirally coiled pods with little hooks to aid dispersal.

✿ Apr–Sep.

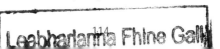

Hop Trefoil
Trifolium campestre
Seamair dhuimhche

Ht. 25cm. **Fls.** 4–5mm long, golden yellow peaflowers (20–30) in dense, rounded clusters up to 15mm across; upper petal broad, sides not folded together, becoming *finely pleated*; on low-growing, hairy stems.

Lvs. Alternate, trifoliate, middle leaflet with longer stalk than lateral leaflets; also *no point* at centre of leaflet.

Hab. Dry grassland, fields, disturbed soil. Native annual found more widely in S half of Ireland.

Fam. Pea/Fabaceae.

☺ Single-seed pods are in hop-like heads after flowering has finished.

✿✿ May–Oct.

Lesser Trefoil
Trifolium dubium | Seamair bhuí

Ht. 20cm. **Fls.** 3–4mm long, yellow peaflowers (5–20) in compact, rounded 8–9mm heads; upper petal narrow, two sides folded together; on hairless stems.

Lvs. Trifoliate with oval leaflets & *no terminal point* at end of midrib.

Hab. Mat-forming species of grassy, dry places. Widespread native annual.

Fam. Pea/Fabaceae.

☺ Seeds are in pods covered by papery dead flowers resembling hops.

☺ This species is known as Shamrock.

☺ To help differentiate from Black Medick (see opposite page), look at end of leaflet's midrib. Black Medick has a point – Lesser Trefoil *does not*.

✿✿✿ May–Oct.

Common Bird's-foot-trefoil
Lotus corniculatus
Crobh éin

Ht. 10cm. **Fls.** 15mm long, bright yellow, occasionally orange, red-streaked, peaflowers (3–6) in clusters; flower buds usually red; calyx teeth *erect* in bud; on slender, *solid*, rarely hairy stems.

Lvs. Alternate, pinnate with oval, almost round, leaflets.

Hab. Roadsides, sandy places, stone walls, open scrub. Widespread native perennial.

Fam. Pea/Fabaceae.

☺ Fruits are in long, dark brown pods arranged like a bird's foot.

☺ Also known as Bird's-foot-trefoil.

✿✿✿ May–Sep.

Greater Bird's-foot-trefoil
Lotus pedunculatus
Crobh éin corraigh

Ht. 50cm. **Fls.** 12mm long, bright yellow peaflowers (5–12) in loose, umbel-like clusters; calyx teeth *reflexed* in bud; on slender, hairy, *hollow*, erect stems.

Lvs. Blue-green, pinnate, oval with 5 leaflets.

Hab. Damp grassy places, marshes, preferring acidic soil. Native perennial, widespread except in centre of Ireland.

Fam. Pea/Fabaceae.

☺ Main differences between Greater & Common Bird's-foot-trefoil are the stem – solid or hollow – numbers of flowers in cluster, height of plant & calyx teeth in bud. Similar fruits.

✿✿✿ Jun–Aug.

Kidney Vetch
Anthyllis vulneraria
Méara Muire

Ht. 40cm. **Fls.** 10–15mm long, yellow, often red-tipped, peaflowers (15–20) in rounded 3cm clusters, each flower surrounded by woolly, inflated calyces creating kidney-shaped flower-head; green leaf-like bracts below head resembling a ruff; on silky stems.

Lvs. Pairs of pinnate leaflets, lower with large end-leaflet, upper with equal-sized narrow leaflets.

Hab. Dunes, shingle, calcareous grassy places. Native perennial, widespread in mainly coastal locations.

Fam. Pea/Fabaceae.

✿✿ May–Sep.

Meadow Vetchling
Lathyrus pratensis
Peasairín buí

Ht. 50cm. **Fls.** 10–18mm long, yellow peaflowers (5–12) in open, long-stalked racemes; on long, hairless, slender, winged & angled stems.

Lvs. Paired grey-green, narrow, parallel-veined; between these is a tendril & below are large stipules with arrow-shaped bases.

Hab. Scrambling over rough, grassy places, hedgerows, coastal grassland. Widespread native perennial.

Fam. Pea/Fabaceae.

☺ Seed-pod (2–4cm long), contains 4–9 seeds & is black when ripe.

☺ Tendrils, used to help plant to climb over other plants, may be branched.

✿✿✿ May–Aug.

Yellow Bartsia
Parentucellia viscosa
Hocas tae buí

Ht. 40cm. **Fls.** 15–25mm long, bright yellow, 2-lipped; lower lip with 3 even lobes, longer than hooded upper lobe; mouth open; in leafy spike on square, erect, unbranched stem.

Lvs. Paired, unstalked, oval-lanceolate, pointed, toothed.

Hab. Damp, grassy, sandy & coastal places. Native annual, common only in N & SW.

Fam. Broomrape/Orobanchaceae.

☺ Stickily-hairy, semi-parasitic plant.

▶ Red Bartsia (p. 204)

✿✿ Jun–Sep.

Semi-parasitic plants, by using haustoria (root-like organs), can absorb water & minerals from neighbouring plants.

Yellow-rattle
Rhinanthus minor
Gliográn

Ht. 45cm. **Fls.** 13–15mm long, yellow, 2-lipped straight petal tube; 2 short, 1mm long, blue-violet teeth on upper lip; in pairs above unstalked, triangular, sharply-toothed bracts; in leafy spikes on 4-angled, erect, sometimes black-spotted stems.

Lvs. Dark green, opposite, oblong, unstalked with rounded teeth.

Hab. Meadows, grassy places, heaths, machair. Widespread native annual.

Fam. Broomrape/Orobanchaceae.

☺ Winged seeds are borne in dry, inflated, enlarged sepals which rattle.

☺ Semi-parasitic plant (see panel above).

✿✿✿ May–Sep.

Marsh Cudweed
Gnaphalium uliginosum
Gnamhlus corraigh

Ht. 20cm. **Fls.** 3–4mm long, numerous yellow disc florets & brown bracts, in dense tufts of 3–10 oval heads, which are themselves in clusters, shorter than surrounding leaves; on upright or sprawling stems covered in white, woolly down.

Lvs. Alternate, greyish, lanceolate-oblong, both sides woolly.

Hab. Damp, sandy, waste & disturbed ground. Native annual, widespread except for the centre of Ireland.

Fam. Daisy/Asteraceae.

✿✿✿ Jul–Oct.

Lesser Meadow-rue
Thalictrum minus
Rú léana beag

Ht. 1.2m. **Fls.** No petals, 4 small, purplish sepals, prominent yellow stamens; flowers drooping at first, erect later; in small panicles on branched, upright, purplish stems.

Lvs. Pinnately divided 3–4 times, end leaflets as broad as long; fern-like.

Hab. Dry grassland, limestone, sand dunes, stony lake shores & mountains. Native perennial, uncommon except in W Connacht, the Burren & SE.

Fam. Buttercup/Ranunculaceae.

☺ Foliage resembles that of Maidenhair Fern with whom it shares its habitat in the Burren.

✿ Jun–Aug.

Lesser Hawkbit
Leontodon saxatilis
Crág phortáin bheag

Ht. 25cm. **Fls.** Flower-heads 20–25mm, with numerous golden-yellow ray florets, end of each being divided into 5 small points, outer rays *streaked grey-violet* beneath; behind each head is circle of bracts; flower-heads solitary on unbranched, leafless stalks which *do not have* scale-like bracts.

Lvs. Stiffly hairy, linear leaves with short, wavy lobes; in a basal rosette.

Hab. Acid soils, grassy places, dunes. Native perennial found widely but less in N.

Fam. Daisy/Asteraceae.

✿✿✿ Jun–Oct.

Autumn Hawkbit
Scorzoneroides autumnalis
Crág phortáin

Ht. 25cm. **Fls.** Flower-heads 15–25mm, bright golden-yellow ray florets, *streaked reddish* below, 5 points at end of ray; involucre or circle of smooth bracts behind florets *tapers gradually* into stem; small scale-leaves just below heads; on erect branched stems.

Lvs. Variable, oblong, deeply-pinnate with narrow wavy lobes.

Hab. Dry grassland, acid soil. Widespread native perennial.

Fam. Daisy/Asteraceae.

☺ Look for *unforked* hairs on underside of leaves; underside of Lesser Hawkbit leaves have *forked* hairs.

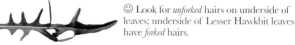

✿✿✿ Jun–Oct.

Carline Thistle
Carlina vulgaris
Feochadán mín

Ht. 60cm. **Fls.** Flower-heads 15–40mm, disc florets only, golden-brown, tinged purple, rayless with conspicuous, spiny, sepal-like, pale, straw-coloured bracts spreading widely apart below; dry flower-heads persist after flowering has finished; on upright, branched or unbranched, densely prickly stems.

Lvs. Alternate, oblong, wavy-lobed, cottony below, with spines.

Hab. Dry grassland, cliffs, sand dunes, not on acid soil. Native biennial, locally frequent in diagonal band from Sligo to Wexford.

Fam. Daisy/Asteraceae.

✿✿ Jul–Sep.

For more information regarding ***ray florets & disc florets*** see p.68.

Nipplewort
Lapsana communis
Duilleog Bhríde

Ht. 90cm. **Fls.** Flower-heads 10–20mm, ray florets only, each ray floret 5-toothed at tip; circle of lance-shaped bracts below flower-heads; in loose panicles on much branched, leggy, upright stems.

Lvs. Basal leaves pinnate with large, oval end lobes; upper lanceolate to diamond-shaped, toothed.

Hab. Cultivated & waste ground, gardens, roadsides. Widespread native annual.

Fam. Daisy/Asteraceae.

☺ Flowers open in sunshine only.

☺ Stems do not produce latex when cut.

✿✿✿ Jul–Oct.

Cat's-ear
Hypochaeris radicata
Cluas chait

Ht. 50cm. **Fls.** Flower-heads 25–40mm, bright yellow ray florets, outer greyish beneath; backed with numerous, *purple-tipped* bracts in 4–5 rows below circle of ray florets; on hairless stems, *slightly swollen* below flower-heads.

Lvs. Oblong-lanceolate, wavy-edged, in basal rosette.

Hab. Pastures, laneways, roadsides, dunes. Widespread native perennial.

Fam. Daisy/Asteraceae.

☺ Tiny bracts (like cat's ears) along stem help to identify this species.

✿✿✿ Jun–Sep.

Colt's-foot
Tussilago farfara
Sponc

Ht. 15cm. **Fls.**
Flower-heads 30–50mm,
numerous narrow,
golden-yellow rays
around centre of darker
disc florets; emerging
from pinkish buds,
solitary on pink-purple,
down-covered, upright
stems; stems are covered in
narrow overlapping scales
or bracts.

Lvs. Appear *after flowers*;
roundish, roughly heart-shaped
with point.

Hab. Waste ground,
roadsides, river-banks,
coastal shingle & sand.
Widespread native
perennial.

Fam. Daisy/Asteraceae.

☺ Seeds are borne in
'clocks'.

✿✿✿ Feb–Apr.

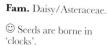

Perennial Sowthistle
Sonchus arvensis
Bleachtán léana

Ht. 1.5m. **Fls.** Flower-heads 40–50mm, tightly-packed rich, deep yellow strap-shaped ray florets; involucres of sticky, pointed bracts, densely covered in yellow, glandular hairs; in branched, loose clusters on stout, hollow, bristly, stems which contain latex.

Lvs. Narrow, alternate, lobed, shiny, with softly spiny margins; auricles at base, clasping stem.

Hab. Patch-forming on coastal cliffs, roadsides, hedgerows, ditches. Widespread, native perennial.

Fam. Daisy/Asteraceae.

☺ Seeds are in a white clock.

✿✿✿ Jul–Sep.

Smooth Sowthistle
Sonchus oleraceus
Bleachtán mín

Ht. 80cm. **Fls.** Flower-heads 20–25mm, pale yellow, strap-shaped ray florets; backed by closely overlapping, lance-shaped bracts; in small clusters on upright, hairless, few-branched stems.

Lvs. Matte, blue-green, softly spiny-toothed, pinnately lobed with triangular lobes, end lobes wider than next pair; clasping stem with arrow-shaped points.

Hab. Waste & cultivated ground. Widespread native annual or biennial.

Fam. Daisy/Asteraceae.

☺ Hollow stems contain latex.

✿✿✿ Apr–Nov.

Prickly Sowthistle
Sonchus asper
Bleachtán colgach

Ht. 1m. **Fls.** Flattish flower-heads
20–25mm, numerous *rich* yellow ray florets;
bracts encircling flower are triangular; in
umbel-like clusters on few-branched, hollow,
erect, *hairless*, stiff stems.

Lvs. Bright, *shiny* green above, wavy, jagged,
spiny margins, clasping stems at bases with
rounded, toothed,
prickly lobes.

Hab. Cultivated land, waste
ground. Widespread native
annual or biennial.

Fam. Daisy/Asteraceae.

☺ Stems contain latex.

☺ Seeds are in a 'clock'.

✿✿✿ Jun–Oct.

Corn Marigold
Glebionis segetum
Buíán

Ht. 50cm. **Fls.** Flower-heads 30–50mm,
daisy-like, flat, golden-orange disc floret centres
surrounded by broad, overlapping deep yellow,
3-notched, ray florets; solitary on upright,
greyish, hairless stems.

Lvs. Lower, slightly fleshy, grey-green, oblong,
deeply lobed, alternate, stalked; upper barely
toothed, clasping stem.

Hab. Arable land, roadsides,
cultivated, lime-free soil.
Introduced annual, found
occasionally throughout,
except for W.

Fam. Daisy/Asteraceae.

☺ Not related to Marsh-
marigold (p. 91).

✿✿ Jun–Oct. 🏃

Goat's-beard
Tragopogon pratensis
Finidí na muc

Ht. 60cm. **Fls.** Flower-heads 20–40mm, yellow florets, 5-toothed with one row of *longer*, narrow, pointed bracts encircling florets; solitary on stiff, upright, blue-green stems.

Lvs. Alternate, narrow, linear-lanceolate, grass-like, clasping stems.

Hab. Grassy places, meadows, coastal, sandy soil. Native annual or perennial, occasional in Midlands, E & SE.

Fam. Daisy/Asteraceae.

☺ Seeds are borne in a large, 8–10cm pappus or 'clock'.

☺ Flower usually closes over at noon.

✿✿ May–Aug.

Bristly Oxtongue
Helminthotheca echioides
Teanga bhó gharbh

Ht. 80cm. **Fls.** Flower-heads 20–25mm, yellow strap-shaped ray florets, outer often with red stripes beneath; flower-heads ringed by slender bracts with 3–5 curved, large, prickly, triangular bracts outside them; in loose clusters, on bristly, sometimes reddish, stems.

Lvs. Distinctive, coarse, oblong, with wavy margins; covered with *swollen, whitish pimple-based bristles*.

Hab. Disturbed, waste ground, often coastal. Introduced annual or biennial, occasional in S, SE & E.

Fam. Daisy/Asteraceae.

☺ Also known as Prickly Oxtongue, this is a very bristly plant.

✿ Jun–Oct.

Dandelion
Taraxacum agg.
Caisearbhán

Ht. 35cm. **Fls.**
Flower-heads 25–50mm,
flattish discs of bright 5-toothed,
strap-shaped ray florets; solitary on
upright hollow stems.

Lvs. Deeply divided into jagged,
triangular lobes, in a basal rosette; seeds
are borne in a 'clock' or pappus.

Hab. Roadsides, gardens, waste
ground, walls. Widespread native
perennial.

Fam. Daisy/Asteraceae.

☺ With over 70 species recorded in
Ireland, the Dandelion is treated in this
book as a single species. Identification of
individual species is *extremely difficult*.

✿✿✿ Mar–Oct.

Smooth Hawk's-beard
Crepis capillaris
Lus cúráin mín

Ht. 80cm. **Fls.** Flower-heads 10–20mm,
bright yellow ray florets, usually reddish
beneath; heads surrounded by *2 rows* of
bracts, outer being shorter than inner; in
branched clusters on slender, hairless or
slightly hairy stems.

Lvs. Irregularly pinnate, basal are
narrow at base & stalked, upper clasp
stem with basal, arrow-shaped lobes.

Hab. Dry, grassy places, banks,
roadsides. Widespread, native annual or
biennial.

Fam. Daisy/Asteraceae.

☺ Fruits are brown & ribbed,
wind-dispersed on pappus
of unbranched hairs.

✿✿✿ Jun–Oct.

Mouse-ear Hawkweed
Pilosella officinarum
Searbh na muc

Ht. 25cm. **Fls.** Flower-heads 20–30mm, lemon-yellow ray florets, red striped beneath, solitary; on hairy, leafless stems rising from centre of rosette.

Lvs. Oval, untoothed, pale green; *long, white hairs* above with soft, shaggy down beneath.

Hab. Dry, grassy places, old stone walls, sand dunes, waste ground. Widespread native perennial.

Fam. Daisy/Asteraceae.

☺ Spreads by creeping runners forming mats, runners decaying after daughter plant is established.

✿✿✿ May–Oct.

Golden-samphire
Inula crithmoides
Ailleann Pheadair

Ht. 75cm. **Fls.** Flower-heads 15–30mm, spreading, narrow yellow ray florets around darker yellow centre of disc florets; in loose, *flat-topped* clusters on upright, branched stems.

Lvs. Bright green, linear, fleshy, untoothed or with 3-toothed top; crowding along stems.

Hab. Rocky places, saltmarshes, cliffs, shingle. Native perennial, uncommon except on part of E & SE coast.

Fam. Daisy/Asteraceae.

☺ Behind rays are green, linear, erect

☺ Not related to Rock Samphire (p. 113).

✿ Jul–Sep.

Common Fleabane
Pulicaria dysenterica
Lus buí na ndreancaidí

Ht. 60cm. **Fls.** Flower-heads
15–30mm, ring of narrow, spreading,
yellow ray florets encircling deeper
yellow centre of tightly-packed disc
florets; in loose clusters on branched,
downy stems.

Lvs. Alternate, green above, grey
beneath; basal leaves oblong,
withering early, stem leaves heart-
shaped, clasping at base.

Hab. Damp places, hedgerows.
Native perennial more common
in S half of Ireland.

Fam. Daisy/Asteraceae.

☺ Entire plant is woolly.

✿✿ Jul–Sep.

Elecampane
Inula helenium
Meacan aillinn

Ht. 2m. **Fls.** Flower-heads 50–80mm,
with long, spreading, narrow
ray florets, each with 3-notched
end, surrounding numerous
deep-yellow disc florets; in groups
of 2–3, on tall, stout, hairy stems.

Lvs. Ovate, basal leaves stalked,
stem leaves unstalked; hairless
above, downy below.

Hab. Roadsides, grassy verges.
Introduced perennial, scattered throughout.

Fam. Daisy/Asteraceae.

☺ Behind flower-heads are cup-like involucres
with hairy, oval, overlapping, spreading bracts.

✿ Jul–Aug. 🏃

Goldenrod
Solidago virgaurea
Slat óir

Ht. 70cm. **Fls.** Flower-heads 15–18mm, few oval-shaped ray florets surround larger number of disc florets; in large branched clusters on upright stems.

Lvs. Basal leaves narrow, spoon-shaped, stalked, only slightly toothed; stem leaves lanceolate, unstalked.

Hab. Heaths, coastal cliffs, dry grassy places. Native perennial, common except for centre & NE.

Fam. Daisy/Asteraceae.

☺ Pappus is brown.

✿✿ Jun–Sep.

Tansy
Tanacetum vulgare
Franclus

Ht. 1m. **Fls.** Flower-heads 7–12mm, bright yellow, *disc florets only*, button-like in flat-topped, loose clusters or corymbs; on stiff, erect, woody stems.

Lvs. Alternate, unstalked, finely divided into lanceolate, toothed segments.

Hab. Hedgerows, grass verges. Introduced perennial, scattered but more common in SE.

Fam. Daisy/Asteraceae.

✿✿ Jul–Sep. 🏃

Cottonweed
Achillea maritima
Cluasach mhara

Ht. 30cm. **Fls.** Flower-heads 8mm, button-like, globose, yellow with disc florets only; with silvery, woolly bracts, in dense terminal clusters on stout, branched stems.

Lvs. Oblong, fleshy, covered in white woolly down; entire plant is covered in a soft, hoary, silvery pubsecence.

Hab. Sand & shingle shore. Now *extremely rare*, only found in SE of Ireland.

Fam. Daisy/Asteraceae.

✿ Aug–Oct. ✚

Pineappleweed
Matricaria discoidea
Lus na hiothlann

Ht. 12cm. **Fls.** Flower-heads 8–12mm, tight, hollow dome of yellow-green disc florets, no ray florets; closely overlapping bracts 'cup' these domes; on upright hairless stems.

Lvs. Blue-green, alternate, feathery, finely pinnately divided, well branched.

Hab. Disturbed ground, tracks, pathways, well-trodden places. Widespread, introduced annual.

Fam. Daisy/Asteraceae.

☺ Strong pineapple scent occurs when this plant is crushed.

✿✿✿ Apr–Nov.

Sticky Groundsel
Senecio viscosus
Grúnlas greamaitheach

Ht. 65cm. **Fls** Flower-heads 12mm long, with yellow disc florets & *recurved* ray florets; *pungent*; long bracts, *not black-tipped*, outer bracts half length of inner; in open clusters on robust upright stems; *entire plant is stickily hairy*, with dense, glandular hairs.

Lvs. Deeply pinnate, lobed & sticky.

Hab. Railway lines, sandy soils, disturbed ground. Introduced annual, occasional in NE & SE, infrequent elsewhere.

Fam. Daisy/Asteraceae.

☺ Sticky hairs can cause plant to be covered in debris.

☺ Seeds are *hairless*, in a pappus.

✿ Jul–Sep.

Groundsel
Senecio vulgaris
Grúnlas

Ht. 40cm. **Fls.** Flower-heads 4–5mm, *cylindrical*, 10mm long, yellow disc florets only, clasped by a circle of short, greenish, *black-tipped* bracts; in clusters on much-branched, upright but weak stems.

Lvs. Bright green, alternate, pinnately lobed, lower stalked, upper stalkless; shiny above, downy below.

Hab. Cultivated, disturbed & waste ground. Widespread native annual.

Fam. Daisy/Asteraceae.

☺ Hairy seeds are borne in pappus of long, white hairs.

✿✿✿ Jan–Dec.

Heath Groundsel
Senecio sylvaticus
Grúnlas móna

Ht. 70cm. **Fls.** Flower-heads 5mm, tight *conical* bundle of disc florets with short, curling ray florets; flower-heads long-stalked; bracts *not black-tipped*; in loose clusters on robust, upright, erect stems.

Lvs. Deeply pinnate, longer-lobed than Groundsel.

Hab. Sandy soils, disturbed ground. Native annual, infrequent, scattered across Ireland.

Fam. Daisy/Asteraceae.

☺ Seeds are *hairy*, in pappus.

☺ Look for *stickily hairy*, *conical* heads in Heath Groundsel & *cylindrical* heads in Groundsel.

✿✿ Jun–Sep.

Common Ragwort
Senecio jacobaea
Buachalán buí

Ht. 1m. **Fls.** Flower-heads
15–25mm, 3-toothed, spreading
ray florets around centre of darker
yellow disc florets; in dense, *flat-topped*
clusters on stout, upright, furrowed,
branched, leafy stems.

Lvs. Dark green, oblong, pinnately lobed,
end lobe blunt; upper unstalked, clasping
stem, lower stalked, withering by flowering
time.

Hab. Cultivated & waste ground,
roadsides, grassland. Widespread native
biennial or perennial.

Fam. Daisy/Asteraceae.

☺ There is a coastal version in which ray
florets are absent, see left.

☺ Listed under the Noxious Weeds Act
1936, this plant is dangerous to animals.

✿✿✿ Jun–Nov.

Marsh Ragwort
Senecio aquaticus
Buachalán corraigh

Ht. 80cm. **Fls.** Flower-heads 20–30mm,
bright yellow ray florets surrounding centre
of darker disc florets; ray florets larger,
more widely spaced than in Common
Ragwort; in loose, spreading, open clusters
which are *not flat-topped*.

Lvs. Pinnate with large end lobe.

Hab. Damp, boggy places, riversides.
Widespread
native biennial or
perennial.

Fam. Daisy/
Asteraceae.

✿✿✿ Jul–Aug.

Oxford Ragwort
Senecio squalidus
Buachalán Pheadair

Ht. 50cm. **Fls.** Flower-heads 15–20mm, *broad*, bright-yellow ray florets around centre of disc florets; all bracts below flower-head *black-tipped*; on straggling, spreading, stems, plant branching from bushy base.

Lvs. Variable, dark green, deeply divided into few narrow lobes, pointed end lobe; lower with winged stalk, upper clasping stem.

Hab. Railway lines, walls, disturbed & waste ground. Introduced annual or perennial, only found occasionally in E & S.

Fam. Daisy/Asteraceae.

✿✿ Apr–Dec.

Silver Ragwort
Senecio cineraria
Buachalán breá

Ht. 80cm. **Fls.** Flower-heads 12–20mm, conspicuous, golden-yellow, well-separated ray florets surrounding large, prominent centre of disc florets; in dense, flat-topped clusters on erect, branching, woolly stems.

Lvs. Pinnate, darker grey-green above, light grey below.

Hab. Coastal areas on E & small part of SE coast only. Scarce introduced perennial.

Fam. Daisy/Asteraceae.

☺ Entire plant is silvery-grey & covered in soft, white, woolly down.

☺ Classed as a potentially invasive species.

✿ Jun–Aug. 🏃🐾

Great Mullein
Verbascum thapsus
Coinnle Muire

Ht. 2m. **Fls.** 15–30mm, 5-lobed, bright yellow; 5 stamens with yellow-white hairs on stalks of *upper 3* stamens, lower 2 stamens almost hairless; in tall, erect, white-woolly spikes on stems with occasional side branches.

Lvs. Distinctive, ovate, covered in thick, soft hairs; clinging to winged stems along spike, basal leaves being ovate, large, withering beneath.

Hab. Roadsides, waste ground, dry, grassy places. Native biennial, scattered, more common in E than W.

Fam. Figwort/ Scrophulariaceae.

✿✿ Jun–Aug.

Common Cow-wheat
Melampyrum pratense
Lus an tsagairt

Ht. 35cm. **Fls.** 15–20mm long, yellow, occasionally pinky-purple, tubular, corolla somewhat flattened; with 2 lips, upper being entire, lower 3-lobed & pointing forward; flower almost closed over; in pairs arising from angle between toothed bracts & stem; on branched stems, sometimes upright, sometimes straggling.

Lvs. Paired, lanceolate, toothed, unstalked.

Hab. Heaths, hills, scrub & grassy places. Native annual, scattered throughout with exception of centre of Ireland.

Fam. Broomrape/Orobanchaceae.

☺ Semi-parasitic plant (see panel on p. 118).

✿✿ May–Sep.

Weld
Reseda luteola
Buí mór

Ht. 1.5m. **Fls.** 4–5mm, yellow-green, *4 deeply-divided petals*, upper petal larger than others; 4 sepals; in long, tapering spikes along stiff, ribbed, hollow, slender stems.

Lvs. Basal rosette of narrow, oblong leaves in first year; unlobed, lanceolate, wavy-edged leaves along stem in second year.

Hab. Grassy places, motorways, dry, lime-rich disturbed ground. Native biennial, common in all but NW.

Fam. Mignonette/Resedaceae.

☺ AKA Dyer's Rocket.

✿✿ Jun–Oct.

Wild Mignonette
Reseda lutea
Buí beag

Ht. 75cm. **Fls.** 6–8mm; *6 raggedy yellow-green petals*, 6 sepals; in compact spikes on *solid*, upright stems.

Lvs. Small, pinnately lobed with 1–2 pairs of lobes & slightly wavy edges.

Hab. Disturbed, cultivated, roadsides, on calcareous ground. Uncommon, introduced biennial or perennial.

Fam. Mignonette/Resedaceae.

☺ Main difference between this species & Weld is that stems in Wild Mignonette are solid, on Weld they are hollow. Weld is usually about twice as tall as Wild Mignonette.

✿ Jun–Aug.

137

Common Toadflax
Linaria vulgaris
Buaflíon

Ht. 80cm. **Fls.** 15–30mm long; pale yellow tube with orange blush on lower 3-lobed lip; upper lip has 2 spreading lobes; corolla tube has long, slender spur; in long racemes on erect, round stems.

Lvs. Grey-green, narrow, slightly fleshy.

Hab. Old walls, meadows, dry grassland. Introduced perennial, occasional through E & S.

Fam. Speedwell/Veronicaceae.

▶ Small Toadflax (p. 171), Ivy-leaved Toadflax (p. 226) & Purple Toadflax (p. 246).

✿ Jun–Oct. 🏃

American Skunk-cabbage
Lysichiton americanus
Geathar buí

Ht. 1.5m. **Fls.** 3–12cm greenish spadix of tiny flowers, opening from bottom of spadix upwards; within a bright yellow spathe; robust plant.

Lvs. Large, ovate-oblong, 35–150cm long & quite broad; hairless & short-stalked.

Hab. In & beside streams, also in wet woodland. Introduced perennial, scattered & uncommon.

Fam. Arum/Araceae.

☺ Originally an introduction into water gardens.

☺ Foul-smelling plant.

☺ Classed as 'Potentially Invasive'.

✿ Apr–May. 🏃 🚫

Agrimony
Agrimonia eupatoria
Marbhdhraighean

Ht. 70cm. **Fls.** 5–8mm, 5
well-separated, slightly wrinkled, pale
yellow petals; in spikes on slender,
sometimes reddish stems, upright but
occasionally curving slightly towards
the top.

Lvs. Lower paired, toothed, pinnate
with smaller toothed leaflets between
them.

Hab. Roadsides, hedgerows,
grassy verges. Frequent native
perennial.

Fam. Rose/Rosaceae.

☺ Fruits are bur-like,
covered with spines.

✿✿ Jun–Aug.

Yellow Corydalis
Pseudofumaria lutea
Giodairiam buí

Ht. 30cm. **Fls.** 12–18mm long; bright-
yellow, 2-lipped with 2 outer & 2 inner
petals, 2 tiny sepals; 6–16 flowers in a
long raceme on greyish-green, branched
stems.

Lvs. Delicate, grey-green, pinnately
lobed ending in leaflet.

Hab. Old walls, rocky ground.
Introduced perennial, occasional in NE.

Fam. Poppy/Papaveraceae.

☺ Garden escape now naturalised in a
few locations.

▶ White Ramping-fumitory (p. 24) &
Common Ramping-fumitory (p. 181).

✿ Jan–Dec. 🏃

Tuberous Comfrey
Symphytum tuberosum
Meacan compair

Ht. 1.2m. **Fls.** 12–18mm long,
creamy-yellow, tubular with corolla
lobes turned back at outer edges; in
curved, arching clusters on *unwinged or
only slightly winged*, hairy stems.

Lvs. Oval, light green, *middle leaves
longest*.

Hab. Waste ground, damp
woodland shade, riverbanks.
Uncommon, scattered,
introduced perennial.

Fam. Borage/Boraginaceae.

▶ White Comfrey (p. 75),
Common Comfrey & Russian
Comfrey (both p. 242).

✿ Apr–Jul. 🏃

Garden Yellow Archangel
Lamiastrum galeobdolon ssp. *argentatum*
Neantóg Mhuire

Ht. 45cm. **Fls.** 20–25mm, bright yellow,
2-lipped corolla; lower lip streaked brown
& divided into 3 lobes, upper lip hooded
& fringed with hairs; in tight whorls at leaf
nodes, on erect stems.

Lvs. Oval, toothed, paired, silvery marks.

Hab. Woodland, hedgerows, roadsides.
Scattered, introduced perennial, found
mainly in S & N.

Fam. Dead-nettle/Lamiaceae.

✿✿ Apr–Jun. 🏃

Ivy Broomrape
Orobanche hederae
Múchóg mhór

Ht. 60cm. **Fls.** 10–20mm long; tubular,
cream-yellow with purple veins; 2 lips –
upper lip notched & lower lip 3-lobed; on
stout, hairy, mauve stems, bulbous at base.

Lvs. Scale-like, brownish, along stem; not
true leaves.

Hab. On calcareous soils mainly &
wherever Ivy grows. Native, perennial,
uncommon & scattered, more frequent in
Munster than elsewhere.

Fam. Broomrape/Orobanchaceae.

☺ This species is parasitic on Ivy by
means of root tubers & totally lacks
chlorophyll. Look for host plant to help
identification.

▶ Common Broomrape (p. 188) &
Thyme Broomrape (p. 206).

✿ May–Jul.

Bog Asphodel
Narthecium ossifragum
Sciollam na móna

Ht. 20cm. **Fls.**
12–15mm, 6 star-like, golden
tepals; anthers orange-red with woolly, orange
filaments; in loose, tapering spike of 6–20
flowers on slender, erect stems.

Lvs. Rigid, sword-shaped, all coming from
roots, becoming bronze in late summer.

Hab. Bogland, heaths, peaty places.
Widespread native perennial.

Fam. Bog Asphodel/Nartheciaceae.

☺ Entire plant becomes orange in autumn,
carpeting bogs with bronze spikes well into
winter.

✿✿ Jun–Aug.

Wild Asparagus
Asparagus prostratus
Lus súgach

Ht. Prostrate. **Fls.** 4–7mm long, greenish-yellow, solitary, bell-shaped; on procumbent, much-branched stems.

Lvs. Small, scale-like, short, in clusters of 4–15; rigid & glaucous.

Hab. Coastal grass, sea-cliffs. Rare, native perennial only found on SE coast.

Fam. Asparagus/Asparagaceae.

☺ Fruit is a red, globose berry.

✿ Jun–Sep. ⊞

Ribbed Melilot
Melilotus officinalis
Crúibín cait

Ht. 1.5m. **Fls.** 4–7mm long, bright-yellow peaflowers, wings & upper petal longer than keel; in loose spikes on slender, erect or spreading stems.

Lvs. Alternate, trefoil with oblong, sharply-toothed leaflets; upper leaves narrower than lower.

Hab. Waste ground, grassland, railway banks, saline soil. Scarce, biennial, introduced species.

Fam. Pea/Fabaceae.

☺ Brown, oval seedpods are wrinkled.

✿ Jun–Sep. 🏃

Gorse
Ulex europaeus
Aiteann gallda

Ht. 2m. **Fls.** 15–20mm long, golden-yellow peaflowers; 4–5mm-long bracts at base of flower; in long, spikes on stems with *blue-green, straight, deeply furrowed*, 15–25mm long spines.

Lvs. Evergreen shrub with trifoliate leaves, only when young.

Hab. Fields, hedgerows, heaths & grassy places. Widespread native shrub.

Fam. Pea/Fabaceae.

☺ Flowers have strong scent of coconut. Seeds are in hairy pods which explode when ripe.

☺ AKA Furze or Whin.

✿✿✿ Feb–May but in some locations, year round.

Broom
Cytisus scoparius
Giolcach shléibhe

Ht. 2m. **Fls.** 25mm long, golden-yellow peaflowers, sometimes tinged red; stamens protrude after pollination; solitary or in pairs along straight, slender, ridged, 5-angled stems.

Lvs. Alternate, trifoliate, short-stalked, untoothed.

Hab. Hedgerows, heaths, open woodland. Native shrub, common in all but centre of Ireland.

Fam. Pea/Fabaceae.

☺ Broom does not have spines.

☺ Seeds are in flat, oblong pods with hair on fringes only.

✿✿✿ Apr–Jun.

Lesser Water-plantain
Baldellia ranunculoides
Corrchopóg bheag

Ht. 20cm. **Fls.** 12–15mm, pale pink, 3 ragged, well-separated petals, yellow towards centre of flower; solitary or in few-flowered clusters on erect, spreading stems.

Lvs. Long, linear-lanceolate, mostly basal, with long stalks.

Hab. Marshes, bogs & lake margins, often on calcareous ground. Native perennial, uncommon except in the W & NW.

Fam. Water-plantain/Alismataceae.

☺ Numerous carpels fill the centre of this flower.

▶ Water-plantain (p. 11).

✿✿ Jun–Sep.

Flowering-rush
Butomus umbellatus
Luachair dhearg

Ht. 1.5m. **Fls.** 16–25mm, 3 pale to deep pink, dark-veined petals, 3 smaller, narrower sepals; on stalks of uneven lengths in single cluster or umbel on leafless stems, leaf-like bracts below cluster.

Lvs. Grey-green, long, slender, triangular in cross-section; all arising from base.

Hab. On creeping underground stems or rhizomes at water margins in lakes, ditches, canals. Native perennial not commonly found except in northern areas, Munster & along R. Shannon.

Fam. Flowering-rush/Butomaceae.

✿ Jul–Aug.

Squinancywort
Asperula cynanchica
Lus na haincise

Ht. 20cm. **Fls.** 3–4mm, pale pink or
white, 4 pointed lobes which spread
from short corolla tube; in dense,
long-stalked, branched clusters on
greyish green, 4-angled, thin, ascending
stems.

Lvs. Narrow, pointed, in whorls of 4,
with 2 long & 2 short.

Hab. Limestone, dry grassy places
& sand dunes. Native perennial only
found in N Kerry, Clare & S Galway.

Fam. Bedstraw/Rubiaceae.

☺ Could be confused with Field
Madder but flowers of that plant are
usually more blue than pink.

✿ Jun–Sep.

Sea Rocket
Cakile maritima
Cearrbhacán mara

Ht. 25cm. **Fls.** 10–15mm; 4 notched, spreading,
pink or pale lilac petals; in dense, terminal
clusters on hairless, blue-grey, branched stems.

Lvs. Shiny, succulent, fleshy, pinnately-lobed.

Hab. Coastal shingle, sandy beaches.
Commonly occurring native annual.

Fam. Cabbage/Brassicaceae.

☺ Fruit is in waisted,
segmented pods, upper
half larger than lower
which has 2 basal
projections.

✿✿✿ Jun–Sep.

Cuckooflower
Cardamine pratensis
Biolar gréagáin

Ht. 50cm. **Fls.** 12–20mm, 4 broad, dark-veined, overlapping, lilac-pink, pink or white petals; yellow anthers; in loose racemes on upright stems.

Lvs. Narrow, pinnate upper leaves; basal rosette of broader, rounder, pinnately-lobed leaves.

Hab. Meadows, bogs, roadsides, damp, grassy places. Widespread native perennial.

Fam. Cabbage/Brassicaceae.

☺ Seeds are borne in smooth, ascending, beaked pods.

☺ AKA Lady's Smock.

✿✿✿ Apr–Jun.

Coralroot
Cardamine bulbifera
Searbh-bhiolar bleibíneach

Ht. 70cm. **Fls.** 12–18mm, 4 rose-pink petals, 6 stamens – 4 long & 2 short; in compact racemes on upright, unbranched stems.

Lvs. Alternate, stalked; lower leaves pinnate with toothed margins; upper leaves lanceolate, untoothed.

Hab. Undisturbed broadleaved woodland. Introduced perennial, found only in E.

Fam. Cabbage/Brassicaceae.

☺ Brown bulbils are borne in leaf axils, dropping off to form new plants.

☺ AKA Coralroot Bittercress.

✿ May–Jun. 🏃

Honesty
Lunaria annua
Sailchuach na gealaí

Ht. 1m. **Fls.** 25–30mm, 4-petalled magenta-pink, rarely white; in dense racemes on erect, branched stems.

Lvs. Heart-shaped, coarsely & irregularly-toothed; lower stalked, upper unstalked.

Hab. Hedgerows, waste ground. Introduced perennial uncommon except for SE & NE.

Fam. Cabbage/Brassicaceae.

☺ Seeds are borne in circular or oval, flattened pods which have silvery lining.

☺ A garden escape, Honesty is usually found close to habitation.

✿ Apr–Jun. 🏃

Dame's-violet
Hesperis matronalis
Feascarlus

Ht. 90cm. **Fls.** 15–20mm, 4-petalled, pale violet or pinkish-white; stigma is 2-lobed; in terminal panicles on erect stems.

Lvs. Alternate, narrow, short-stalked & pointed, upper smaller than lower.

Hab. Damp places, river-banks, hedgerows, waste ground. Introduced biennial or perennial, commonly found throughout.

Fam. Cabbage/Brassicaceae.

☺ Dame's-violet carries a scent quite similar to that of Violets.

✿✿ May–Aug. 🏃

Rosebay Willowherb
Chamerion angustifolium
Lus na tine

Ht. 1.5m. **Fls.** 15–25mm, 4 notched, slightly unequal, magenta or rose-purple petals, 4 long, narrow, darker sepals; in tall, tapering racemes, each flower with long, red stalk; on erect, usually unbranched stems.

Lvs. Alternate, hairless, narrow, pointed with slightly toothed margin.

Hab. Margins of woodland, bogs, railway embankments, roadsides. More widespread in E than W. Perennial, native to some counties, introduced into others.

Fam. Willowherb/ Onagraceae.

✿✿✿ Jun–Sep.

*The **Willowherb** family is quite varied. Look for the stigma as its shape can be quite vital in identifying the species – whether it is lobed or club-shaped. Also look at the leaf – its shape, whether hairy, clasping, toothed, short or long-stalked, opposite or alternate. Examine the stem – does it have raised lines, is it winged, ridged, square or hairy?*

Hoary Willowherb
Epilobium parviflorum
Saileachán liath

Ht. 75cm. **Fls.** 6–10mm; 4 pale pink, notched petals, *4-lobed stigma*; on erect, round, *downy* stems.

Lvs. Grey-green, oval, hairy, leaf bases *not clasping* stem.

Hab. Damp habitats, waste ground. Widespread native perennial.

Fam. Willowherb/Onagraceae.

☺ Look for non-clasping leaves.

☺ Long pods contain cottony seeds.

✿✿✿ Jul–Sep.

Great Willowherb
Epilobium hirsutum
Lus na Tríonóide

Ht. 1.8m. **Fls.** 15–25mm, 4 notched, magenta or purplish-pink petals, pale at centre of flower; cream stigma has *4 arching lobes*; on robust, hairy, erect stems.

Lvs. Opposite, oval-lanceolate, hairy, *clasping* & stalkless.

Hab. Hedgerows, waste ground, lake margins, in open aspects. Widespread native, patch-forming perennial.

Fam. Willowherb/Onagraceae.

☺ Occasionally a plant bearing white flowers occurs.

✿✿✿ Jun–Sep.

Marsh Willowherb
Epilobium palustre
Saileachán corraigh

Ht. 60cm. **Fls.** 4–7mm, pale pink or white; notched petals, *club-shaped* stigma; flower drooping or held horizontally; on slender, upright, *round, smooth* stems.

Lvs. Opposite, grey-green, strap-shaped, unstalked, toothed, narrowing at either end.

Hab. Damp places, mainly acid soils, marshes. Widespread native perennial.

Fam. Willowherb/Onagraceae.

☺ This plant is stoloniferous, rising from creeping stems. These stolons develop small bulbs at their tips which break off in autumn, floating to new ground where they form fresh plants.

✿✿ Jul–Aug.

Short-fruited Willowherb

Epilobium obscurum | Saileachán caol

Ht. 80cm. **Fls.** 6–8mm, 4 notched, pink petals, *club-shaped* stigma; calyx tube has sparse glandular hairs; on upright stem with 4 *raised* ridges.

Lvs. Opposite, almost hairless, stalkless, ovate-lanceolate with *rounded* base.

Hab. Damp woodland, marshes, ditches. Commonly found native perennial.

Fam. Willowherb/Onagraceae.

☺ Fruits are less than 6cm long.

✿✿✿ Jul–Aug.

Broad-leaved Willowherb

Epilobium montanum | Saileachán leathan

Ht. 60cm. **Fls.** 6–9mm, 4 notched, pale pink petals, *4-lobed stigma*; on round, upright stem.

Lvs. Oval-lanceolate, toothed, usually opposite, occasionally alternate or in whorls of 3.

Hab. Roadsides, gardens, waste ground. Widespread, native perennial.

Fam. Willowherb/Onagraceae.

✿✿✿ Jun–Aug.

Rockery Willowherb

Epilobium pedunculare | Saileachán reatha

Ht. Prostrate to 20cm. **Fls.** 3–7mm, 4 deeply-notched pink or white petals, *club-shaped* stigma; on long, upright stalks rising from mat-forming stems.

Lvs. Round, loosely toothed green-bronze.

Hab. Bare, damp ground, wet mountains. Introduced perennial, in few NW locations.

Fam. Willowherb/Onagraceae.

✿ Jun–Aug. 🏃

American Willowherb
Epilobium ciliatum
Saileachán sráide

Ht. 75cm. **Fls.** 8–10mm, 4 deeply-notched pink petals, *club-shaped* stigma & calyx tube barely hairy; on reddish upright stems which have 4 raised lines & spreading *glandular* hairs.

Lvs. Short-stalked, opposite, hairless, lancolate-oval, loosely toothed.

Hab. Disturbed ground, gardens, roadsides, damp woodland. Introduced perennial, widespread in E & S.

Fam. Willowherb/Onagraceae.

☺ Very similar to Short-fruited Willowherb – look for glandular hairs on stem.

☺ Hairy pods contain cottony seeds.

☺ No stolons.

✿✿✿ Jun–Sep.

New Zealand Willowherb
Epilobium brunnescens
Saileachán sraoilleach

Ht. Creeping. **Fls.** 6–8mm, pale pink or white, with 4 notched petals; *club-shaped* stigma; solitary, on curved stalks ascending to 10cm; flower stalks arise from leaf-axils of creeping, pinkish stems which root at nodes; mat-forming plant.

Lvs. In opposite pairs, round-ovate, bronze tinted with central stem indented.

Hab. Damp, hilly regions, tracks, quarries, gravelly ground. Introduced perennial, frequent except for centre.

Fam. Willowherb/Onagraceae.

✿✿ Jun–Aug.

Heather
Calluna vulgaris
Fraoch mór

Ht. 80cm. **Fls.** 5mm long, 4 pink-purple petals, fused at base only, calyx similar colour but larger than corolla; bell-shaped; in slender, branched racemes on spreading, evergreen, woody stems.

Lvs. Scale-like, *paired*, overlapping on younger shoots, margins rolled back.

Hab. Acid soil, mountains, moorland. Widespread native perennial.

Fam. Heather/Ericaceae.

☺ Flowers can also be white.

☺ AKA Ling.

✿✿✿ Aug–Sep.

St Dabeoc's Heath
Daboecia cantabrica
Fraoch na haon choise

Ht. 60cm. **Fls.** 10–14mm long, pink to magenta, urn-shaped, 4 lobes turning back slightly; stamens do not protrude; each flower has a bract; in loose, terminal racemes on straggly, wiry stems.

Lvs. Alternate, lanceolate, narrow, dark green above, white felty undersides, margins rolled back.

Hab. Dry heaths, acid soils, rocky moors. Native perennial, only found in parts of Counties Galway & Mayo.

Fam. Heather/Ericaceae.

☺ A member of the Lusitanian flora (see p. 51).

✿ Jun–Oct. ✚

152

Bell Heather
Erica cinerea
Fraoch cloigíneach

Ht. 50cm. **Fls.** 5–6mm long, magenta-purple, bell-shaped; stamens not projecting; in clusters along upright, wiry stems, hairy when young, woody when mature.

Lvs. Needle-like, narrow, hairless, dark green, sometimes bronzy, in *whorls of 3* at intervals along stem.

Hab. Hills, moorland, dry acid soils. Native perennial, widespread except for centre of Ireland.

Fam. Heather/Ericaceae.

☺ Look for groups of flowers along stems & not clusters at the top as in Cross-leaved Heath.

✿✿✿ Jun–Sep.

Cross-leaved Heath
Erica tetralix
Fraoch naoscaí

Ht. 50cm. **Fls.** 7–9mm long, pale pink to magenta, globular with almost-closed mouths; stamens do not protrude; in tight, one-sided, terminal clusters on thin, woody, wiry, greyish branches.

Lvs. Grey, needle-like, narrow, in *whorls of 4* along the stems.

Hab. Heaths, wet moors, bogs, mountains. Fairly widespread native perennial.

Fam. Heather/Ericaceae.

☺ More commonly found on waterlogged, acid soil than Bell Heather.

✿✿✿ Jun–Oct.

Greater Sea-spurrey
Spergularia media
Cabróis mhara mhór

Ht. 40cm. **Fls.** 7–12mm, pale pink-mauve, 5-petalled; flowers have white centres with 10 stamens; *petals longer than sepals*; on hairless, fleshy, prostrate to ascending stems.

Lvs. Fleshy, opposite, linear with short points; triangular stipules are pale but not silvery.

Hab. Saltmarshes, brackish, muddy shores. Native perennial found commonly in coastal habitats.

Fam. Pink/Caryophyllaceae.

☺ Could be confused with Lesser Sea-Spurrey but that species has only *4 to 8 stamens* & petals *shorter* than sepals.

✿✿ Jun–Sep.

Lesser Sea-spurrey
Spergularia marina
Cabróis mhara bheag

Ht. Prostrate. **Fls.** 6–9mm, deep pink becoming paler towards centre of corolla; purple-tipped sepals *longer than petals*; 4–8 stamens; in loose clusters on sticky, trailing, fleshy stems.

Lvs. Yellowish-green, opposite, narrow, fleshy, slightly pointed with sheath-like stipule at their base.

Hab. Upper reaches of saltmarshes. Native annual, widespread in coastal habitats.

Fam. Pink/Caryophyllaceae.

☺ Occasionally biennial.

✿✿ May–Aug.

Rock Sea-spurrey
Spergularia rupicola
Cabróis na gcloch

Ht. 20cm. **Fls.**
8–12mm, pink (or white)
petals, *colour remaining same throughout*;
sepals & petals *equal*, 10 stamens; on
unridged, often purple, stems.

Lvs. Fleshy, narrow, flattened with
fine point; silvery stipules.

Hab. Coastal cliffs, rocks, scree, old
walls near sea. Native perennial quite
commonly found in coastal locations.

Fam. Pink/Caryophyllaceae.

☺ This is a stickily hairy plant unlike
Greater Sea-spurrey which is hairless.
Lesser Sea-spurrey is occasionally
stickily hairy.

✿✿ Jun–Sep.

> ***Spurreys*** *are low-growing, sprawling plants
> with fleshy leaves, stipules & small pink or white
> flowers. They have 5 uncleft petals, 5 sepals, 3 or 5
> styles. Mainly coastal, on walls or sandy soil.*

Sand Spurrey
Spergularia rubra
Cabróis dhuimhche

Ht. Prostrate.
Fls. 3–5mm,
pink petals,
paler at base,
*slightly shorter than
sepals*; 10 stamens;
in loose clusters on
sprawling stems.

Lvs. Grey-green, not fleshy, thin,
pointed; stickily hairy above;
silvery lanceolate stipules.

Hab. Open, dry sandy ground.
Rare native annual or biennial.
Only found occasionally in W,
SE & N.

Fam. Pink/Caryophyllaceae.

✿ May–Sep.

Ragged-robin
Silene flos-cuculi
Lus síoda

Ht. 70cm. **Fls.** 30–40mm, 5 pink, or sometimes white, petals, each divided into 4 narrow, pointed lobes; reddish sepals fused into 5-toothed, 10-veined tube; in loose clusters on erect, slender, red stems.

Lvs. Basal leaves oval & stalked; stem leaves opposite, narrow-lanceolate, unstalked.

Hab. Marshes, damp meadows, fens. Native perennial found frequently throughout.

Fam. Pink/Caryophyllaceae.

☺ Petals have been modified into strips to cope with harsh weather.

✿✿✿ May–Aug.

Red Campion
Silene dioica
Coireán coilleach

Ht. 1m. **Fls.** 20–30mm, 5 rose-pink, deeply cleft petals; very short, white inner ring stands erect around centre; dark-red calyx is 10-veined; dioecious – male flowers smaller than female flowers (from which stigma protrudes); in loose cymes on erect, hairy stems.

Lvs. Opposite, untoothed, oblong-oval, pointed, hairy, lower stalked, upper unstalked.

Hab. Shady hedgerows, grassy banks, woods. Native biennial or perennial, uncommon except in NE.

Fam. Pink/Caryophyllaceae.

☺ Hybridises with White Campion (p. 35)

✿✿ Mar–Oct.

Bog Pimpernel
Anagallis tenella
Falcaire corraigh

Ht. Creeping to 5cm. **Fls.** 6–10mm long, bell-shaped with 5 pink lobes, each finely veined with crimson; upright & solitary on long, slender stems from leaf axils.

Lvs. Opposite, round, short-stalked, untoothed on long, trailing stems.

Hab. Wet, peaty ground, marshes, mainly on acid soil. Native perennial, more common in W & S than elsewhere.

Fam. Primrose/Primulaceae.

☺ Mat-forming plant which roots at nodes.

▶ Yellow Pimpernel (p. 96) & Scarlet Pimpernel (p. 200).

✿✿ Jun–Aug.

Soapwort
Saponaria officinalis
Garbhán creagach

Ht. 70cm. **Fls.** 25–35mm, pale pink, unnotched petals, sepals joined together in smooth tube; in crowded heads on upright, thick, brittle, hollow, hairless stems.

Lvs. Opposite, bright or pale green, smooth, narrow with 3–5 conspicuous veins.

Hab. Roadsides, waste ground, grassy places. Introduced perennial, more commonly found near habitation.

Fam. Pink/Caryophyllaceae.

☺ Flowers have a heavy fragrance.

☺ Stamens protrude from single flowered version but not from double-flowered.

✿✿ Jun–Aug. 🏃

Common Mallow
Malva sylvestris
Lus na meall Muire

Ht. 1.5m. **Fls.** 20–50mm,
pink-purple, 5 widely-notched,
well-separated, dark-veined petals,
about 4 times longer than sepals;
in clusters at leaf axils; on erect or
spreading stout stems.

Lvs. Rounded at base of plant,
palmate stem leaves with 5, toothed
lobes.

Hab. Roadsides, waste ground,
railway embankments. Introduced
perennial, common
in E, SE & S.

Fam. Mallow/
Malvaceae.

✿✿✿ Jun–Oct.

Tree-mallow
Malva arborea
Hocas ard

Ht. 3m. **Fls.** 30–50mm; 5 overlapping
petals, pink towards outer edge,
becoming dark purple at centre of flower;
petals united at centre, considerably
longer than sepals; numerous stamens;
in clusters of 2–7 at upper leaf axils; on
stout stems; very downy plant.

Lvs. Palmately lobed, long-stalked,
velvety, folding like a fan.

Hab. Coastal, rocky areas & waste
ground. Native to some areas, introduced
into others, a biennial found on coasts in
E, SE, S & SW.

Fam. Mallow/
Malvaceae.

✿✿ Jun–Sep.

Musk-mallow
Malva moschata
Hocas muscach

Ht. 80cm. **Fls.** 30–50mm, rosy-pink or white; 5 notched, slightly overlapping petals; solitarily in leaf axils or in loose terminal clusters on stiff, erect stems.

Lvs. Lower long-stalked, kidney shaped, divided; upper cut deeply into 5–7 narrow, feathery lobes.

Hab. Roadsides, hedgerows, well-drained field margins. Introduced perennial, scattered but only common in SE.

Fam. Mallow/Malvaceae.

✿ Jul–Oct.

Pale Butterwort
Pinguicula lusitanica
Leith uisce beag

Ht. 10cm. **Fls.** 5–8mm, pale pink-lilac, with yellow throat, darker pink spur; lobes of upper lip are rounded, spur cylindrical, blunt, short; on long, slender stem.

Lvs. Basal rosette of pale olive-green, thick, purple-veined leaves; margins are rolled in & sticky.

Hab. Bogs, wet heaths. Native perennial found occasionally in damp habitat, rarer in Midlands.

Fam. Bladderwort/Lentibulariaceae.

☺ Sticky leaves trap small insects to supplement meagre nutrition found in bogland.

▶ Common & Large-flowered Butterwort (p. 227).

✿ Jun–Sep.

Water Avens
Geum rivale
Macall uisce

Ht. 50cm. **Fls.** 8–15mm long, nodding, bell-shaped, dusty-pink; striped petals & dark red-purple sepals; arched, hairy, red stems.

Lvs. Basal leaves pinnate with trifoliate leaves further up stem; small stipules at base of stem leaves.

Hab. Damp riversides, marshes, mountain ledges. Native perennial, occasional; more common in N.

Fam. Rose/Rosaceae.

☺ Seeds are in fluffy, feathery bur-like heads which contain hooked styles.

✿✿ May–Aug.

*Most members of the **Rose** family have 5 petals, 5 sepals & numerous stamens. Leaves are alternate, almost always with stipules.*

Bramble
Rubus fruticosus agg. *
Dris

Ht. 3m. **Fls.** 20–30mm, pink or white, 5 petals & 5 sepals which fold back when flower opens; numerous stamens surrounding cluster of carpels; in loose panicles on tough, arching, prickly, angled stems which root at shoot tips.

Lvs. Alternate, grey-green, 3–5 toothed, oval leaflets often whitish beneath.

Hab. Hedgerows, railway tracks, scrub. Widespread native shrub.

Fam. Rose/Rosaceae.

☺ Fruit is our familiar 'blackberry'.

* Very complex aggregate or group of very closely related species.

▶ Dewberry (p. 46).

✿✿✿ May–Sept.

Dog-rose
Rosa canina
Feirdhris

Ht. 3m. **Fls.** 30–50mm, pink or white, wide, saucer-shaped, scented corolla; numerous stamens stand well clear of styles; sepals bend back after flowering; in small clusters on stiff, long, arching stems.

Lvs. Pinnate with 5–7 broad, hairless leaflets.

Hab. Hedgerows, scrubland, woodland margins. Native shrub more common in E half of Ireland than W.

Fam. Rose/Rosaceae.

☺ Stems bear curved thorns.

☺ Fruit is a red, egg-shaped hip.

▶ Burnet Rose & Field-rose (both p.47).

✿✿ Jun–Jul.

Japanese Rose
Rosa rugosa
Rós rúscach

Ht. 1.5m. **Fls.** 60–90mm, 5 slightly wrinkled, deep pink or white petals surrounding centre which is crowded with golden stamens; sweetly scented; on downy stalks & densely prickly, thicket-forming, suckering branches.

Lvs. Shiny, furrowed, dark, pinnate with 5–9 oval leaflets.

Hab. Hedgerows, roadsides. Introduced shrub, occasional.

Fam. Rose/Rosaceae.

☺ Branches carry thorns which are almost straight.

☺ Distinctive red hips are covered in little bristles.

☺ Classed as 'potentially invasive'.

✿ Jun–Aug. 🏃 🌀

Common Centaury
Centaurium erythraea
Dréimire Muire

Ht. 50cm. **Fls.** 10–12mm; 5 (occasionally 6) spreading, pink petals fused into a long tube; orange anthers & tightly-clasping, long, toothed sepals; in flat-topped clusters at top of erect, hairless stems & also from side shoots, only opening in full sunshine.

Lvs. Opposite, pale green, oval, 3–7 veined, lower forming *basal rosette*, upper being narrower.

Hab. Damp woodland paths, scrub, dunes & on short coastal turf. Widespread native annual or biennial.

Fam. Gentian/Gentianaceae.

☺ These flowers only open in full sunshine.

✿✿✿ Jun–Sep.

Lesser Centaury
Centaurium pulchellum
Dréimire beag

Ht. 15cm. **Fls.** 5–8mm, pink with 5 (occasion-ally 4) narrow lobes & long corolla-tube; calyx closely gripping corolla-tube; in open clusters on very short, hairless, slender, ridged stems.

Lvs. Opposite, lanceolate, pointed, untoothed, 3–7 veined; *only on stem*.

Hab. Damp grassy places, sandy coastal ground, dry saltmarshes. Rare, native annual, only found in a few locations in SE.

Fam. Gentian/Gentianaceae.

☺ Lesser Centaury *lacks a basal rosette*.

☺ This is a protected species.

✿ Jun–Sep. ⊞

Pink Purslane
Claytonia sibirica
Nuaireacht dhearg

Ht. 30cm. **Fls.** 15–20mm; 5 dark-veined, notched, pink petals, small yellow markings towards centre of flower; in small clusters on erect, hairless stems.

Lvs. Basal leaves oval, stalked; stem leaves opposite, veined, stalkless.

Hab. Damp woodland, sandy soil. Introduced annual or perennial, very occasional in NE & SE.

Fam. Blinks/Montiaceae.

☺ Stamens are tipped with *pink pollen*.

☺ Look for *2 cup-shaped* sepals.

✿ Apr–Jul. 🏃

Pink-sorrel
Oxalis articulata
Seamsóg ghlúineach

Ht. 30cm. **Fls.** 15–25mm, 5 spreading, unnotched, pink petals with deep purple veins, making flower seem slightly twisted; in loose umbels on long, slender stems.

Lvs. Trifoliate, each segment heart-shaped, downy with orange or brown spots below; on long, slender stems arising from base.

Hab. Road banks, waste & coastal ground. Introduced perennial, frequent in NE & SE.

Fam. Wood-sorrel/Oxalidaceae.

☺ Garden escape now naturalised.

✿✿ May–Oct. 🏃

Cut-leaved Crane's-bill
Geranium dissectum
Crobh giobach

Ht. 50cm. **Fls.** 8–10mm; 5 notched, pink-purple petals, each with 3 dark purple veins; blue anthers; on short, straggling, downy stalks.

Lvs. Divided almost to base; *narrow* lobes.

Hab. Bare or grassy places, cultivated & disturbed soil. Widespread native annual.

Fam. Crane's-bill/Geraniaceae.

☺ Downy seeds are encased in long pointed seedpod which ejects seeds when ripe.

✿✿✿ May–Sep.

Crane's-bill flowers have 5, usually pink or mauve, separate petals & 5 sepals, 5 or 10 stamens & alternate, usually pinnate or palmate leaves with stipules. The Crane's-bill family distinguishes itself by having fruits which resemble cranes' beaks & these 'beaks' roll up & expel the seeds.

Dove's-foot Crane's-bill
Geranium molle
Crobh bog

Ht. 20cm. **Fls.** 5–10mm; 5 notched, pink petals, barely longer than sepals; anthers blue; in pairs on spreading, branched, hairy stems.

Lvs. Grey-green, *rounded*, hairy, deeply-etched, divided into 5–7 lobes.

Hab. Cultivated & waste ground, roadsides. Common native annual.

Fam. Crane's-bill/Geraniaceae.

☺ Seedpods are hairless.

✿✿✿ Apr–Aug.

Bloody Crane's-bill
Geranium sanguineum
Crobh dearg

Ht. 30cm. **Fls.** 20–30mm, 5 magenta-reddish-purple, slightly notched, heart-shaped petals, hairy sepals; usually solitary, nodding when in bud, on long, hairy, slender stems which bear a small pair of bracts halfway up.

Lvs. Round but deeply divided, almost to base, into 5–7 lobes.

Hab. Calcareous grassland, sand-dunes, limestone pavement. Native perennial found in Counties Clare, Galway & Dublin.

Fam. Crane's-bill/Geraniaceae.

☺ Leaves turn red in autumn.

✿ Jun–Aug.

Hedgerow Crane's-bill
Geranium pyrenaicum
Crobh na bhfál

Ht. 60cm. **Fls.** 12–18mm, 5 deeply-notched, veined, purple-pink petals, each fading to lighter shade of pink towards centre of flower; sepals bristle-tipped; drooping in bud; in pairs on downy, branched stems.

Lvs. Bright-green, rounded, *divided halfway* into 5–7 lobes, *only* toothed at ends.

Hab. Scrambling over rough hedges, roadsides & waste ground. Introduced perennial, common in Leinster & parts of S. Munster.

Fam. Crane's-bill / Geraniaceae.

☺ Hairy, beaked fruit splits when ripe.

✿✿ Jun–Aug.

Long-stalked Crane's-bill
Geranium columbinum
Crobh coilm

Ht. 60cm. **Fls.** 12–18mm, 5 unnotched, veined, pink petals; striped, bristle-tipped sepals; on long stalks (to 6cm) which stand clear of leaves; sometimes nodding when in bud; scrambling plant, often red-tinged.

Lvs. Divided to base into long, narrow lobes; lower leaves *long-stalked*.

Hab. Scattered, native annual, found mainly in S half of Ireland.

Fam. Crane's-bill / Geraniaceae.

☺ Fruit almost hairless.

☺ Long flower stalks help to differentiate this species.

✿ Jun–Aug.

Herb-Robert
Geranium robertianum
Ruithéal rí

Ht. 40cm. **Fls.** 12–18mm, 5 unnotched, pink petals; each is *clawed* (having narrow, stalk-like base) & has paler pink lines; *yellow-orange* pollen; in loose clusters on straggly, hairy, often red, stems.

Lvs. Hairy, stalked, bright green & often tinged red, with 3–5 deeply cut lobes; upper leaves mostly 3-lobed.

Hab. Banks, bases of walls, shingle, shady places. Widespread native annual.

Fam. Crane's-bill /Geraniaceae.

☺ Strong, *unpleasant* smelling.

✿✿✿ Apr–Oct.

Shining Crane's-bill
Geranium lucidum
Crobh geal

Ht. 30cm. **Fls.** 10–15mm, 5 unnotched, round pink petals with marked claws; sepals are *inflated, hairless & keeled*; on branched, almost hairless stems; similar to Herb-Robert but smaller.

Lvs. Round, glossy, long-stalked, cut halfway into 5–7 lobes, each cut further; often red tinged.

Hab. Shady banks, limestone walls. Widespread but local annual, native to County Clare & parts of Munster, introduced elsewhere.

Fam. Crane's-bill / Geraniaceae.

✿✿ Apr–Aug.

Pencilled Crane's-bill
Geranium versicolor | Crobh stríocach

Ht. 60cm. **Fls.** 20–30mm, 5 notched, pale pink or white petals, delicate tracery of dark violet-coloured veins; petals curved outwards; flowers in pairs on erect downy stems.

Lvs. Downy, 3–6 quite broad, toothed lobes.

Hab. Hedgerows, shady damp woodland. Introduced perennial, scattered in E & SE.

Fam. Crane's-bill /Geraniaceae.

☺ Easily confused with Druce's Crane's-bill.
✿ Jun–Jul. 🟩

Druce's Crane's-bill
Geranium x oxonianum | Crobh gallda

Ht. 60cm. **Fls.** 18–25mm, 5 shallowly-notched, pink petals, purple-veined in similar way to Pencilled Crane's-bill; petals not curved outwards as much as in that species; anthers tipped purple; on erect downy stems.

Lvs. Palmate, divided into 5 lobes; deeply veined.

Hab. Grassy verges, hedgerows, not too far from gardens. Introduced perennial, uncommon except in SE.

Fam. Crane's-bill /Geraniaceae.

☺ This is a hybrid between *Geranium endressii* & *G. versicolor.*

✿ May–Sep. 🏃

Dusky Crane's-bill
Geranium phaeum | Crobh odhar

Ht. 60cm. **Fls.** 15–20mm, 5 deep maroon, somewhat reflexed, slightly pointed petals; stamens in a tightly-packed cluster; on hairy stems.

Lvs. Rounded, divided into 5–7 lobes.

Hab. Grassy verges, woodland edges. Introduced perennial, uncommon except in NE.

Fam. Crane's-bill /Geraniaceae.

✿ May–Jul. 🏃

Round-leaved Crane's-bill
Geranium rotundifolium
Crobh cruinn

Ht. 40cm. **Fls.** 10–12mm, 5 pink, barely-notched petals; *sepals not bristle-tipped*; mostly in pairs, on glandular-hairy, much-branched, trailing stems.

Lvs. Kidney-shaped, only shallowly lobed & not round as name suggests.

Hab. Dry, grassy places, calcareous soil & waste ground. *Rare* native annual only found in parts of E & S.

Fam. Crane's-bill / Geraniaceae.

☺ Fruit hairy & smooth.

✿ Jun–Jul. ⊞

Common Stork's-bill
Erodium cicutarium
Creagach

Ht. 30cm. **Fls.** 10–15mm, 5 unlobed, round rose-pink (or sometimes white), *unequal* petals; base of each of larger, upper 2 petals has dark spot; in loose umbels on stickily hairy, spreading stems.

Lvs. Feathery, lobes pinnately cut; conspicuous, pointed, whitish stipules.

Hab. Sandy soil, bare, grassy, coastal places. Native annual or biennial, locally widespread.

Fam. Crane's-bill / Geraniaceae.

☺ Fruit is a long, hairy beak.

✿✿ May–Aug.

Musk Stork's-bill

Erodium moschatum
Creagach muscach

Ht. 60cm. **Fls.** 10–20mm, 5
pink-mauve petals, 5 hairy sepals with
long tip; in clusters of 4–10, on *stickily-
hairy*, much-branched stems; stems carry
3 broad, papery stipules at the base of
each branch.

Lvs. Pinnate, divided less than halfway
with toothed lobes.

Hab. Waste ground, coastal dunes, field
margins. Annual, probably introduced
into Ireland, this plant is quite rare,
found mainly on coastal sites in S half.

Fam. Crane's-bill/Geraniaceae.

☺ Smells strongly of musk.

✿ May–Aug.

Sea Stork's-bill

Erodium maritimum
Creagach mara

Ht. Prostrate. **Fls.** 3–4mm,
palest-pink petals *frequently absent*,
falling off early in the day, 5
hairy sepals remaining; solitary
or paired, on hairy, sprawling
stems.

Lvs. Lobed, hairy, oval in
outline.

Hab. Coastal dunes, waste
ground. Rare native annual
found only in coastal areas of
E & SE.

Fam. Crane's-bill/Geraniaceae.

☺ Little petals are *rarely seen*.

☺ Fruit is long & beak-like.

✿ May–Jul. ✚

Common Vetch

Vicia sativa ssp. *segetalis*
Peasair chapaill

Ht. 80cm. **Fls.** 18–30mm long,
pink-mauve peaflowers; calyx teeth equal;
singly or in pairs in leaf axils; on clambering,
downy stems.

Lvs. 3–8 pairs, ovate, trefoil, bristle-
tipped; toothed stipules at base, often with
dark spot; tendrils sometimes unbranched.

Hab. Dry grasslands, hedgerows. Native
annual, common except for NW.

Fam. Pea/Fabaceae.

☺ Fruits are pods with 4–12 smooth
seeds; pods ripen brown to black.

▶ Bush Vetch (p. 250), Bitter &
Tufted Vetch (both p. 251).

✿✿ Apr–Sep.

Small Toadflax

Chaenorhinum minus
Buaflíon beag

Ht. 25cm. **Fls.** 6–8mm long, pale
pink-lilac, 2-lipped corolla with
short spur; upper lip 2-lobed, lower
lip 3-lobed; slight yellow flush around
opening; solitary, on long, stickily-
hairy, erect stalks arising from leaf axils.

Lvs. Oblong, alternate, untoothed.

Hab. Arable fields, dry banks, walls, waste
ground & along railway tracks. Introduced
annual, not very common.

Fam. Speedwell/Veronicaceae.

▶ Common Toadflax (p. 138), Ivy-leaved
Toadflax (p. 226) & Purple Toadflax (p. 246).

✿✿ May–Oct.

Sea Bindweed
Calystegia soldanella
Plúr an phrionsa

Ht. Prostrate. **Fls.** 30–50mm, trumpet-shaped, pink, 5 equally-spaced white lines running into centre; epicalyx bracts shorter than sepals; solitary on hairless, creeping stems arising from rhizomes; not climbing.

Lvs. Fleshy, shiny, kidney-shaped, long-stalked.

Hab. Sandy sea-shores, dunes, shingle. Native perennial, common on E & S coasts.

Fam. Bindweed/Convolvulaceae.

▶ Hedge & Large Bindweed (p. 49).

✿✿ Jun–Aug.

Field Bindweed
Convolvulus arvensis
Ainleog

Ht. Climbing to 3m.
Fls. 20–30mm, trumped-shaped, pink or white with broad, white stripes; sepals 5-lobed, without epicalyx; on twining stems arising from fleshy rhizomes.

Lvs. Arrow-shaped, stalk shorter than blade.

Hab. Roadsides, grassland, railway tracks, seen as an aggressive garden weed. Native perennial, fairly common throughout.

Fam. Bindweed/Convolvulaceae.

▶ Hedge & Large Bindweed (p. 49).

✿✿✿ Jun–Sep.

Bog-rosemary
Andromeda polifolia
Lus na móinte

Ht. 40cm. **Fls.** 8–10mm long, urn-shaped, with 5 joined lobes which roll back slightly at mouth; initially rose-pink, turning paler; with 5 small, pink sepals & pink petioles; drooping in small clusters of 5 or so, on upright, hairless stems.

Lvs. Alternate, untoothed; dark green above with tracery of veins etched into surface & pronounced mid-rib.

Hab. Acid soil, raised & blanket bogs, always beside *Sphagnum* moss. Native evergreen shrub, frequent in the Midlands.

Fam. Heather/Ericaceae.

✿✿ May–Sep. ⊞

Meadow Saffron
Colchicum autumnale
Cróch an fhómhair

Ht. 20cm. **Fls.** 40mm long, pink-purple, occasionally white; 6 lobes or tepals, *6 stamens* with yellow anthers; each flower solitary on weak, white perianth tube, appearing like a stem, directly from ground.

Lvs. Bright green, broad, long, on short stems; erect in spring, dying away before flower blooms.

Hab. Damp meadows, close to rivers. Rare, native perennial, only found in SE.

Fam. Meadow Saffron/Colchicaceae.

✿ Aug–Oct. ⊞

Thrift
Armeria maritima
Rabhán

Ht. 30cm. **Fls.** 8mm, 5-petalled, pink or white, papery, fragrant, in dense, roundish heads 15–25mm across; brownish, tubular, membranous sheath below each flower-head; on erect, slender, leafless stalks.

Lvs. Linear, grass-like, one-veined, basal, in loose rosettes; cushion-forming.

Hab. Mainly coastal, on cliffs, saltmarshes. Locally frequent native perennial.

Fam. Thrift/Plumbaginaceae.

✿✿✿ Apr–Aug.

Common Valerian
Valeriana officinalis
Caorthann corraigh

Ht. 70cm. **Fls.** 2–5mm, pale-pink corolla, tubular with 5 lobes & 3 protruding stamens; in dense umbels 40–70mm across; on thick, erect stems, branching in upper part; unpleasantly scented.

Lvs. Opposite, pinnate, lanceolate-oval with toothed leaflets; lower leaves long-stalked, upper short-stalked.

Hab. Rivers, canals, meadows, damp hedgerows. Widespread native perennial.

Fam. Valerian/ Valerianaceae.

▶ Red Valerian (p. 202).

✿✿✿ Jun–Aug. 🏃

Wild Angelica
Angelica sylvestris
Gallfheabhrán

Ht. 2m. **Fls.** White, often flushed pink, in *domed* umbels to 15cm across; numerous rays, bracts absent or few; on robust, hollow, ridged, stems, branching towards top & purple tinged.

Lvs. Inflated sheathing bases connect leaves to main stems; 2–3 pinnate with oval to oblong segments.

Hab. Roadsides, river banks & damp, grassy places. Widespread native perennial.

Fam. Carrot/Apiaceae.

☺ Fruits oval, flattened, 4 winged.

☺ Wild Angelica has a sweet scent.

✿✿✿ Jun–Aug.

Upright Hedge-parsley
Torilis japonica
Fionnas fáil

Ht. 1m. **Fls.** 2–3mm, pale pink to purple; notched petals, outer longer than inner; in terminal, long-stalked umbels, 20–40mm across, each umbel with *up to 12 rays*; on hairy, rough, ridged, solid, unspotted, branched stems with downward-pointing, straight hairs, pressed close to stem.

Lvs. Coarsely toothed, hairy, lanceolate, 1–3 pinnate, upper leaves small & often trifoliate.

Hab. Hedgerows, laneways, woodland margins. Widespread native annual.

Fam. Carrot/Apiaceae.

☺ Fruits are egg-shaped & covered with tiny, curved hooks.

✿✿✿ Jul–Aug.

Mountain Everlasting
Antennaria dioica
Catluibh

Ht. 20cm. **Fls.** *Dioecious* species, both sexes having tightly-packed flower-heads of florets; female flower-heads 12mm, pink-tipped bracts, male flower-heads 6mm, white-tipped bracts, spreading outward; flower-heads in clusters of up to 8; on upright, downy, unbranched stems.

Lvs. Basal rosette spoon-shaped, stem leaves narrow, downy below.

Hab. Limestone, cliffs, sand-dunes. Native perennial frequent in N half.

Fam. Daisy/Asteraceae.

☺ AKA Cat's-paw, due to shape.

✿✿ Jun–Aug.

Alsike Clover
Trifolium hybridum
Seamair Lochlannach

Ht. 30cm. **Fls.** Small, white peaflowers in dense, packed 16mm heads; flowers turning pink or brown; on long stalks.

Lvs. Trifoliate, toothed, *without* markings.

Hab. Verges, waste & cultivated ground. Introduced perennial, local in SE & NE.

Fam. Pea/Fabaceae.

☺ Differs from White Clover in having erect stems which *do not root*.

▶ Strawberry Clover (see opposite page).

✿✿ Jun–Oct.

Hare's-foot Clover
Trifolium arvense
Cos mhaideach

Ht. 25cm. **Fls.** 20–30mm long, egg-shaped
heads of tiny, pale pink peaflowers, each
surrounded by long sepal tube with fine,
hairy teeth giving flower-heads soft, silky
appearance; heads stalked, some axillary,
most terminal; on slender, erect hairy stems.

Lvs. Trefoil with narrow, oval, scarcely-
toothed leaflets.

Hab. Dry, mostly coastal, sandy soil.
Occasional native annual in S, E
& NE.

Fam. Pea/Fabaceae.

☺ Heads lengthen, becoming
cylindrical.

✿✿ Jun–Sep.

Strawberry Clover
Trifolium fragiferum
Seamair mhogallach

Ht. Creeping to 15cm.

Fls. 10–15mm, round, clustered head
of tiny, pale pink peaflowers; on creeping
stems, *rooting at nodes*.

Lvs. Trifoliate with oval lobes, *without* white
marks; on long stems.

Hab. Coastal areas, grassland,
old pasture. Scarce, native
perennial, found mainly in SE
& SW.

Fam. Pea/Fabaceae.

☺ Densely hairy calyx
which swells in fruit, forming
round, pink bladders which makes
flower-head resemble small, pink strawberry.

▶ White Clover (p. 55).

✿ Jul–Sep.

For more about
Peaflowers see p. 114.

Babington's Leek

Allium ampeloprasum var. *babingtonii* | Cainneann

Ht. 2m. **Fls.** 5–8mm mauve, cup-shaped in dense, globular, 5–9cm heads; forming 6–8mm *bulbils* which detach; heads initially sheathed in papery spathe; on erect, stout stems.

Lvs. Long, glaucous, grass-like, keeled.

Hab. Roadsides, sandy places. Native perennial found occasionally in W.

Fam. Onion/Alliaceae. ✿ Jun–Sep.

Wild Leek

Allium ampeloprasum var. *ampeloprasum*
Cainneann fhiáin

Ht. 1.75m. **Fls.** 8–15mm long, dark-pink to mauve, bell-shaped & almost closed, with yellow anthers; in tightly-packed round heads on robust, stout stems.

Lvs. Long, glaucous, grass-like, keeled, tending to wither.

Hab. Roadside banks, ditches. Introduced perennial found occasionally in SE only.

Fam. Onion/Alliaceae.

☺ Before plant blooms, cluster is covered with papery sheath with long, pointed tip. ✿ Jun–Sep.

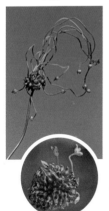

Crow Garlic

Allium vineale | Gairleog Mhuire

Ht. 60cm. **Fls.** 2–4mm, pink or green-white, wide bell-shape, protruding stamens, on 1–2cm long stalks arising from round cluster of bulbils; protected by papery bract initially; on round, stiff, smooth, often blotched stems.

Lvs. Grey-green, half-cylindrical, hollow.

Hab. Dry grassland, disturbed ground, hedgerows. Native perennial, occasional in E, SE & SW.

Fam. Onion/Alliaceae.

☺ Bulbils detach & fall to the ground to become new plants. AKA Wild Onion.

✿ Jun–Jul.

Lousewort
Pedicularis sylvatica
Lus an ghiolla

Ht. 20cm. **Fls.** 20–25mm long, pink,
2-lipped, *upper lip with **2 teeth** at tip only*;
emerging from inflated, 5-sided, purplish,
veined & lobed calyx; in small spikes on
numerous branching stems.

Lvs. Small, pinnate, fern-like with toothed,
lobed segments.

Hab. Damp, peaty soil & bogland. Native
perennial, common
throughout.

Fam. Broomrape/
Orobanchaceae.

☺ A plant which is
semi- parasitic on roots
of other plants.

✿✿✿ Apr–Jul.

Marsh Lousewort
Pedicularis palustris
Milseán móna

Ht. 60cm. **Fls.** 20–25mm long, reddish-
pink, 2-lipped; ***4 teeth** on narrow, upper lip*;
lower lip is hairy-edged; on erect stems,
often a bushy plant with many branches &
flowers, frequently at *right-angles* to stem.

Lvs. Feathery, divided deeply into toothed
lobes.

Hab. Marshes, fens & bogs. Native
annual, not as commonly found as
Lousewort.

Fam. Broomrape/
Orobanchaceae.

☺ Note ***4 teeth*** on upper lip.

☺ Also Semi-parasitic.

✿✿✿ May–Sep.

Water-pepper
Persicaria hydropiper
Biorphiobar

Ht. 70cm. **Fls.** 3–4mm long, pale pink to green-white with 4–5 lobes; in graceful, arched, slender spikes, nodding at tip; on upright, branched hairless stems.

Lvs. Alternate, lanceolate, untoothed, peppery tasting; around leaf base is a tubular, sheath-like brown or silver ochrea.

Hab. Damp, waste ground, shallow lake margins & marshes. Widespread native annual.

Fam. Knotweed/ Polygonaceae.

✿✿✿ Jul–Sep.

Amphibious Bistort
Persicaria amphibia
Glúineach uisce

Ht. 40cm. **Fls.** 2–3mm long, pink, 5-lobed with 2 styles, 5 protruding stamens; in dense, oval, terminal spikes.

Lvs. Two forms of this plant exist: aquatic has hairless, floating leaves, truncate at base; terrestrial form has hairy, narrow leaves, round at base, short-stalked.

Hab. Slow moving streams, marshes, ponds, damp fields & ditches. Native perennial, found throughout in specific habitat.

Fam. Knotweed/ Polygonaceae.

✿✿ Jun–Sep.

Redshank
Persicaria maculosa
Glúineach dhearg

Ht. 80cm. **Fls.** 3–4mm long, pink,
bell-shaped, 5 tepals fused halfway;
in dense, cylindrical terminal spikes
& in spikes in leaf axils; on upright or
sprawling reddish stems, swollen at leaf
bases.

Lvs. Alternate, lanceolate-oval, often with
dark blotch.

Hab. Arable land, roadsides, cultivated
land. Widespread native annual.

Fam. Knotweed/
Polygonaceae.

✿✿✿ Jun–Oct.

Common Ramping-fumitory
Fumaria muralis
Camán searraigh balla

Ht. 10cm. **Fls.** 9–11mm long, tubular,
pink with deep purple tips; upper petals
compressed, spoon-shaped with broad
wings; lower petal with almost parallel
sides, slightly up-turned, not paddle-
shaped; in loose spikes on spreading or
upright stems.

Lvs. Lobed, floppy, feathery, weak.

Hab. Arable land, gardens, waste ground,
hedgerows. Introduced annual, common
in E & S.

Fam. Poppy/Papaveraceae.

▶ White Ramping-
fumitory (p. 24).

✿✿ Apr–Sep.

Sea-milkwort
Glaux maritima
Lus an tsailte

Ht. 10cm. **Fls.** 5–6mm, no petals, 5 pale pink sepals, 5 stamens; on very short stalks solitarily in leaf axils; on upright shoots from low-growing, mat-forming, creeping stems.

Lvs. Opposite, ovate, fleshy, unstalked.

Hab. Saltmarshes, damp sand & shingle. Native perennial, common in coastal regions.

Fam. Primrose/Primulaceae.

☺ This plant creeps on stems which root down at nodes.

✿✿✿ May–Sep.

Flowering Currant
Ribes sanguineum
Cuirín

Ht. 2m. **Fls.** 6–10mm, 5 spreading, deep pink sepals & 5 small, pale pink petals, almost forming tube; at centre of flower tube is a 2-branched style & 5 yellow stamens; in racemes of 6–30 flowers, borne in drooping bunches from tips of branches.

Lvs. Bright green, unpleasantly scented, palmate 5-lobed.

Hab. Hedgerows, roadsides, woodland. Introduced deciduous shrub, common in NE & SE mainly.

Fam. Currant/Grossulariaceae.

☺ Fruits are dark purple berries, not poisonous but bitter.

✿✿ Mar–May. 🏃

Snowberry
Symphoricarpos albus
Póirín sneachta

Ht. 3m. **Fls.** 4–6mm,
funnel-shaped, 4–5 lobed;
outer side of corolla is pink with
white inside; in short, dense,
terminal racemes of 5–15 on arching
branches.

Lvs. Oval, hairless, untoothed.

Hab. Thicket-forming in hedgerows,
roadsides, woodland, scrub.
Introduced deciduous shrub.

Fam. Honeysuckle/Caprifoliaceae.

☺ Fruits are soft, round, white
berries, poisonous to humans but
eaten by pheasants.

☺ Potentially invasive species.

✿✿ Jun–Sep.

Himalayan Honeysuckle
Leycesteria formosa
Féithleann álainn

Ht. 2m. **Fls.** 10–20mm, pale pinkish-
purple, funnel-shaped with central,
long stigma & 5 short stamens; in
whorls in axis of larger, maroon
bracts; in drooping spikes on woody,
red stems.

Lvs. Large, opposite, lanceolate,
red-stemmed.

Hab. Hedgerows, woodland,
roadsides. Introduced deciduous
shrub, scattered in E & SE mainly.

Fam. Honeysuckle/
Caprifoliaceae.

☺ AKA Pheasant-berry due
to berries which are red at first
becoming black & eaten by birds.

✿✿ Jul–Sep.

Field Woundwort
Stachys arvensis
Cuislín gan duaire

Ht. 30cm. **Fls.** 12–20mm long, pale pink, 2-lipped, with faint purple markings on flat 3-lobed lower lip; in leafy whorls of 2–6, each emerging from 5-toothed, extremely hairy calyx; on creeping, upright, hairy, square stems.

Lvs. Opposite, heart-shaped, bluntly toothed; lower stalked, upper not stalked.

Hab. Arable, sandy, disturbed soil. Introduced annual, common in S & SE.

Fam. Dead-nettle/Lamiaceae.

✿✿ Apr–Oct.

Marsh Woundwort
Stachys palustris
Cabhsadán

Ht. 1m. **Fls.** 12–15mm long, pale, pinkish-purple; 2-lipped with concave upper lip & spreading, white-patterned lower lip; in whorls on open spikes; on square, hairy, creeping, maroon-coloured stems.

Lvs. Opposite, narrow, oblong-lanceolate, mostly with stalk.

Hab. Damp hedgerows, marshes, ditches. Widespread native perennial.

Fam. Dead-nettle/Lamiaceae.

▶ Hedge Woundwort (p. 204).

✿✿✿ Jun–Sep.

Wild Thyme
Thymus polytrichus
Tím chreige

Ht. Creeping to 8cm. **Fls.** 3–4mm long, pink-purple, 4 unequal-sized lobes; in dense, round heads; on sprawling, square stems, 2 sides being hairy, 2 sides almost hairless.

Lvs. Opposite, oval, short-stalked, with bristles at margins.

Hab. Dry grasslands, dunes, cliffs. Native perennial, common in coastal areas mainly.

Fam. Dead-nettle/Lamiaceae.

☺ Sweet & delicate fragrance, stronger when crushed.

▶ Basil Thyme (p. 246).

✿✿ Jun–Sep.

Wild Marjoram
Origanum vulgare
Máirtín fiáin

Ht. 70cm. **Fls.** 6–8mm long, pinkish-mauve, 2-lipped; lower lip is 3-lobed; 4-pointed calyx, red-tinged & shorter than flower tube; on reddish, downy, erect stems, branched in upper part.

Lvs. Opposite, oval, pointed, untoothed; leaf surface covered in tiny glands.

Hab. Mostly on lime, roadsides, dry grassland. Native perennial, scattered & uncommon except for Midland region.

Fam. Dead-nettle/Lamiaceae.

☺ Leaves have aromatic smell.

✿✿ Jul–Sep.

Red Dead-nettle
Lamium purpureum
Caochneantóg dhearg

Ht. 30cm. **Fls.** 10–18 mm long,
pink-purple, 2-lipped; upper lip hooded,
lower lip toothed with purple markings;
corolla tube is straight, longer than
calyx & has ring of hairs near base; in
whorls on erect, downy, dark-red stems,
branched near base.

Lvs. Opposite, oval-heart-shaped, downy,
coarsely toothed; lower long-stalked,
upper short-stalked, frequently purple
tinged; slightly aromatic.

Hab. Arable, cultivated &
disturbed soil, waste ground,
gardens. Widespread annual, now
considered to be an introduction.

Fam. Dead-nettle/Lamiaceae.

✿✿✿ Mar–Dec.

Cut-leaved Dead-nettle
Lamium hybridum
Caochneantóg dhiosctha

Ht. 30cm. **Fls.** 10–20mm long, pale
pink-purple, 2-lipped similar to Red
Dead-nettle except that corolla-tube is often
shorter than calyx & lacking ring of hairs
near base; in whorls on erect, square, slender
stems.

Lvs. Opposite, short-stalked, oval; leaves &
bracts *more deeply toothed* than those of Red
Dead-nettle; less downy plant also.

Hab. Dry, arable, waste & cultivated
ground. Annual, possibly introduced
into Ireland & not occurring as
commonly as Red Dead-nettle.

Fam. Dead-nettle/Lamiaceae.

▶ White Dead-nettle (p. 72).

✿✿ Apr–Oct.

Hen-bit Dead-nettle

Lamium amplexicaule
Caochneantóg chirce

Ht. 25cm. **Fls.** 12–18mm long, pink-purple, 2-lipped; lower lip hairy, large purple markings; 2 types exist – long, narrow corolla tube *or* very short corolla tube, encased in calyx; in loose, well-spaced whorls on hairy, slender stems.

Lvs. Opposite, round-oval, cordate at base, blunt-toothed; upper unstalked, lower long-stalked.

Hab. Cultivated soil & waste ground. Native annual only in E & SE.

Fam. Dead-nettle/Lamiaceae.

✿ Mar–Sep.

Toothwort

Lathraea squamaria
Slánú fiacal

Ht. 25cm. **Fls.** 15–20mm long, pale pink, tubular, 2-lipped; upper lip folded, lower lip 3-lobed; hairy 4-lobed calyx, shorter than corolla; in 1-sided spike on white, downy stems.

Lvs. Creamy-white, clasping scales, alternate & untoothed.

Hab. Woodlands with base-rich soils. Rare native perennial.

Fam. Broomrape/Orobanchaceae.

☺ Completely without chlorophyll, Toothwort is entirely parasitic on roots of shrubs & trees, especially Hazel, using creeping, underground rhizomes which insert themselves into tree roots, gaining nutrients.

✿ Apr–May.

Common Broomrape
Orobanche minor
Múchóg bheag

Ht. 40cm. **Fls.** 12–18mm long, purple-veined pink-yellow, tubular, 2-lipped; upper lip 2-lobed, lower lip 3-lobed; back of tube is arched in smooth curve; between flowers are pointed bracts, roughly similar in size to flowers; in loose spikes on rough, hairy, erect stems.

Lvs. Oval, pointed, brown, not true leaves.

Hab. Meadows, roadsides, hedgerows. Introduced annual, scattered in SE & E.

Fam. Broomrape/Orobanchaceae.

☺ Parasitic on roots of members of Pea family.

▶ Ivy Broomrape (p. 141) & Thyme Broomrape (p. 206).

✿✿ Jun–Sep.

Hemp-agrimony
Eupatorium cannabinum
Cnáib uisce

Ht. 1.5m. **Fls.** Flower-heads 2–5mm across, dusty pink, 5–6 florets in each; each floret is tubular with 5 short teeth & protruding stamens; in dense, flat-topped, terminal clusters, 3–6cm across; on robust, hairy, erect, red stems.

Lvs. Basal ovate, stalked; stem leaves 3–5 lobed, opposite, unstalked.

Hab. Riverbanks, ditches, sea-cliffs. Native perennial common in E, SE & Midlands.

Fam. Daisy/Asteraceae.

☺ Hemp-agrimony is very heavily scented & attracts butterflies, moths & other insects.

☺ Not related to Agrimony (p. 139).

✿✿ Jul–Sep.

Winter Heliotrope
Petasites fragrans
Plúr na gréine

Ht. 25cm. **Fls.** Tiny, 5 lobed pale pink, in tight heads 10–15mm, outside flowers having strap-shaped petals; in loose racemes on upright, hairy stems; smells of liquorice.

Lvs. Bright green, shiny, kidney-shaped, hairless above, hairy below, regularly toothed; long-stalked.

Hab. Waste & cultivated ground, damp places, embankments, shady roadsides. Widespread, introduced, patch-forming perennial.

Fam. Daisy/Asteraceae.

☺ Classed as 'Potentially Invasive'.

✿✿✿ Nov–Mar. 🏃 ⚘

Winter Heliotrope & *Butterbur* are dioecious, having separate-sex plants. In Ireland we generally only have male plants, which spread vegetatively, by means of rhizomes rather than by sexual propagation through seeds.

Butterbur
Petasites hybridus
Gallán mór

Ht. 40cm. **Fls.** Flower-heads 7–12mm, initially maroon, then pink-lilac, brush-like; individual florets are 5-lobed, outer florets opening before inner; flower-heads in cylindrical, loose spikes on stout pinkish stems, many narrow bracts.

Lvs. Large (to 90cm across), rounded, heart-shaped, pale-green with robust hollow stalks, softly hairy below, appearing after flowers.

Hab. Wet ground, roadsides, riverbanks. Common native perennial.

Fam. Daisy/Asteraceae.

✿✿✿ Mar–May.

Fragrant Orchid
Gymnadenia conopsea
Lus taghla

Ht. 45cm. **Fls.** 8–12mm, pale rosy-pink to lilac-purple; outer lateral sepals pointed, upper sepal & petals forming hood, lower lip with 3 blunt, equal lobes, descending backward into long spur (8–17mm); in cylindrical spikes, bracts as long as flowers; on erect stems.

Lvs. Linear, grooved, glossy, 4–8 near base, decreasing in size up stem.

Hab. Stabilised dunes, alkaline soil. Native perennial, more common in N.

Fam. Orchid/Orchidaceae.

☺ Strong fragrance of cloves.

✿✿ Jun–Aug.

Orchids are complex & often hybridise, therefore making identification difficult. Some are very rare, many take years to produce flowers. As with all rare species, please take photographs – not specimens. N.B. Flower measurements are across unless otherwise specified.

Heath Fragrant Orchid
Gymnadenia borealis
Lus taghla na móna

Ht. 30cm. **Fls.** 8–10mm, pink-purple; lateral sepals ovate, upper 3 tepals incurved & wide, 3-lobed lip, central lobe longest; spur 11-14mm; in loose spike on erect green stems, redder towards top.

Lvs. Narrow basal leaves, unspotted, keeled; small along stem.

Hab. Acidic heaths, poor hilly soil, eskers. Native perennial, uncommon in S.

Fam. Orchid/Orchidaceae.

☺ Carnation-scented flowers.

✿✿ Jul–Sep.

Common Spotted-orchid
Dactylorhiza fuchsii ssp. *fuchsii*
Nuacht bhallach

Ht. 60cm. **Fls.** 8–10mm, pale pink to mauve, lateral sepals spreading slightly upwards; 2 petals & 1 sepal forming small hood; lower lip spotted & streaked purple, 3-lobed, *central lobe slightly longer* than other pair; lip extends back into short spur; in open spikes on upright stem becoming cylindrical as flowers open.

Lvs. Dark, transverse spots, oblong-lanceolate, keeled.

Hab. Calcareous soil, meadows. Locally common, native perennial.

Fam. Orchid/Orchidaceae.

▶ O'Kelly's Spotted-orchid (p. 78).

✿✿✿ May–Aug.

Heath Spotted-orchid
Dactylorhiza maculata
Na circíní

Ht. 75cm. **Fls.** 8–10mm, white, pale pink or purple; 2 lateral spreading sepals; 2 sepals & 1 petal forming hood; lower lip 3-lobed with shorter, smaller central lobe & 2 frilly, flared outer lobes; markings on lower lip streaked & looped; in conical spikes on erect stems.

Lvs. Lanceolate, pointed, circular spots.

Hab. Damp, acid soil, heaths. Locally common, native perennial.

Fam. Orchid/Orchidaceae.

☺ Main identification points between these 2, *very variable*, Spotted-orchids are:

- size of central lobe of lip
- markings on petals & leaves
- type of soil where plant is found.

✿✿✿ Jun–Aug.

191

Pyramidal Orchid
Anacamptis pyramidalis
Magairlín na stuaice

Ht. 50cm. **Fls.** 3–6mm, deep pink to rosy-purple; laterally spreading outer sepals, upper tepals hood-like; lower lip, with 3 deeply cut & ridged lobes, descending back into downward-pointing spur; in conical spike on leafy stems.

Lvs. Lanceolate lower leaves, sheath-like on stem; foxy smelling.

Hab. Grassy, coastal paths, stabilised dunes, mostly calcareous soil, eskers. Native perennial, locally common in Midlands & coastal regions of E, SE & NW.

Fam. Orchid/Orchidaceae.

✿✿ Jun–Aug.

Early-purple Orchid
Orchis mascula
Magairlín meidhreach

Ht. 40cm. **Fls.** 8–12mm long, pink-purple, occasionally white, with 3-lobed lower lip, fading to white into throat, sprinkled with purple dots; 2 outer petals & rear sepal form 'hood'; 2 outer sepals spread; long *upturned* spur; in loose spike on erect stem.

Lvs. Glossy, dark green, oblong-lanceolate, dark-spotted or occasionally unspotted.

Hab. Neutral or calcareous soil. Native perennial, fairly frequent throughout.

Fam. Orchid/Orchidaceae.

☺ Scented quite strongly of cat's pee.

✿✿ Apr–Jun.

Bee Orchid
Ophrys apifera
Magairlín na mbeach

Ht. 40cm. **Fls.** 25–30mm, 3
spreading, deep-pink sepals; 2
short, stumpy, narrow, greenish
petals; large, furry, bee-like lip,
brown with light green-yellow
markings & 2 small side-lobes;
2 bright-yellow pollinia* above
'bumblebee'; no spur; in loose
spikes of 2–11 on slender, erect
stems.

Lvs. Grey-green, oblong-
lanceolate, forming loose rosette;
inrolled edges to stem leaves.

Hab. Sand dunes, meadows,
mainly calcareous. Scarce native
perennial.

Fam. Orchid/Orchidaceae.

✿✿ Jun–Jul. ✚

* These are 2 pollen masses which are located at back of flower. They
have sticky bases which can stick to visiting insects' heads. See also p. 275.

☺ Occasionally a white variety of this species, *Ophrys apifera* var. *chlorantha*,
can be found. Without colourful pink sepals, it still retains the 'bee-like'
furry pouch.

Indian Balsam
Impatiens glandulifera
Lus na pléisce

Ht. 1.8m. **Fls.** 25–40mm long, pinkish-purple, appearing as 2-lipped; upper lip helmet-like, frilly, 2 lower petals forming lower lip; spotted in 'throat'; with short, curved spur; in long-stalked racemes growing from leaf axils, on hairless, reddish stems.

Lvs. Lanceolate-oval, pointed, finely toothed, in whorls of 3.

Hab. River banks, ditches, waste ground. Introduced annual, becoming more common, mainly in N & SE.

Fam. Balsam/Balsaminaceae.

☺ This species is classed as 'Invasive'.

☺ AKA Himalayan Balsam

✿✿ Jul–Sep. 🏃 🐝

Sainfoin
Onobrychis viciifolia
Goirm choiligh

Ht. 60cm. **Fls.** 10–14mm long, pink peaflowers, upper petal (or standard) veined deep maroon, lower petals (wings & keel) tinged violet towards tip; calyx teeth long, pointed; in long-stalked spikes on slender, erect stems.

Lvs. Pinnate, 6–12 pairs oblong, untoothed leaflets.

Hab. Dry grassland, roadsides. Rare introduced perennial.

Fam. Pea/Fabaceae.

✿ Jun–Aug. 🏃

Common Restharrow
Ononis repens
Fréamhacha tairne

Ht. Creeping to 60cm. **Fls.**
10–20mm long, pink peaflowers;
wings & keel of equal length; very
hairy calyx; in loose, irregular,
leafy clusters on creeping, reddish
stems which are usually *spineless* &
glandular-hairy all around.

Lvs. Alternate, trifoliate with sticky,
toothed, oval leaflets; crushed leaves give an
unpleasant smell.

Hab. Calcareous soil, grassy places,
meadows, coastal grassland. Native
perennial frequent in E & S.

Fam. Pea/Fabaceae.

For more about *Peaflowers* see p. 114.

☺ Trailing stems often root at intervals towards
the base.

✿✿ Jul–Sep.

Broad-leaved Everlasting-pea
Lathyrus latifolius
Peasairín leathanduilleach

Ht. 2m. **Fls.** 20–30mm long, bright
magenta-pink peaflowers; in long-stalked
racemes of 5–15 flowers; on clambering,
winged, downy or hairless, zigzagging stems
which terminate in branched tendrils.

Lvs. One pair of veined, blue-green, oval
or rounded, blunt leaflets; pointed, leaf-like
stipules occur at branching.

Hab. Coastal grassland, embankments, waste
ground, hedgerows. Introduced perennial,
occasional on E & SE coast.

Fam. Pea/Fabaceae.

☺ Pale pink & pure white flowers also occur.

✿ Jun–Sep. 🏃

Bog-myrtle
Myrica gale
Raideog

Ht. 1m. **Fls.** Usually dioecious species; male flowers with red stamens, borne in ovoid, orange-yellow catkins (7–15mm); females with red-purple styles in pendulous red-brown catkins (4–5mm); on red-brown, woody stems.

Lvs. Grey-green, oval-lanceolate, downy below, almost hairless above; fragrance of resin.

Hab. Bogs, fens, wet heaths. Native shrub, common in NW, W & SW.

Fam. Bog-Myrtle/Myricaceae.

✿✿ Apr–May.

Babington's Orache
Atriplex glabriuscula
Eilifleog chladaigh

Ht. Prostrate. **Fls.** Miniscule flowers; mostly monoecious plants; male has 5 tepals, female has no tepals but 2 bracteoles (leaf-like structures) 4–10mm; bases of bracteoles are thick, spongy & *knobbly or warty*; on reddish, mealy stems.

Lvs. Triangular or diamond-shaped.

Hab. Shingle, sand, coastal sites only. Native annual, uncommon except on coasts.

Fam. Goosefoot/Amaranthaceae.

▶ Oraches (pp. 196, 256–7).

✿ Jul–Sep.

Common Sorrel
Rumex acetosa
Samhadh bó

Ht. 60cm. **Fls.** Under 2mm; dioecious plants; male often red, 6 tepals, 6 stamens; female flowers in 2 whorls of 3 flowers; outer whorl green & erect; inner whorl greenish or red; in spikes on tall, slender stems.

Lvs. Shiny, arrow-shaped, stem leaves with basal lobes *pointed & converging.*

Hab. Grassland, roadsides, dunes. Widespread native perennial.

Fam. Knotweed/Polygonaceae.

☺ Leaves taste of vinegar.

✿✿✿ May–Jul.

Sheep's Sorrel
Rumex acetosella
Samhadh caorach

Ht. 30cm. **Fls.** Dioecious plants; male plants have 6 tepals, red-tinged or greenish & 6 large, red stamens; female similar except with ovary at centre, no stamens; in loose, branched spikes on slender spreading or erect stems.

Lvs. More than twice as long as wide, linear, untoothed with pair of *spreading, pointed* basal lobes.

Hab. Bare acid soils, heaths; rarely on lime. Widespread native perennial.

Fam. Knotweed/Polygonaceae.

☺ Leaves are acid-tasting.

✿✿✿ May–Aug.

197

Mugwort
Artemisia vulgaris
Mongach meisce

Ht. 1.2m. **Fls.** 2–4mm, oval, tubular, nodding red-brown heads of rayless florets; in leafy, tapering spikes on downy, reddish, stems.

Lvs. Alternate, dark-green above, silver below, pinnately lobed; aromatic; lower stalked, upper unstalked.

Hab. Waste places, roadsides, embankments. Native perennial, occasional throughout.

Fam. Daisy/Asteraceae.

✿✿ Jul–Sep.

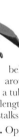

Fuchsia
Fuchsia magellanica
Fiúise

Ht. 2m. **Fls.** 20mm long, bell-shaped, 4 bright red-pink sepals around 4 small, violet petals which form a tube; 8 long, red stamens unequal in length; hanging down on long reddish stalks; on deciduous, much-branched stems.

Lvs. Opposite, ovate, toothed.

Hab. Hedgerows, scrub, coastal sites. Introduced shrub, widespread except in centre of Ireland.

Fam. Willowherb/Onagraceae.

☺ Produces black, fleshy berries.

☺ Well-known garden escape.

✿✿✿ Aug–Oct. 🏃

Common Poppy
Papaver rhoeas
Cailleach dhearg

Ht. 60cm. **Fls.** 60–80mm, 4 deep
scarlet, overlapping, silky, petals,
often with black blotch at base; deep
blue-black anthers; buds nodding;
solitary on slender, hairy stems.

Lvs. Deep green, hairy, toothed, lobed;
lower stalked, upper sessile.

Hab. Embankments, roadsides,
arable fields, waste ground. Annual,
probably introduced. Common in S, E
& Midlands.

Fam. Poppy/
Papaveraceae.

☺ Seeds are in *ovoid*,
flat-topped capsules.

✿✿✿ Jun–Aug.

Long-headed Poppy
Papaver dubium
Cailleach fhada

Ht. 60cm. **Fls.** 30–70mm, 4
orange-red, overlapping petals,
seldom with dark blotches at
base; anthers blue-black;
on 4-angled stems with
appressed, *upward-pointing*
hairs.

Lvs. Alternate, stalked,
hairy, blue-green, much
divided.

Hab. Roadsides, waste ground,
arable land. Introduced annual, more
commonly found in E, S & Midlands.

Fam. Poppy/Papaveraceae.

☺ Seeds are held in capsules which
are hairless & *more than twice as long* as
they are wide.

✿✿ Jun–Aug.

Scarlet Pimpernel
Anagallis arvensis
Falcaire fiáin

Ht. Prostrate. **Fls.** 10–15mm, 5 scarlet petals with *hairy margins;* purple tint at base of petal; 5 sharply-pointed sepals, solitary on creeping, hairless stems.

Lvs. Opposite, untoothed, shiny, oval shaped, with little black dots on underside; on square stems.

Hab. Arable, sandy, coastal & disturbed soil. Common native annual.

Fam. Primrose/Primulaceae.

☺ Flowers only open in bright sunshine & always close when it rains.

☺ Flowers may occasionally be blue or pink.

▶ Yellow Pimpernel (p. 96) & Bog Pimpernel (p. 157). ✿✿✿ Jun–Aug.

Escallonia
Escallonia macrantha
Tomóg ghaelach

Ht. 3m. **Fls.** 10–15mm, pink to dark red, 5 corolla lobes spreading back, longer than calyx; in terminal racemes on evergreen branches.

Lvs. Evergreen, dark, glossy, oval, toothed; glandular below.

Hab. Hedgerows, banks, roadsides, cliffs, walls. Introduced shrub, more common in S & SE.

Fam. Escallonia/Escalloniaceae.

☺ Originally planted for hedging, this shrub has naturalised & is frequently found near coasts.

▶ Young twigs are quite sticky.

✿✿ Jun–Sep.

Marsh Cinquefoil
Comarum palustre
Cnó léana

Ht. 35cm. **Fls.** 20–25mm, 5 large maroon sepals, backs covered with down; 5 small, pointed, purple petals, *half as long* as sepals; numerous stamens; in few-flowered clusters on slightly hairy, erect stems.

Lvs. Grey-green; pinnately divided, toothed.

Hab. Marshes, bogs, wet meadows. Locally common native perennial.

Fam. Rose/Rosaceae.

☺ Sepals close after fertilisation & protect developing seeds.

✿✿ May–Jul.

Bilberry
Vaccinium myrtillus
Fraochán

Ht. 60cm. **Fls.** 4–6mm long, greenish to pale red, urn-shaped with 5 tiny, reflexed teeth; stigma slightly projecting; mostly solitary on 3-angled, branched stems.

Lvs. Bright green, oval, deciduous.

Hab. Damp mountainsides, acid heaths, dry peat bogs. Native shrub, locally frequent but scattered & uncommon except for Midland region.

Fam. Heather/Ericaceae.

☺ Fruit is a spherical berry, black with a whitish bloom when ripe.

☺ Commonly known as '*Frochan*'.

✿✿✿ Apr–Jun.

201

Red Valerian
Centranthus ruber
Slán iomaire

Ht. 80cm. **Fls.** 8–10mm long, red, pink or white; corolla is a slender tube with lobed, unequal petals & spur at its base; in dense, terminal clusters; on upright, hairless stems.

Lvs. Opposite, grey-green, ovate, untoothed, slighty fleshy.

Hab. Stone walls, cliffs, waste ground, railway tracks, coastal ground. Introduced perennial, more common in NE & S half of Ireland.

Fam. Valerian/Valerianaceae.

▶ Common Valerian (p. 174).

✿✿✿ May–Sep.

Hound's-tongue
Cynoglossum officinale
Teanga chon

Ht. 65cm. **Fls.** 5–7mm, deep red, 5-lobed, funnel-shaped flowers; in elongated, one-sided racemes on arching to erect, leafy stems.

Lvs. Soft, grey, alternate, lanceolate-oblong, untoothed, hairy; lower leaves stalked; upper leaves unstalked, clasping stem.

Hab. Dry grassland, coastal dunes, shingle. Native biennial, quite scarce, only found in E.

Fam. Borage/ Boraginaceae.

☺ Fruits are flattened nutlets covered in hooked bristles.

✿ Jun–Aug. ✚

Fox-and-cubs
Pilosella aurantiaca
Searbh dearg

Ht. 50cm. **Fls.** 15–30mm, orange-red ray florets; below each flower-head are linear flower-bracts, covered in closely-overlapping black hairs; in tight clusters of 2–12 on upright, leafy stems.

Lvs. Basal rosette of extremely hairy, lanceolate leaves; small, bract-like upper leaves.

Hab. Grassy places, churchyards, cultivated & waste ground. Uncommon, introduced perennial.

Fam. Daisy/Asteraceae.

☺ Spreading, stoloniferous plant.

✿ Jun–Jul. 🏃

Red Clover
Trifolium pratense
Seamair dhearg

Ht. 40cm. **Fls.** Heads 12–25mm; a dense, round cluster of small, red-pink peaflowers; sessile, leaves directly below inflorescence; on downy, spreading stems.

Lvs. Trifoliate with oval-elliptical leaflets, each with *white*, *V-shaped* mark; stipules triangular towards tip, with fine, brown bristly point.

Hab. Grassy places, waste ground, meadows & verges. Widespread native perennial.

Fam. Pea/Fabaceae.

☺ Peaflowers restore nitrogen into the soil.

✿✿✿ May–Oct.

Hedge Woundwort
Stachys sylvatica
Créachtlus

Ht. 75cm. **Fls.** 12–18mm long, 2-lipped, deep red-purple, paler markings on lower lip; calyx with rigid, triangular, teeth; in loose, terminal, whorled spike on erect, square stems.

Lvs. Ovate, opposite, toothed; lower long-stalked, upper short-stalked.

Hab. Hedgerows, ditches, mostly in shade. Widespread, native perennial.

Fam. Dead-nettle/Lamiaceae.

☺ Unpleasant-smelling when bruised.

▶ Marsh & Field Woundwort (p. 184).

✿✿✿ Jun–Oct.

Red Bartsia
Odontites vernus
Hocas tae

Ht. 50cm. **Fls.** 8–10mm long, reddish-pink, occasionally white, *very hairy*; 2-lipped, open mouth; upper lip hooded, lower lip 3-lobed; stamens slightly protruding; calyx 4-toothed; in leafy, one-sided, curved spikes on straggly, branched reddish stems.

Lvs. Narrow, toothed, sessile; alternate above, opposite below.

Hab. Bare, disturbed ground, arable field margins, tracks, roadsides. Widespread native annual.

Fam. Broomrape/Orobanchaceae.

▶ Yellow Bartsia (p. 118).

✿✿✿ Jun–Sep.

Common Figwort
Scrophularia nodosa
Donnlus

Ht. 70cm. **Fls.**
10mm long, 2-lipped;
maroon 2-lobed upper
lip, greenish-red 3-lobed
lower lip; 4 stamens *with* anthers,
1 stamen *without* anthers; 5 calyx
lobes have *very narrow*, white,
membranous borders; in open,
stalked clusters on square, *unwinged*
stems.

Lvs. Oval, pointed, coarsely
toothed, lower stalked, upper
unstalked.

Hab. Ditches, hedgerows
roadsides. Common native
perennial.

Fam. Figwort/Scrophulariaceae.

✿✿✿ Jun–Sep.

Water Figwort
Scrophularia auriculata
Donnlus uisce

Ht. 70cm. **Fls.** 10mm long,
2-lipped; brown-maroon jutting
upper lip, lower lip paler; with *broad*,
white border to sepal lobes; in loose
clusters on square stems which have
narrow wings at angles.

Lvs. Oval with blunt tips, rounded
teeth, often *having 2 lobes* at bases; on
broad, winged stalks, *wings far more
pronounced* than on square stalks of
Common Figwort.

Hab. Damp ground, beside fresh water.
Native perennial, common except for N.

Fam. Figwort/
Scrophulariaceae.

✿✿ Jul–Sep.

Thyme Broomrape
Orobanche alba
Múchóg dhearg

Ht. 25cm. **Fls.** 15–20mm long, red-brown, tubular, 2-lipped, wrinkled; stamens attached above base of corolla tube; stigmas reddish; in short spikes on upright, downy, red stems with numerous reddish bracts.

Lvs. No true leaves but alternate brownish scales.

Hab. Limestone, maritime cliffs, calcareous grassland. Scarce native annual or perennial found in the Burren, Aran Is. & N coast.

Fam. Broomrape/Orobanchaceae.

☺ Lacks chlorophyll & is parasitic on roots of Wild Thyme (p. 185).

▶ Ivy Broomrape (p. 141) & Common Broomrape (p. 188).

✿ May–Jul. ⊞

Montbretia
Crocosmia x crocosmiiflora
Feileastram dearg

Ht. 60cm. **Fls.** 25–55mm, reddish-orange corolla, funnel-shaped, spreading into 6 unequal lobes; 3 stamens protrude along with style; in one-sided, loose panicle on stiff, erect, stems.

Lvs. Sword-shaped, long, narrow, bright green.

Hab. Hedgerows, waste ground, woods, cliffs. Widespread, introduced perennial hybrid.

Fam. Iris/Iridaceae.

☺ Classed as 'Potentially Invasive'.

☺ This is a hybrid between *Crocosmia aurea* & *C.pottsii*.

✿✿✿ Jul–Aug. 🏃 🚫

Lesser Twayblade
Neottia cordata
Dédhuilleog bheag

Ht. 20cm. **Fls.**
2–3mm long, reddish-
green with 5 tepals & lip
which has long tapering
lobes; in short, loose spike of
6–12 on upright, reddish stem.

Lvs. *One pair* of basal, shiny, ovate
leaves, 1/3 of way up stem.

Hab. Damp, shady, mossy
woodland. Rare native perennial,
mainly in N.

Fam. Orchid/Orchidaceae.

▶ Common Twayblade (p. 274).

✿ Jun–Aug. ✤

Dark-red Helleborine
Epipactis atrorubens
Cuaichín dearg

Ht. 40cm. **Fls.** 8–12mm,
3 petals & 3 sepals, all deep,
red-purple; lower lip is cup-like
with 2 bosses or bumps; nodding
in long spikes on erect, solitary, downy,
unbranched stems.

Lvs. Alternate,
oval-lanceolate,
pointed, parallel-
veined.

Hab. Limestone,
calcareous soil.
Rare Burren native
perennial, worthy of
protection.

Fam. Orchid/
Orchidaceae.

☺ Vanilla-scented flowers.

✿ Jun–Jul. ✤

207

Early Marsh-orchid
Dactylorhiza incarnata ssp. *coccinea*
Magairlín dearg

Ht. 20cm. **Fls.** 8–10mm, deep,
brick red; each flower with 2 outer
tepals erect & lip folded back
causing it to appear very narrow;
lip decorated with U-shaped line
enclosing dots & squiggles; spur
downward-pointing; in dense,
cylindrical spike on hollow stems.

Lvs. Yellow-green, lanceolate,
keeled, unspotted, tapering into
hooded tip.

Hab. Dune slacks, marshes,
fens & damp grassland. Rare,
scattered, native perennial.

   Fam. Orchid/Orchidaceae.

▶ *Dactylorhiza incarnata* ssp.
cruenta (p. 252).

▶ *Dactylorhiza incarnata* ssp.
pulchella (p. 253).

✿ May–Jul.

Some **Orchid** facts:
- Flowers are usually in spikes or racemes
- Outer 3 sepals usually alike, usually coloured
- Inner 3 petals have 1 petal very different from others
- This different petal forms a lip or '*labellum*'
- Labellum is usually on lower side of flower
- It may be lobed, furry, pouch-like
- It can be elaborately decorated
- Spur is a modified petal extending behind flower
- Stamens & stigmas are borne on a '*column*' at centre of flower
- 2 pollen masses called '*pollinia*' are located at back of flower. These have sticky bases which can stick to visiting insects' heads.

I.D. tips:
- Type of soil is a key factor in identification process
- Scent is a distinguishing feature in some cases
- Take note of the angle of the spur
- Colours can vary immensely.

Marsh Helleborine
Epipactis palustris
Cuaichín corraigh

Ht. 50cm. **Fls.** 15mm, 3 purple-red sepals, 2 narrow, red-streaked white upper petals & frilled, white lower lip; lower lip is notched, has red veins & central platform with yellow crinkled splotch above the white frills; each flower is on a dark-red, drooping stalk; in loose spike of up to 14 flowers on upright reddish stems.

Lvs. Lanceolate, keeled, spirally arranged, decreasing in size up stem.

Hab. Marshes, fens, dune slacks. Native perennial, worthy of protection; scattered but rarely in S except for County Wexford.

Fam. Orchid/Orchidaceae.

✿✿ Jul–Aug. ✚

Heath Milkwort
Polygala serpyllifolia
Na deirfiúiríní

Ht. 20cm. **Fls.** 5–6mm long, usually deep blue, rarely pink or white; similar in shape to Common Milkwort; in short spikes of 3–10; on spreading stems.

Lvs. Narrow, oval-lanceolate; lower stem leaves to a *certain extent* are opposite.

Hab. Acid grassland, heaths, mountains. Native perennial, common except in parts of Midlands.

Fam. Milkwort/Polygalaceae.

✿✿✿ May–Sep.

These two species are difficult to tell apart – look for leaves or leaf scars at base of stem & note habitat.

Common Milkwort
Polygala vulgaris
Lus an bhainne

Ht. 30cm. **Fls.** 5–8mm long with 3 tiny outer sepals & 2 larger, coloured, pointed, wing-like, veined sepals; corolla is 3 petals, fused into a little tube with fringed margins; blue, pink or white; in lax terminal spikes of 10–35 on erect stems.

Lvs. *All alternate*, oval-elliptical, untoothed; lowest leaves shorter & broader.

Hab. Calcareous soil, grassland but not on acid soil. Common native perennial.

Fam. Milkwort/Polygalaceae.

✿✿✿ May–Sep.

Field Madder

Sherardia arvensis

Dearg faille

Ht. Creeping to 40cm.

Fls. 2–3mm, pale lilac-purple, funnel-shaped with 4 spreading, star-like corolla lobes; in small clusters of up to 10; surrounded by whorl of 4–6 leaf-like bracts; on square, grooved stems.

Lvs. Upper leaves narrow, elliptical, with prickly edges; in whorls of 4–6; lower leaves wither early.

Hab. Bare, cultivated, arable ground & walls. Occasional native annual.

Fam. Bedstraw/Rubiaceae.

▶ Wild Madder (p. 106).

✿✿ May–Sep.

Opium Poppy

Papaver somniferum

Codlaidín

Ht. 90cm. **Fls.** 8–18cm, 4 silky, white to lilac-coloured petals with dark purple blotches towards centre of flower; bowl-shaped, solitary on erect, glaucous stems.

Lvs. Waxy-grey, oblong, coarsely-toothed, shallowly-lobed, upper clasping stem.

Hab. Waste & cultivated ground. Introduced annual, scattered in NE, E & SE.

Fam. Poppy/Papaveraceae.

☺ Seeds are in large, spherical capsule. Stems contain latex from which opium is derived.

✿✿ Jun–Aug. 🏃

Germander Speedwell
Veronica chamaedrys
Lus cré talún

Ht. 20cm. **Fls.** 10–12mm, 4 bright blue lobes with dark blue lines, lowest lobe being smallest; *white 'eye' at centre* & 2 slightly curved stamens; on long, slender stalks in loose racemes of 10–20 in axils of upper leaves; on creeping & ascending stems.

Lvs. Opposite, oval, toothed, dark green, on short stalks.

Hab. Grassy places, meadows, grass verges. Widespread, native perennial.

Fam. Speedwell/Veronicaceae.

☺ Stems have 2 *opposite rows of long, white hairs*.

☺ Fruit heart-shaped, shorter than calyx.

✿✿✿ Apr–Jun.

*All **Speedwells** have 4-petalled flowers – usually blue – 4 sepals & 2 stamens. The upper petal is the largest, the lower petal the smallest. Look at: flower colour, leaf shape, whether stalked or not, hairiness, whether stem has 2 lines of hairs or hairs all around, plant is creeping, rooting at nodes or erect, & note fruit shape.*

Wood Speedwell
Veronica montana
Lus cré coille

Ht. 20cm. **Fls.** 7–9mm, 4 pale-lilac lobes with purple lines, lowest lobe smallest; in small racemes of 2–5, bracts are shorter than flower stalks; on creeping, rooting stems.

Lvs. Oval, toothed, pale green.

Hab. Damp woodland, less acid soil. Native perennial, common except in Connacht.

Fam. Speedwell/Veronicaceae.

☺ Stems *hairy all around*.

☺ Fruit kidney-shaped, longer than calyx.

✿✿✿ Apr–Jul.

Heath Speedwell
Veronica officinalis
Lus cré

Ht. 10cm. **Fls.** 6–8mm, corolla 4-lobed, lilac-blue with darker veins; in long-stalked, dense, tapering, upright spikes; on delicate stems, creeping & *rooting at nodes*.

Lvs. Oval, toothed, hairy on both sides, lower leaves stalked; flowering stem rises from opposite pair of leaves.

Hab. Heaths, open woods, acid soil. Common native perennial.

Fam. Speedwell/Veronicaceae.

☺ Stems are hairy all around.

☺ Fruits are heart-shaped capsules, longer than calyx.

✿✿✿ May–Aug.

Common Field-speedwell
Veronica persica
Lus cré garrai

Ht. Prostrate to 20cm. **Fls.** 8–12mm bright blue, *lower lobe pale*; 2 stamens; calyx lobes oval, pointed, hairy; solitary in leaf axils on slender stalks, longer than leaves; on spreading, hairy, branched stems.

Lvs. Fresh, pale green, oval, toothed, hairy underneath.

Hab. Bare, cultivated soil, disturbed ground. Introduced annual, common in all but NE.

Fam. Speedwell/ Veronicaceae.

☺ Fruits are hairy, broad, flattened capsules with keeled lobes.

✿✿✿ Jan–Dec.

Green Field-speedwell
Veronica agrestis
Lus cré léana

Ht. Prostrate. **Fls.** 3–5mm, very *pale* blue with white lower lip; 2 stamens; calyx lobes oblong, blunt; flower stalks short; solitary in leaf axil, on low-growing, straggling stems.

Lvs. Opposite, short-stalked, ovate, shallowly lobed.

Hab. Fields, gardens, waste ground. Occasional, introduced perennial.

Fam. Speedwell/Veronicaceae.

☺ Fruit capsule has erect, rounded lobes.

☺ Stems & leaves hairy.

✿✿ Jun–Aug.

Thyme-leaved Speedwell
Veronica serpyllifolia
Lus an treacha

Ht. 20cm. **Fls.** 5–8mm, 4-lobed corolla, white or pale-blue with dark blue lines; in terminal racemes, bracts longer than flower-stalks; on creeping, more or less hairless, erect stems.

Lvs. Opposite, oval, rounded, untoothed, dark-green, *thyme-like*; deep central groove, short-stalked.

Hab. Lawns, cultivated & bare ground, damp acid soils. Widespread native perennial.

Fam. Speedwell/Veronicaceae.

☺ Stems & leaves have minute hairs, only visible through hand lens.

☺ Fruit is flattened, oval capsule.

✿✿✿ Apr–Oct.

Ivy-leaved Speedwell
Veronica hederifolia
Lus cré eidhneach

Ht. Prostrate. **Fls.** 4–5mm, pale blue or lilac with dark lines, corolla *shorter* than calyx; sepals ovate & extremely hairy; solitary on long stalks in leaf axils; on hairy, spreading, branched stems.

Lvs. Kidney-shaped, 1–3 deep lobes, edged with white, *bristly hairs;* shaped somewhat like ivy leaves.

Hab. Cultivated & bare, waste ground, woodlands, arable land. Introduced annual, common in NE, E & S.

Fam. Speedwell/Veronicaceae.

☺ Fruits are flattened, broad, hairless capsules.

✿✿✿ Mar–Aug.

Marsh Speedwell
Veronica scutellata
Lus cré corraigh

Ht. 20cm. **Fls.** 6–7mm, pale lilac to white with purple lines on *lower* corolla lobe; flower-stalks much longer than bracts, in long-stalked, alternate, few-flowered racemes on creeping or ascending stems.

Lvs. Linear-lanceolate, pointed, stalkless, few-toothed, yellowish-green but often purplish tinged.

Hab. Damp, boggy, acid ground, ponds, muddy land. Common native perennial.

Fam. Speedwell/Veronicaceae.

☺ Fruits are flattened, notched capsules, broader than long.

✿✿✿ Jun–Aug.

Wall Speedwell
Veronica arvensis
Lus cré balla

Ht. 15cm. **Fls.** 2–4mm, brilliant blue with white centre & 2 white stamens; flowers have *very* short stalks & are almost completely hidden by leaf-like bracts; in terminal racemes on erect, softly hairy stems.

Lvs. Upper leaves oval, toothed, unstalked, lower leaves coarsely round-toothed & short-stalked.

Hab. Dry, bare ground, tilled fields, old walls, open grassland. Widespread native annual.

Fam. Speedwell/Veronicaceae.

☺ Fruits hairy, heart-shaped, as long as broad.

✿✿✿ Mar–Oct.

Slender Speedwell
Veronica filiformis
Lus cré réileán

Ht. Prostrate. **Fls.** 8–10mm, purplish-blue with paler, *narrow lower lobe*; petals narrowing towards centre of flower, showing sepals; on long, slender, downy stalks from leaf axils.

Lvs. Toothed, round, kidney-shaped; alternate on flowering stems, opposite on non-flowering stems.

Hab. Mat-forming on low-creeping stems over lawns, pasture, short grass. Introduced perennial, common in N, E & S.

Fam. Speedwell/Veronicaceae.

✿✿ Apr–Jul.

Brooklime
Veronica beccabunga
Lochall

Ht. Creeping to 30cm. **Fls.** 7–8mm, 4-lobed, deep blue; narrow bracts same length as flower stalks; in paired racemes in leaf axils of upper stems; on hairless, fleshy, prostrate to ascending, rooting stems.

Lvs. Opposite, oval-oblong, rounded at base, shallowly toothed, thick.

Hab. Shallow, standing water, muddy places, ditches. Widespread native perennial.

Fam. Speedwell/Veronicaceae.

☺ Fruit is flattened, rounded capsule.

✿✿✿ May–Sep.

Columbine
Aquilegia vulgaris
Colaimbín

Ht. 90cm. **Fls.** 30–40mm long, 5 petals, 5 petal-like sepals of similar purple colour; occasionally white or pink; petals have curved, hooked spurs; many yellow stamens; flowers are nodding on long, stiff stems.

Lvs. Grey-green, large, twice trifoliate, mainly basal.

Hab. Calcareous soil, damp meadows, scrub, open woodland. Occasional introduced perennial, possibly native to some areas.

Fam. Buttercup/Ranunculaceae.

✿✿ May–Jul. 🏃

Autumn Gentian
Gentianella amarella
Muilcheann

Ht. 25cm. **Fls.** 12–14mm, mauve, purple or pink, usually 5-lobed (occasionally 4-lobed); centre of flower fringed with short, erect hairs; calyx lobes narrowly lanceolate & all roughly *equal* in size; in branched clusters on thin, erect stems.

Lvs. Opposite, oval-lanceolate, untoothed; basal leaves in rosette in first year.

Hab. Calcareous soil, sand dunes, grassy meadows, dry banks. Native annual or biennial, occasional in centre & parts of W.

Fam. Gentian/Gentianaceae.

☺ AKA Felwort.

✿ Jun–Sep.

Spring Gentian
Gentiana verna
Ceadharlach Bealtaine

Ht. 7cm. **Fls.** 15–25mm, deepest, richest blue; 5 oval corolla lobes spreading wide, white centre to flower; each lobe has small fringed blue & white scales protruding at centre of flower; long calyx tube; usually solitary on upright, hairless stems.

Lvs. Oval-elliptical, bright-green, in basal rosette & opposite pairs on stem.

Hab. Limestone grassland, calcareous flushes, peat hummocks. Rare native perennial, confined to the Burren.

Fam. Gentian/Gentianaceae.

☺ Stunning flower – treat with care as this is a really rare plant in Ireland. It is usually found in alpine regions & is typical of the amazing, fascinating Burren flora.

✿ Apr–Jun.

219

Pale Flax
Linum bienne | Líon beag

Ht. 60cm. **Fls.** 12–20mm, pale blue, silky petals with darker blue lines toward centre of flower; petals fall off soon after flower opens; sepals all ovate, pointed, half as long as petals; club-shaped stigmas; in leafy racemes on wiry, hairless, branched stems.

Lvs. Alternate, narrow, 3-veined, pointed.

Hab. Dry hedgerows, calcareous soil, grassy meadows, frequently near coast. Native perennial, scarce except for SE & S.

Fam. Flax/Linaceae.

▶ Fairy Flax (p. 40). ✿✿ May–Jul.

Greater Periwinkle
Vinca major | Fincín mór

Ht. 1m. **Fls.** 30–50mm, violet-blue, petals fused toward centre, fading to white into 5-angled centre; sepals narrow, margins densely hairy; solitary in leaf axils on slender, trailing stems, often rooting at tip.

Lvs. Evergreen, opposite, ovate, shiny, dark-green.

Hab. Hedgerows, open woodland, scrub. Occasional introduced perennial.

Fam. Periwinkle/Apocynaceae.

✿✿ Mar–Jun. 🏃

Borage
Borago officinalis | Borráiste gorm

Ht. 60cm. **Fls.** 20–25mm, star-shaped, 5 narrow blue petals reflexed & pointed backwards; extremely hairy purple calyx whose teeth show between petals; column of purple-black anthers at centre of flower; in loose inflorescence with leaf-like bracts on bristly, robust, branched stems.

Lvs. Oval-lanceolate, rough.

Hab. Dry, waste & arable ground. Introduced perennial, occasional E & SE.

Fam. Borage/Boraginaceae. ✿✿ Jun–Jul.🏃

Bugloss
Anchusa arvensis
Boglas

Ht. 60cm. **Fls.** 5–7mm, bright blue,
5-lobed corolla which has a short,
curved tube; throat of corolla closed
by 5 hairy scales; in branched clusters
on rough, bristly stems.

Lvs. Rough, alternate, lanceolate-
oblong with toothed, wavy margins;
lower leaves stalked, upper clasping
stem with heart-shaped bases.

Hab. Waste, bare ground coastal,
arable land. Uncommon native
annual.

Fam. Borage/Boraginaceae.

▶ Viper's-bugloss (p. 243).

✿✿ May–Sep.

Green Alkanet
Pentaglottis sempervirens
Boglas spáinneach

Ht. 60cm. **Fls.** 8–10mm, 5 blue,
spreading, saucer-shaped lobes;
corolla has short tube closed over
by hairy, white scales; in dense
clusters in leaf-axils; on erect, bristly,
branched stems.

Lvs. Oval-lanceolate, pointed,
untoothed; basal leaves narrowing
into long petiole or leaf-stalk; stem
leaves unstalked.

Hab. Shady hedgerows, waste
ground, woodland margins.
Introduced perennial scattered in E
half of country.

Fam. Borage/Boraginaceae.

☺ Basal leaves can sometimes have
little blisters.

✿✿ Apr–Jun. 🏃

Water Forget-me-not
Myosotis scorpioides
Ceotharnach uisce

Ht. 50cm. **Fls.** 8–12mm, sky-blue with yellow & white centre; flat, 5-lobed, united in short tube; in slowly-uncoiling cymes on spreading, branching, ascending stems from creeping rootstock.

Lvs. Alternate, untoothed, pointed tips, stems covered in closely-pressed hairs.

Hab. Wet places, marshes, damp fields. Widespread native perennial.

Fam. Borage/Boraginaceae.

☺ Hairs are *closely pressed* into stems & leaves.

☺ Calyx teeth short & triangular.

✿✿✿ May–Sep.

Creeping Forget-me-not
Myosotis secunda
Ceotharnach reatha

Ht. 12cm. **Fls.** 4–8mm, blue with slightly-notched lobes, yellow eye; leafy bracts on lower part of inflorescence; in clusters on creeping stems, rooting at intervals.

Lvs. Pale, oblong on occasionally reddish stems.

Hab. Damp, acid soil, marshes & bogs. Native perennial, widespread except for centre.

Fam. Borage/Boraginaceae.

☺ Hairs on flowering stems are *appressed*, hairs on lower stems are *spreading*.

☺ Calyx tube is divided more than halfway into calyx teeth.

✿✿✿ Jun–Aug.

Field Forget-me-not
Myosotis arvensis
Lus míonla goirt

Ht. 25cm. **Fls.** 3–4mm, pale to bright blue with yellow eye, saucer shaped; corolla tube shorter than calyx tube; in coiled clusters, elongating as fruit develops; on erect, branching stems with spreading hairs.

Lvs. Broadly ovate, stalked, forming basal rosette; stem leaves alternate, elliptical.

Hab. Dry grassland, arable & disturbed land. Widespread native annual.

Fam. Borage/Boraginaceae.

☺ Calyx bell-shaped with hooked hairs.

✿✿✿ Apr–Jun.

Changing Forget-me-not
Myosotis discolor
Lus míonla buí

Ht. 20cm. **Fls.** 2mm, 5-lobed, initially creamy-yellow, then pink, then blue, changing as cluster slowly uncoils, only new flowers opening cream; petals flat, corolla tube *twice as long* as calyx; on downy, branched stems; hairs on upper stems *appressed*, hairs on lower stems *spreading*.

Lvs. Basal leaves tapering, upper unstalked, oblong-lanceolate.

Hab. Dry, bare soil; occasionally in wet habitats. Native annual, common in all but parts of Connacht.

Fam. Borage/Boraginaceae.

☺ Calyx has hooked, curly hairs & erect teeth.

✿✿✿ May–Sep.

Common Dog-violet

Viola riviniana

Fanaigse

Ht. 12cm. **Fls.** 15–25mm, violet-blue; dark purple lines run over light patch & into throat which is white-fringed; with pale purple or white, slightly curved spur which is *notched* at tip; sepals with *square* appendages; solitary on long, slightly downy stalks.

Lvs. Dark-green, heart-shaped, narrow stipules at base of leaf-stalks.

Hab. Woodland, grassy hedgerows, heaths & dunes. Widespread native perennial.

Fam. Violet/Violaceae.

☺ Unscented species.

✿✿✿ Mar–May.

Early Dog-violet

Viola reichenbachiana

Sailchuach luath

Ht. 15cm. **Fls.** 12–20mm, violet with 2 upper petals *narrower* than Common Dog-violet; dark veined throat & *straight*, *dark*, *unnotched* spur; sepals with *short* appendages; solitary on almost hairless stems.

Lvs. Alternate, heart-shaped with toothed margin; on long stalks; stipules are fringed & narrower than those of Common Dog-violet.

Hab. Woods, hedgerows, shady places. Native perennial scattered throughout except in W Munster.

Fam. Violet/Violaceae.

✿✿ Mar–May.

Marsh Violet
Viola palustris
Sailchuach chorraigh

Ht. 15cm. **Fls.** 10–15mm, pale-lilac, rarely white, with dark veins & short, *blunt*, pale lilac spur & rounded petals; solitary on stems which arise *directly* from creeping underground stolons or runners.

Lvs. Kidney or heart-shaped, long stalked, oval-shaped stipules at base.

Hab. Wet places, acid marshes, damp fields. Native perennial, common in N, W & SE.

Fam. Violet/ Violaceae.

✿✿✿ Apr–Jul.

Wild Pansy
Viola tricolor ssp. *tricolor*
Goirmín searraigh

Ht. 15cm. **Fls.** 10–25mm, blue-violet upper petals, yellow or white lower petals with dark lines leading into throat; colours can vary; upper part of throat opening is fringed; petals longer than sepals; on erect or spreading stems.

Lvs. Alternate, oblong-elliptical, shallowly toothed margin; lower leaves rounded; stipules pinnately lobed.

Hab. Acid or neutral soil, arable & disturbed ground. Occasional native annual in E & SE.

Fam. Violet/Violaceae.

▶ Field Pansy (p. 42) & Sand Pansy (p. 104).

✿✿ Apr–Aug.

Sharp-leaved Fluellen
Kickxia elatine
Buaflíon Breatnach

Ht. Prostrate. **Fls.** 6–10mm, 2 purple
upper lobes, 3 yellow lower lobes with
faint purple smudges on each lobe & 2
round bosses or bumps under opening of
mouth; straight spur; on slender stalks from
leaf-axils of creeping, branching stems.

Lvs. Arrow-shaped, triangular, sharply-
pointed, stalked.

Hab. Cultivated ground, stubble fields.
Rare native annual found in SE & S
mainly.

Fam. Speedwell/Veronicaceae.

☺ This plant, being extremely scarce, is
worthy of protection.

✿ Jul–Oct. ✚

Ivy-leaved Toadflax
Cymbalaria muralis
Buaflíon balla

Ht. Creeping to 10cm. **Fls.** 8–15mm,
2 lilac upper lobes, 3 paler lilac lower
lobes with 2 round, yellow-white bosses or
bumps above; occasionally white; curved
spur; on trailing, red-purple, hairless stems.

Lvs. Alternate, fleshy, ivy-shaped, purplish
beneath, light green above, often edged
purple.

Hab. Old walls, pavements, stony waste
ground. Introduced perennial, widespread
in all but extreme W.

Fam. Speedwell/Veronicaceae.

☺ Stems bearing seeds curve, pushing
seed into cracks in walls.

▶ Common Toadflax (p. 138), Small
Toadflax (p. 171) & Purple Toadflax
(p. 246).

✿✿✿ Mar–Sep. 🏃

Large-flowered Butterwort
Pinguicula grandiflora
Leith uisce

Ht. 20cm. **Fls.** 20–30mm, 5-lobed, deep violet with long, white throat, streaked with dark-purple; lower lobes slightly overlapping; backward-directed spur; solitary on stems from centre of basal rosette.

Lvs. Yellow-green, ovate-oblong, sticky, in basal rosette.

Hab. Bogs, damp flushes. Rare native perennial confined to Counties Cork, Kerry, Limerick & the Burren.

Fam. Bladderwort/Lentibulariaceae.

☺ Carnivorous plant with sticky glands on leaves to trap insects.

▶ Pale Butterwort (p. 159).

✿ May–Jul. ✚

Common Butterwort
Pinguicula vulgaris
Bodán meascáin

Ht. 15cm. **Fls.** 10–12mm, violet coloured 2-lipped; upper lip 2-lobed, lower lip 3 well-separated, flat lobes; fringed; white throat & slender, backward-pointing, pointed spur; solitary on slender, erect stems.

Lvs. Yellow-green, sticky, fleshy, elliptical with *inrolled* leaf margins; in star-shaped basal rosette.

Hab. Nitrogen deficient bogs, wet rocks & mountain heaths. Native perennial, common in NW, W & Midland areas of habitat.

Fam. Bladderwort/Lentibulariaceae.

☺ When an insect lands on sticky leaf, enzymes are exuded aiding plant's digestion of insect.

▶ Pale Butterwort (p. 159).

✿✿ May–Aug.

Harebell
Campanula rotundifolia
Méaracán gorm

Ht. 40cm. **Fls.** 15mm long, pale blue, bell-shaped with sharp, triangular lobes, spreading slightly; calyx teeth deep purple, narrow; nodding on *very* slender stalks in few-flowered, loose, branched clusters; on erect, dark, wiry stems.

Lvs. Basal leaves round-ovate, cordate-based, long-stalked; stem leaves narrow, linear, sessile.

Hab. Calcareous & acid soil, dunes, cliffs. Native perennial found in NW & W mainly.

Fam. Bellflower/Campanulaceae.

☺ Basal leaves wither quite soon, stem leaves remaining longer.

✿✿ Jul–Oct.

Bittersweet
Solanum dulcamara
Fuath gorm

Ht. 1m. **Fls.** 10–15mm, purple corolla with 5 reflexed, pointed, lobes; yellow stamens projecting in long narrow cone; in loose clusters on scrambling, downy stems.

Lvs. Oval with pointed tip, spreading lobes at base.

Hab. Hedgerows, scrub, shingle. Native perennial, more common in E half of country.

Fam. Nightshade/Solanaceae.

☺ Fruits are *poisonous*, egg-shaped red berries in hanging clusters.

☺ AKA Woody Nightshade due to woody nature of lower stems.

✿✿✿ May–Sep.

Nettle-leaved Bellflower
Campanula trachelium
Scornlus

Ht. 75cm. **Fls.** 30–40mm long, blue-violet, bell-shaped corolla with 5 short, spreading lobes; calyx has erect, pointed, triangular lobes; on short stalks & in branched, leafy panicles on erect, stiff, hairy, sharply-angled stems.

Lvs. Rough, coarsely-toothed, heart-shaped at base; lower leaves are stalked & oval; nettle-like stem leaves are short-stalked; leaves are rich green above but a paler shade of green below.

Hab. Hedgerows, scrub, calcareous soil. Rare native perennial found only in SE & Midlands.

Fam. Bellflower/Campanulaceae.

☺ Nettle-leaved Bellflower is a protected species & falls into the 'Endangered' category.

✿ Jul–Aug. ✚

Blue-eyed-grass
Sisyrinchium bermudiana
Feilistrín gorm

Ht. 20cm. **Fls.** 15–20mm, 6 bright blue tepals, each bearing 3 dark stripes & each ending in a short *bristle-like* point; at centre of flower is a dark-blue 'eye' surrounding a small yellow centre; in small clusters on erect, hairless, *flattened* stems.

Lvs. All basal, linear, grass-like.

Hab. Damp, muddy ground, lake shores. Rare perennial, possibly introduced; found in Kerry & Clare.

Fam. Iris/Iridaceae.

☺ Fruit is a globular capsule.

✿ Jun–Aug.

Spring Squill
Scilla verna
Sciolla earraigh

Ht. 12cm. **Fls.** 10–15mm, lilac-blue, star-shaped with 6 pointed tepals; each flower has a blue-purple bract longer than flower's stalk; in 2–12 flowered, terminal clusters on hairless, upright stems.

Lvs. Linear, basal, curly, appearing before flowers.

Hab. Coastal sites, rocky sea cliffs, short grass. Native perennial only found on N (inc. Rathlin Is.), NE & E coasts.

Fam. Asparagus/Asparagaceae.

☺ Fruit is a small, 3-part capsule.

✿ Apr–Jun.

Water Mint
Mentha aquatica
Mismín mionsach

Ht. 60cm. **Fls.** 3–4mm long, lilac-mauve 4-lobed flowers; stamens protrude & calyx tube is hairy; in dense, globular, *terminal heads* with more heads below; on erect, stiff, hairy, red-tinged stems.

Lvs. Opposite, oval, hairy, toothed.

Hab. Wet places, marshes, fens, lake margins. Widespread native perennial.

Fam. Dead-nettle/Lamiaceae.

☺ Strong minty fragrance.

☺ Plant often flushed with purple.

✿✿✿ Jul–Oct.

Corn Mint
Mentha arvensis
Mismín arbhair

Ht. 40cm. **Fls.** 3–4mm long, lilac, 2-lipped, stamens protruding; calyx bell-shaped, hairy, with short triangular teeth; in dense whorls at intervals along stem, emerging from axils of leaves which are longer than leaf bases; on erect, square, stems which terminate in *leaves & not flowers*.

Lvs. Oval-elliptical, short-stalked, hairy on both sides, toothed.

Hab. Arable ground, paths, woodland tracks. Native perennial or annual locally frequent.

Fam. Dead-nettle/Lamiaceae.

☺ Aroma is peppery & pungent.

✿✿ May–Oct.

231

Keeled-fruited Cornsalad
Valerianella carinata
Ceathrú uain dhroimneach

Ht. 30cm. **Fls.** 1–2mm, pale blue, 5-lobed; 3 stamens & very small, 1-toothed calyx; in dense terminal heads on repeatedly branching stems.

Lvs. Lower leaves spoon-shaped, upper leaves oblong.

Hab. Walls, arable ground, paths, cracks in pavements. Introduced annual, scattered, more common in E & SE.

Fam. Valerian/Valerianaceae.

✿✿ Jun–Jul.

Sheep's-bit
Jasione montana
Duán na gcaorach

Ht. 40cm. **Fls.** 15–25mm, round, blue, densely-packed flower-heads; each corolla 5mm long, 5-lobed, with 5 stamens & 2 protruding, stout *stigmas*; on sparsely branched, spreading, downy stems.

Lvs. Basal leaves in rosette, wavy-edged, linear-lanceolate; stem leaves are narrower, short, stalkless, many together towards lower part of plant's stem.

Hab. Coastal dunes, dry grassland, heaths. Native biennial, more common in coastal counties.

Fam. Bellflower/ Campanulaceae.

✿✿✿ May–Sep.

Field Scabious
Knautia arvensis
Cab an ghasáin

Ht. 75cm. **Fls.** 30–40mm blue-lilac flower-heads; each tiny corolla has 4 unequal lobes; smaller flowers at centre of head, larger flowers at outer margins; on long, hairy stems, often spotted.

Lvs. Basal leaves unlobed, spoon-shaped, hairy, blunt-toothed; stem leaves pinnately divided.

Hab. Dry grassland, hedgerows. Native perennial, more common in E half.

Fam. Teasel/Dipsacaceae.

✿✿✿ Jun–Oct.

Devil's-bit Scabious
Succisa pratensis
Odhrach bhallach

Ht. 75cm. **Fls.** 15–25mm, domed, violet-blue flower-heads; funnel-shaped corollas have 4 equal lobes & protruding *stamens* with pink, *angled* anthers; inner & outer florets all same size; calyx cup-shaped with 5 teeth; on slender, long, erect, hairy stems.

Lvs. Deep green, oval, opposite, lower long-stalked, untoothed; upper narrower & sometimes toothed.

Hab. Marshes, pastures & hedgerows. Widespread native perennial.

Fam. Teasel/Dipsacaceae.

✿✿✿ Jun–Oct.

Rhododendron
Rhododendron ponticum | Róslabhras

Ht. 3m. **Fls.** 40–60mm long, bell-shaped, pinkish-purple with 5 long, unequal lobes & 10 stamens; in rounded clusters on erect, spreading branches.

Lvs. Evergreen, hairless, shiny, elliptical, dark green above, light green below.

Hab. Damp, acid, peaty soil, hillsides. Common introduced shrub.

Fam. Heather/Ericaceae.

☺ Highly invasive species posing great threat to native oak woodland. ✿✿ May–Jun. 🏃 ⊛

Chicory
Cichorium intybus | Siocaire

Ht. 1m. **Fls.** 25–40mm clear, bright blue flower-heads, *all ray* florets, strap-shaped & spreading, toothed tips; in loose spikes on branched, grooved, stiff stems, producing latex when broken or cut.

Lvs. Basal leaves pinnately lobed, roughly spoon-shaped in outline; stem leaves lanceolate, clasping stem.

Hab. Bare places, roadsides, mostly calcareous soils. Uncommon introduced perennial, mostly in E & SE.

Fam. Daisy/Asteraceae.

☺ Flowers usually open in the morning & in sunny weather. ✿ Jun–Sep. 🏃

Seaside Daisy
Erigeron glaucus | Nóinín cladaigh

Ht. 30cm. **Fls.** 15–25mm flower-heads, purple-mauve ray florets surrounding circle of golden disc florets; on short, upright, hairy stems.

Lvs. Glaucous, spoon-shaped, stalked & fleshy; sometimes leaves have a few teeth.

Hab. Coastal cliffs, rocky places, dry waste ground, old stone walls. Introduced perennial, uncommon except for some SE coastal areas.

Fam. Daisy/Asteraceae.

☺ AKA Seaside Fleabane, this species spreads by means of stout rhizomes. ✿ Jul–Sep. 🏃

234

Sea-holly
Eryngium maritimum
Cuileann trá

Ht. 60cm. **Fls.** 6mm, powder-blue in dense, globular umbels, 40mm long; flower-heads surrounded by large, blue-tinged, spiny, leaf-like bracts; on tough, hairless, blue-green, branched stems.

Lvs. Waxy, blue-green, 3–5 lobed with wavy margin; white-veined, white edged, spiny.

Hab. Shingle, sandy soil, coastal sand-dunes. Native perennial common in coastal regions except in NE & N Connacht.

Fam. Carrot/Apiaceae.

☺ Not related to Holly (p. 24).

✿✿ Jul–Sep.

Blue Fleabane
Erigeron acris
Lus gorm na ndreancaidí

Ht. 30cm. **Fls.** 12–18mm flower-heads of erect, pale purple ray florets encircling tuft of slightly-shorter, pale yellow disc florets; bristly, pointed bracts *closely surround* flower-heads; in loose clusters on hairy, branched stems.

Lvs. Basal leaves stalked, spoon-shaped; stem leaves untoothed & clasping.

Hab. Calcareous grasslands, coastal shingle, eskers. Rare native annual or biennial found in Midlands, Kilkenny, Carlow & Wexford.

Fam. Daisy/Asteraceae.

✿ Jun–Aug. ⊞

For more information regarding ray florets & disc florets see p. 68.

Spear Thistle
Cirsium vulgare
Feochadán colgach

Ht. 1m. **Fls.** 20–40mm flower-heads of bright purple florets clustered tightly above an ovoid ball of long, cottony, spine-tipped bracts; solitary or in small clusters on upright, cottony stems with spiny, *interrupted* wings.

Lvs. Alternate, dull, *upper surface with small bristles*, pale undersides; basal rosette of matt, deeply-pinnate spiny leaves, *end lobe* with long, sharp point.

Hab. Disturbed ground, roadsides. Common native biennial.

Fam. Daisy/Asteraceae.

☺ Seeds are in a feathery pappus.

✿✿✿ Jul–Sep.

Slender Thistle
Carduus tenuiflorus
Feochadán caol

Ht. 1m. **Fls.** 6–10mm mauve-pink, narrow, unstalked flower-heads; tapered bracts behind flower-heads curve outwards; in dense, prickly, terminal clusters of 3–10; on upright, grey-green, narrowly-branched stems; broad, *spiny wings running entire length*.

Lvs. Alternate, elliptical, spiny, deep green above, white & cottony below; sharply-spiny margins.

Hab. Coastal habitats, dry, grassy ground. Native annual or biennial, rare apart from E & SE coastal areas.

Fam. Daisy/Asteraceae.

☺ Occasionally found inland.

✿ Jun–Aug.

Marsh Thistle
Cirsium palustre
Feochadán corraigh

Ht. 1.5m. **Fls.**
10–15mm short-
stalked flower-heads
of purple-red,
occasionally white,
florets; outer bracts
dark purple with
pointed tips; in crowded
clusters of 2–8, on upright
branched stems, *continuously spiny-
winged;* plant often tinged red.

Lvs. Pinnately lobed, linear-
lanceolate wavy & spiny; hairy on
upper surface.

Hab. Marshes, hedgerows,
woods. Widespread native biennial.

Fam. Daisy/Asteraceae.

✿✿✿ Jul–Sep.

*Most **Thistles** have heads of purple flowers
surrounded by sharply-pointed bracts. Check
for creeping runners, shape of leaves – are
they pinnate or simple, stem wings – are they
continuous or interrupted & look at the number
of flower-heads together.*

Creeping Thistle
Cirsium arvense
Feochadán reatha

Ht. 1m. **Fls.**
10–15mm lilac-pink
or white, narrow, *fragrant,*
short-stalked flower-heads;
purplish bracts, erect with sharp
tips; solitary or in small clusters on
unwinged, erect, mainly spineless stems.

Lvs. Alternate, oblong-lanceolate,
hairless above, cottony below; spiny
on wavy, edges.

Hab. Grassland, arable, waste
ground. Widespread native perennial.

Fam. Daisy/Asteraceae.

☺ Persistent weed, creeping on
rhizomes & producing a lot of seeds.

✿✿✿ Jun–Sep.

237

Meadow Thistle
Cirsium dissectum
Feochadán móna

Ht. 75cm. **Fls.** 15–30mm purple flower-heads; lanceolate bracts dark purple, pressed close below florets, outer ones spine-tipped; solitary on long, erect, unbranched, *unwinged*, downy, grooved stems.

Lvs. Basal leaves elliptical, toothed, green & hairy above, white & cottony below; margins have soft spines only.

Hab. Damp, peat bogs, limestone, fens. Native perennial, more common in W & N than E & S.

Fam. Daisy/Asteraceae.

☺ AKA Bog Thistle, this thistle creeps on rhizomes.

✿✿ Jun–Jul.

Sea Aster
Aster tripolium
Luibh bhléine

Ht. 1m. **Fls.** 10–20mm, blue-mauve ray florets spreading around bright yellow disc florets; in umbel-like clusters on erect, branched stems.

Lvs. Fleshy, basal leaves are oblong; stem leaves are dark green, untoothed, linear-oblong with prominent midrib.

Hab. Coastal salt-marshes, sea cliffs. Native perennial, common in given habitat.

Fam. Daisy/Asteraceae.

☺ Salt-tolerant plant which closely resembles garden escape, Michaelmas Daisy.

✿ Jul–Sep.

Greater Knapweed
Centaurea scabiosa
Mínscoth mhór

Ht. 1m. **Fls.** 30–50mm red-purple
flower-heads; *outer larger* florets
radiating, inner florets smaller; florets
are slender tubes with 5 *narrow* lobes;
swollen base with bracts overlapping
closely, with bristly teeth; solitary on
erect, stiff, grooved stems, branching
in upper part.

Lvs. Lower leaves oblong, *deeply
pinnate*; upper stalkless, less deeply
lobed.

Hab. Grassy, calcareous soil.
Native perennial found in parts
of SE, Clare & Galway.

Fam. Daisy/Asteraceae.

✿ Jun–Sep.

Common Knapweed
Centaurea nigra
Mínscoth

Ht. 1m. **Fls.** 20–40mm
purple-red flower-heads,
all florets equal length; on
globular heads covered by
closely overlapping bracts with
deeply fringed dark tips; solitary
on ridged, hairy, erect stems.

Lvs. Oblong-linear, alternate, *not
pinnate*.

Hab. Grassland, arable, waste
ground, walls. Widespread native
perennial.

Fam. Daisy/Asteraceae.

☺ AKA Hardheads.

✿✿✿ Jun–Sep.

239

Lax-flowered Sea-lavender

Limonium humile | Lus liath na mara

Ht. 40cm. **Fls.** 6–7mm, 5 lilac petals, 5 stamens, 5 styles, red-brown anthers; purple-green calyx; in open clusters which branch *below middle* into upright stems; woody rootstock.

Lvs. Narrow, untoothed, long-stalked; *pinnately veined*.

Hab. Saltmarshes. Scattered native perennial, uncommon in NW.

Fam. Thrift/Plumbaginaceae.

✿✿ Jul–Sep.

Rock Sea-lavender

Limonium binervosum | Lus liath aille

Ht. 30cm. **Fls.** 6–7mm, 5 lilac petals; in spiked clusters on stems which branch *low down*.

Lvs. Glaucous, *3-veined, winged* stalks.

Hab. Coastal cliffs. Rare native perennial of E & SE.

Fam. Thrift/Plumbaginaceae.

✿ Jul–Sep. 🔲

Western Sea-lavender

Limonium recurvum ssp.
pseudotranswallianum | Lus liath na Boirne

Ht. 20cm. **Fls.** 5–6mm, lilac, papery calyx; in clusters on tough, branched stems.

Lvs. Basal rosette of fleshy, spoon-shaped leaves.

Hab. Limestone rocks, coastal cliffs. Rare native perennial of the Burren.

Fam. Thrift/Plumbaginaceae.

✿ Jul–Aug. 🔲

Purple-loosestrife
Lythrum salicaria
Créachtach

Ht. 1.5m. **Fls.** 10–15mm
red-purple with 6 crumpled,
narrow petals; in dense
whorls on upright spikes
with dark red, leafy bracts;
stems sometimes ridged,
clasped by long, *unstalked*
narrow leaves.

Lvs. Oval-lanceolate, pointed,
paired below flowers or in whorls
of 3.

Hab. Fens, damp ditches, river banks, wet
ground. Widespread native perennial.

Fam. Purple-loosestrife/Lythraceae.

☺ Not related to Yellow Loosestrife or
Dotted Loosestrife (p. 97).

✿✿✿ Jun–Aug.

Eyebright
Euphrasia officinalis agg.
Glanrosc

Ht. 25cm. **Fls.** 5–10mm long, 2-lipped
white, often tinged pink or violet, with
purple veins, yellow blush within corolla;
upper lips hooded, 2-lobed, lower lips
spread, lobed; in erect, branched, leafy
terminal spikes.

Lvs. Oval, sharply-toothed.

Hab. Undisturbed, grassy places.
Widespread native annual.

Fam. Broomrape/Orobanchaceae.

☺ Being semi-parasitic plants,
Eyebrights obtain their nutrition from
roots of Clovers, Plantains, grasses.

☺ There are many species of
Eyebright & hybrids occur.

✿✿✿ May–Sep.

Common Comfrey
Symphytum officinale
Compar

Ht. 1.5m. **Fls.** 12–18mm long, tubular, bell-shaped, purple, pink or white; edges slightly upturned as 5 tiny lobes; in branched, coiled clusters; on erect, hairy, stems with downward-pointing, tapering hairs & *wings which continue from one leaf axil to next.*

Lvs. Upper clasping, oval, hairy; basal leaves large, oval-lanceolate, stalked, untoothed & softly hairy.

Hab. Damp grassland, riverbanks, waste ground, marshes. Scattered perennial, probably introduced.

Fam. Borage/Boraginaceae.

▶ White Comfrey (p. 75) & Tuberous Comfrey (p. 140).

✿✿ May–Jul.

Russian Comfrey
Symphytum x uplandicum
Compar Rúiseach

Ht. 1.2m. **Fls.** 12–15mm long, bell-shaped tubes, pink in bud, turning purple-violet with 5 tiny turned-back lobes; in coiled clusters on *slightly winged*, rough, bristly stems.

Lvs. Upper leaves oval, stalkless, short, *wings only running short distance* down stem; lower leaves hairy, oval & veined.

Hab. Rough, waste ground, roadsides, verges. Introduced perennial, more common in E than W.

Fam. Borage/Boraginaceae.

☺ This is a hybrid between *Symphytum asperum* & *S.officinale.*

✿✿ May–Aug.

Viper's-bugloss
Echium vulgare
Lus nathrach

Ht. 90m. **Fls.**
15–20mm long,
funnel-shaped, bright
blue, 5 unequal lobes with
5 unequal violet-coloured stamens, 4
protruding & 1 shorter than corolla;
buds usually pink; in coiled cymes in
leaf-axils on erect, *bristly*, spotted stems.

Lvs. Narrow, pointed; basal leaves
stalked & with prominent mid-rib; stem
leaves sessile.

Hab. Coastal grassland, dunes & sea
cliffs. Uncommon native biennial,
mainly found in E & S coastal regions.

Fam. Borage/Boraginaceae.

▶ Bugloss (p. 221).

✿ May–Sep.

Butterfly-bush
Buddleja davidii
Tor an fhéileacáin

Ht. 5m. **Fls.** 3–4mm, mauve-
violet, 4-lobed tube with orange
'eye'; 4 stamens, 4 sepals fused
into tube; in dense, long, tapering,
conical spikes on arching branches.

Lvs. Opposite, long, narrow; light
& downy beneath.

Hab. Waste, disturbed ground,
railways, urban sites. Introduced
shrub, common in all but W of
Ireland.

Fam. Figwort/Scrophulariaceae.

☺ Flowers are heavily scented
& very attractive to insects.

✿✿ Jun–Sep. 🏃

Vervain
Verbena officinalis
Beirbhéine

Ht. 70cm. **Fls.** 4–5mm, blue-pink, 2-lipped with 5 lobes, 4 stamens; colour lighter towards centre; calyx half length of corolla; in long, tapering spikes on stiff, branched, square, rough, hairy stems.

Lvs. Paired, deep green, lower leaves deeply cut; upper leaves small, unstalked, hardly divided.

Hab. Dry, grassy places, waste ground, chalky soil. Introduced perennial, found in SE mainly.

Fam. Vervain/ Verbenaceae.

✿✿ Jun–Sep.

Ground-ivy
Glechoma hederacea
Athair lusa

Ht. 20cm. **Fls.** 15–20mm, blue-violet, two-lipped, lower lip quite flat & lobed with purple spots; fringing on lower lip at 'mouth' of flower; calyx 2-lipped; in whorls arising from leaf axis, usually all facing in *same direction*; on softly hairy, upright stalks arising from creeping, rooting stems.

Lvs. Downy, round, kidney-shaped, toothed, long-stalked.

Hab. Woods, grassland, hedgerows, waste & cultivated ground. Native perennial, widespread in all but extreme W.

Fam. Dead-nettle/Lamiaceae.

☺ Not related to Atlantic Ivy (p. 264).

✿✿✿ Mar–Jul.

Bugle
Ajuga reptans
Glasair choille

Ht. 30cm. **Fls.** 15mm
long, blue-violet; corolla
with tiny upper lip &
long, veined, 4-lobed lower
lip; 4 stamens protrude from
mouth of corolla; in whorls on
leafy spikes on erect, 4-angled stems
which are hairy on *two opposite sides*.

Lvs. Opposite, ovate, shiny, green-
bronzy; basal rosette & unstalked stem
leaves.

Hab. Deciduous woods, damp
grassland. Widespread native perennial.

Fam. Dead-nettle/Lamiaceae.

☺ Spreads *on stolons* – above-ground runners, which root at nodes.

✿✿✿ Apr–Jun.

Pyramidal Bugle
Ajuga pyramidalis
Glasair bheannach

Ht. 10cm. **Fls.** 15mm long,
blue-violet, 2-lipped; lower lip lobed,
purple-veined, pale toward centre of
flower; stamens slightly protruding;
above downy, purplish, leafy, bristle-
edged bracts, much longer than
flowers; in cone-shaped spike on *short*,
upright stems, *hairy all around*.

Lvs. Oval, bluntly-toothed, stalked,
basal rosette.

Hab. Grassy, calcareous, rocky soil.
Very rare native perennial of Burren
region & Rathlin Is.

Fam. Dead-nettle/Lamiaceae.

☺ This species has *no stolons*, but
spreads by rhizomes (horizontal
underground stems).

✿ Apr–Jun. ✛

Basil Thyme
Clinopodium acinos
Lus mhic rí Breatan

Ht. 20cm. **Fls.** 8–10mm long, violet,
2-lipped; 3-lobed bottom lip has white
horse-shoe pattern with fringing towards corolla
opening; 2-lobed upper lip smaller, jutting
forward; in few-flowered whorls of 4–6
in leaf bases; on square, branching, hairy
stems.

Lvs. Paired, oval, shallowly-toothed with
network of veins.

Hab. Dry, grassy places, calcareous soil.
Rare annual, probably introduced, found
mainly in centre & SE.

Fam. Dead-nettle/Lamiaceae.

▶ Wild Thyme (p. 185).

✿✿ May–Aug. ✚

Purple Toadflax
Linaria purpurea
Buaflíon corcra

Ht. 90cm. **Fls.** 8–12mm long, purple,
2-lipped; lower lip is 3-lobed, centre
lobe slightly overlapping outer 2; smaller
2-lobed upper lip; rear of corolla is
a long, downward-pointing spur; in
tapering spikes on slender, upright stems.

Lvs. Pointed, narrow, grey-green,
untoothed; lower leaves in whorls, upper
alternate.

Hab. Embankments, bare, waste
ground, old walls. Introduced perennial,
occasional in E half of Ireland.

Fam. Speedwell/Veronicaceae.

▶ Common Toadflax (p. 138), Small
Toadflax (p. 171) & Ivy-leaved Toadflax
(p. 226).

✿ Jun–Aug. 🏃

246

Betony
Betonica officinalis
Lus beatha

Ht. 60cm. **Fls.** 12–18mm
long, red-purple, 2-lipped;
3-lobed lower lip with central lobe
largest; 4 stamens, 2 short, 2 long;
corolla tube longer than calyx which
has *pointed teeth*; in whorls on 4-sided
stems.

Lvs. Oval-oblong, roundly-toothed,
opposite; narrower stem leaves.

Hab. Grassy banks, woodland,
hedgerows. Rare, native
perennial, mainly found
in Counties Kerry &
Wexford.

Fam. Dead-nettle/
Lamiaceae.

✿✿ Jun–Sep. ✚

Selfheal
Prunella vulgaris
Duán ceannchosach

Ht. 20cm. **Fls.** 10–15mm long, violet-
purple; 2-lipped with *concave* upper lip;
lower lip has toothed margin; calyx
is bell-shaped & persists after flowers
have finished; in dense, cylindrical
heads with hairy, purple-red bracts, on
upright, square stems.

Lvs. Opposite, oval-diamond shaped,
below flower-heads.

Hab. Grassy places, woodland, waste
ground, neutral & calcareous soils.
Widespread native perennial.

Fam. Dead-nettle/Lamiaceae.

☺ Occasionally white.

✿✿✿ Apr–Jun.

Foxglove
Digitalis purpurea
Lus mór

Ht. 1.5m. **Fls.** 40–55mm long, mauve-purple, tubular or bell-shaped with lower edge of corolla slightly prominent; inside corolla are dark purple spots on larger white spots; in erect, leafy, terminal racemes on downy, stems.

Lvs. Oval-lanceolate, grey-green, downy, wrinkled; basal rosette in year 1, stem leaves in year 2.

Hab. Woodland, on acid soil, mountains, hedgerows. Widespread native biennial.

Fam. Speedwell/Veronicaceae.

☺ White forms often occur.

✿✿✿ Jun–Sep. ⚠

Fairy Foxglove
Erinus alpinus
Méirín sí

Ht. 30cm. **Fls.** 8–12mm, pink-purple tubular corolla with 5 notched petal-lobes, upper 2 narrower than lower 3; in loose, short-stalked clusters which elongate as seed capsules develop; on erect stems.

Lvs. Fleshy, long, wedge-shaped & lobed at tip; mainly in basal rosette.

Hab. Old stone walls, rocky places. Uncommon, introduced perennial.

Fam. Speedwell/Veronicaceae.

✿✿ May–Sep. 🏃

Wild Teasel
Dipsacus fullonum
Leadán úcaire

Ht. 2m. **Fls.** 60–80mm
long, prickly, egg-shaped
flower-heads encircled by
tiny pink-purple florets; thin,
spiny bracts form a whorl below flower-
heads, usually longer than flower-head;
on prickly, ridged, angled stems.

Lvs. Basal rosette of oblong leaves in
year 1, sharp spines at rear of midrib; in
year 2, opposite leaves join across stem,
forming cup which fills with rainwater.

Hab. Grassy places, meadows,
embankments. Native biennial,
more common in E half of
Ireland.

Fam. Teasel/Dipsacaceae.

✿✿ Jul–Aug.

Bluebell
Hyacinthoides non-scripta
Coinnle corra

Ht. 50cm. **Fls.** 14–20mm long,
violet-blue, drooping, tubular, with
6 *recurved* lobes & *cream* anthers; each
flower has 2 blue-purple bracts; 4–15
flowers in long, one-sided raceme,
curving gracefully; on hairless,
drooping stems.

Lvs. All basal, narrow, hooded at tip.

Hab. Carpet-forming in old
woodlands & hedgebanks. Common,
native perennial.

Fam. Asparagus/Asparagaceae.

☺ *H.* x *massartiana* (near right),
hybrid between native & Spanish
Bluebell has blue anthers & erect
stems & is potentially invasive.

✿✿✿ Apr–Jun.

Hairy Tare
Vicia hirsuta
Peasair arbhair

Ht. 40cm. **Fls.** 2–4mm long, pale lilac peaflowers, in long, stalked, one-sided clusters of 1–9; on slender, scrambling, downy stems.

Lvs. Pinnate; linear-oblong leaflets in 4–10 pairs, ending in *branched tendrils*.

Hab. Grassy places, neutral & calcareous soil. Native annual, uncommon except in NE, SE, S & Midlands.

Fam. Pea/Fabaceae.

☺ Seedpods are covered in fine hairs & contain 2 seeds.

✿✿ May–Aug.

For more about
Peaflowers *see p. 114.*

Bush Vetch
Vicia sepium
Peasair fhiáin

Ht. 1m. **Fls.** 15mm long, dull mauve-purple which fades; upper 2-lobed petal dark-veined; calyx teeth unequal, upper shorter; in clusters of 2–6 on slender, scrambling stems.

Lvs. Pinnate; linear-ovate leaflets, widest at base, tip blunt with bristle-point; in 3–9 pairs with *branched tendrils*.

Hab. Hedgerows, grassy places, meadows. Widespread native perennial.

Fam. Pea/Fabaceae.

☺ Seeds are in black, hairless pods.

▶ Common vetch (p. 171).

✿✿✿ Apr–Oct.

Tufted Vetch
Vicia cracca
Peasair na luch

Ht. 2m. **Fls.** 8–12mm long, blue-purple, in narrow, crowded, 1-sided spike of 10–30; calyx teeth unequal, upper tiny; on downy stems, scrambling & slightly ridged.

Lvs. Pinnate; narrow-oblong leaflets in 6–12 pairs, ending in *branched tendrils*.

Hab. Hedgerows, scrub. Widespread native perennial.

Fam. Pea/Fabaceae.

☺ Seedpods are brown & hairless.

✿✿✿ Jun–Aug.

Bitter-vetch
Lathyrus linifolius
Corra meille

Ht. 40cm. **Fls.** 10–15mm long, crimson-purple, dark-veined, changing to blue or green as they mature; blue-purple, fused, cap-like, sepals have 5 teeth; in long-stalked racemes of 2–6 on upright, almost hairless, *winged* stems.

Lvs. Pinnate; narrow, untoothed; in 2–4 pairs *ending in a point – not a tendril*.

Hab. Scrub, woodland, heathy hedge banks; often acid soil. Native perennial, common except in centre of Ireland.

Fam. Pea/Fabaceae.

☺ Seedpod is brown & hairless.

✿✿ Apr–Jul.

Flecked Marsh-orchid
Dactylorhiza incarnata ssp. *cruenta*
Magairlín craorag

Ht. 30cm. **Fls.** 8–12mm long, mauve with purple pattern on lower, 3-lobed lip; *downward-pointing* spur & 2 erect, spreading sepals on either side of 3 centre tepals which curve to form a hood; in spikes on upright stems.
Lvs. Erect, keeled, usually *spotted on both sides.*
Hab. Marshes, limestone. Rare native perennial only found in Clare & Galway.
Fam. Orchid/Orchidaceae.

▶ *Dactylorhiza incarnata* ssp. *coccinea* (p. 208).

▶ *Dactylorhiza incarnata* ssp. *pulchella* (p. 253).

✿ May–Jul.

Narrow-leaved Marsh-orchid
Dactylorhiza traunsteinerioides
Magairlín caol

Ht. 45cm. **Fls.** 8–10mm long, narrow, pinkish-purple, each with well-marked lower 3-lobed lip, central lobe narrower but longer than outer 2; side sepals spreading; slender, straight spur; in open spikes, tending to be one-sided, on slender, erect stems.
Lvs. Few, very narrow, keeled, slightly hooded tip; unspotted or only spotted at tip.
Hab. Fens & marshes. Scarce, native perennial.
Fam. Orchid/Orchidaceae.

✿ May–Jun. ⊞

Northern Marsh-orchid
Dactylorhiza purpurella
Magairlín corcra

Ht. 40cm. **Fls.** 8–12mm long, deep, rich purple with darker purple designs & squiggles; lower petal is *diamond-shaped* with barely upturned edge & *slight* central lobe; stout *down-turned spur;* outer sepals spreading & erect; in dense, cylindrical, *flat-topped* spikes on erect stems.

Lvs. *Narrow*, flat, often spotted near hooded tip.

Hab. Wet meadows, dune slacks. Native perennial, mainly N & SE.

Fam. Orchid/Orchidaceae.

✿✿ Jun–Jul.

Early Marsh-orchid
Dactylorhiza incarnata var. *pulchella*
Magairlín álainn

Ht. 30cm. **Fls.** 8–12mm long, light purple; labellum narrow, reflexed, shallowly-lobed; 2 outer, lateral sepals erect & spreading; upper 3 tepals forming incurved hood; pattern of dots & loops throughout; downward-pointing, slightly curved, stout spur; in dense head becoming longer & cylindrical on narrow stem.

Lvs. Unspotted, linear-lanceolate, hooded slightly at apex.

Hab. Lakeshores, bogs, marshes, fens. Native perennial, scattered but more frequent in Galway & Clare.

Fam. Orchid/Orchidaceae.

▶ *Dactylorhiza incarnata* ssp. *cruenta* (p. 252).

▶ *Dactylorhiza incarnata* ssp. *coccinea* (p. 208).

✿ May–Jul.

Marsh Pennywort
Hydrocotyle vulgaris
Lus na pingine

Ht. Prostrate. **Fls.** 1–2mm, green-pink, with 5 triangular lobes & 5 stamens with 5 bright yellow anthers; in *tiny* whorls on creeping, pink stems, usually hidden below distinctive leaves.

Lvs. Hairless, circular, veined, shallowly-toothed, peltate i.e. with stem attached behind *centre* of leaf.

Hab. Damp meadows, marshes, bogs, fens, stream margins. Widespread native perennial.

Fam. Pennywort/Hydrocotylaceae

☺ Hand lens recommended.

✿✿✿ Jun–Aug.

Fat-hen
Chenopodium album
Blonagán bán

Ht. 1m. **Fls.** 2mm, green-white, 5 tepals, *very mealy*; in dense, leafy, grey-green spikes on erect stems which are often red-tinged.

Lvs. Oval to diamond-shaped, grey-green, with dull, matt appearance.

Hab. Arable, cultivated, waste ground & roadsides. Introduced annual plant, common throughout except for NW.

Fam. Goosefoot/Amaranthaceae.

☺ Similar to Common Orache (p. 257) but that species has *conspicuous bracteoles* & *forward-pointing* lobes to *lower* leaves.

✿✿✿ Jun–Oct.

Pellitory-of-the-wall
Parietaria judaica
Feabhraíd reatha

Ht. 30cm. **Fls.** Minute, green-red;
male & female flowers separate;
reddish male flowers (in close-up
below) in leaf axils, female flowers
nearer tip of stem; on softly hairy,
red, spreading branched stems
which do not root at nodes.

Lvs. Alternate,
oval-lanceolate, stalked &
untoothed.

Hab. Rocks, old walls. Native
perennial, more common in S
half of Ireland.

Fam. Nettle/Urticaceae.

✿✿✿ Jun–Oct.

Sea-purslane
Atriplex portulacoides
Lus an ghaill

Ht. 80cm. **Fls.** *Tiny*,
green-yellow with 5 tepals
& 5 unstalked stamens; in
dense, branched spikes on
brownish, much-branched stems,
woody near ground.

Lvs. Mostly opposite, oblong,
silver-green, untoothed, fleshy &
stalked; upper leaves
narrow; all mealy.

Hab. Drier reaches
of saltmarshes, coastal
walls & rocks. Native
perennial shrub,
common on E & S
coasts.

Fam. Goosefoot/
Amaranthaceae.

✿✿ Jul–Oct.

Frosted Orache
Atriplex laciniata
Eilifleog phlúrach

Ht. Prostrate to 20cm. **Fls.** Tiny, yellow-green, in dense, lateral clusters at leaf axils; on sprawling, dusty-pink stems.

Lvs. Silvery, fleshy, wavy-edged, toothed, diamond-shaped.

Hab. Coastal sand & shingle, above high-tide mark. Native annual common on all but W coast.

Fam. Goosefoot/ Amaranthaceae.

✿✿ Jul–Sep.

☺ *Oraches are fleshy plants with tiny, separate male & female flowers, the latter having a pair of triangular bracteoles or tiny leaf-like structures which swell in fruit.* ▶ *Babington's Orache (p. 196).*

Grass-leaved Orache
Atriplex littoralis
Eilifleog thrá

Ht. 1m. **Fls.** Tiny, greenish; male flowers have 5 tepals & 5 stamens; female flowers have 2 large triangular bracts; in long, branched spikes which are leafy towards the base; on *erect*, ridged stems.

Lvs. Linear-lanceolate; lower leaves short-stalked, upper leaves unstalked.

Hab. Coastal sites, saltmarshes. Scarce, native annual found on some E & SE coasts.

Fam. Goosefoot/ Amaranthaceae.

✿ Jul–Sep.

Common Orache
Atriplex patula
Eilifleog chaol

Ht. 60cm. **Fls.** Tiny, greenish, inconspicuous; male flowers with 3–5 sepals, female flowers with 2 bracteoles; in leafy spikes on prostrate *or* erect, much-branched, ridged, often reddish stems.

Lvs. Lower leaves arrow or diamond shaped, with *forward-pointing* lower lobes; upper leaves narrow, slightly toothed.

Hab. Arable, coastal & disturbed ground. Widespread introduced annual.

Fam. Goosefoot/Amaranthaceae.

☺ Triangular bracteoles are fused to *half* of length.

✿✿✿ Jul–Sep.

Spear-leaved Orache
Atriplex prostrata
Eilifleog leathan

Ht. 70cm. **Fls.** Tiny, yellow-green tinged pink; male flowers have 4–5 tepals; female flowers have 2 erect, mealy, *unstalked* bracts; in clusters on erect, reddish stems.

Lvs. Triangular; base of leaf at right angle to stem; upper leaves narrower.

Hab. Waste ground inland, saltmarshes, coastal sand & shingle. Native annual common on all coasts.

Fam. Goosefoot/Amaranthaceae.

☺ Bracteoles only joined for about *one quarter* of length.

✿✿✿ Jul–Sep.

Annual Sea-blite
Suaeda maritima
Blide mhara

Ht. 50cm. **Fls.** 1–2mm, green, in groups of 1–3 in upper leaf axils; on green-red, hairless, succulent, branched, often prostrate stems.

Lvs. Alternate, linear, fleshy, half-cylindrical, pointed.

Hab. Middle & lower levels of saltmarshes, creeks. Native annual, fairly common in coastal areas.

Fam. Goosefoot/Amaranthaceae.

☺ Could be mistaken for Glasswort (see p. 74) but leaves of Annual Sea-blite are not fused into a mass with stems.

✿✿ Aug–Oct.

Water Dock
Rumex hydrolapathum
Copóg uisce

Ht. 2m. **Fls.** 4–5mm, green, becoming red; inner tepals have short teeth, are long & each has a long wart; in dense, crowded whorls on tall, much-branched, erect, robust stems.

Lvs. Lanceolate-oval, leathery, *reaching 1m long*, tapering at base.

Hab. Marshes, ditches, margins of rivers, ponds, canals. Common native perennial, absent from parts of W.

Fam. Knotweed/Polygonaceae.

☺ Unmistakeable because of its habitat & height.

✿✿ Jul–Sep.

Slender Parsley-piert
Aphanes australis
Mionán Muire caol

Ht. Prostrate. **Fls.** 1mm, no petals but 4 green, sepals *which are not erect*, 1 stamen; surrounded by *oblong stipule-lobes*; in dense, unstalked clusters in leaf-axils along downy stems.

Lvs. Downy, green, fan-shaped, divided into 3, deeply-lobed segments.

Hab. Sandy soil, tracks, bare, cultivated places. Native annual, more common in S half of Ireland.

Fam. Rose/Rosaceae.

☺ Hand lens necessary.

✿✿ Apr–Oct.

Sea-buckthorn
Hippophae rhamnoides
Draighean mara

Ht. 3m. **Fls.** 3mm, green, petals absent, 2 sepals; male & female flowers on separate shrubs; in short spikes in leaf axils; on much-branched, *thorny*, suckering stems.

Lvs. Alternate, narrow, untoothed, grey-green, covered in silvery scales.

Hab. Coastal sand dunes, planted & self-sown. Uncommon, introduced shrub.

Fam. Sea-buckthorn/Elaeagnaceae.

☺ Potentially invasive species.

☺ Not related to Buckthorn (p. 261).

✿ Mar–Apr. 🏃 🌀

Yew
Taxus baccata
Iúr

Ht. 20m. **Fls.** Male & female flowers on separate trees; male flower has many yellow stamens; tiny green female flower, borne singly in leaf axils, is followed by berry-like cone; on upright, red-brown, scaly, flaky stems, often branching from base of trunk.

Lvs. Linear, dark green above, flat, in 2 rows.

Hab. Limestone, scrub, hedgerows. Native, evergreen shrub or tree, more common in E half.

Fam. Yew/Taxaceae.

☺ Leaves & berries are poisonous.

✿✿ Mar–Apr. ⚠

Juniper
Juniperus communis
Aiteal

Ht. Prostrate, *occasionally* with erect branches. **Fls.** Male & female flowers are on separate shrubs; male flowers small, yellow, releasing pollen; tiny female flowers are yellowish-green clusters of scales; in groups of 3 in leaf axils; on stiff, low-growing stems.

Lvs. Green, keeled below & single band above; sharply-pointed, narrow, stiff, in groups of 3.

Hab. Limestone, scrub. Native, evergreen shrub confined mainly to NW & W of Ireland.

Fam. Juniper/Cupressaceae.

☺ Produces berries – green in year 1, blue-black when ripe.

✿ May–Jun.

Spindle
Euonymus europaeus
Feoras

Ht. 4m. **Fls.** 8–10mm,
greenish-white, 4 *well-separated*
petals, 4 sepals; in small, branched
clusters in leaf-axils; on square-sided twigs
on much-branched, upright stems.

Lvs. Opposite, ovate-lanceolate, hairless,
pointed & scarcely-toothed.

Hab. Scrub, hedges, limestone. Native
deciduous shrub, scattered widely
throughout.

Fam. Spindle/Celastraceae.

☺ Fruits are coral pink, 4-lobed,
with fleshy, orange succulent
covering to seeds.

✿✿ May–Jun.

Buckthorn
Rhamnus cathartica
Paide bréan

Ht. 5m. **Fls.** 4–6mm, green,
star-shaped flowers with 4
widely-spaced, *pointed* petals; sepals
longer than petals; male & female
flowers on separate shrubs; in small
clusters at base of upper leaves; on
branches which can be twisted &
have scattered thorns.

Lvs. Opposite, ovate, finely-
toothed; *2–4 pairs veins curve into tip.*

Hab. Scrub, woodland, mainly
calcareous soil. Native perennial
shrub mainly found in Midlands &
mid-west.

Fam. Buckthorn/Rhamnaceae.

☺ Not related to Sea-buckthorn
(p. 259).

✿✿ May–Jun.

Procumbent Pearlwort
Sagina procumbens
Mongán sínte

Ht. Prostrate. **Fls.** 2–3mm, long stalked; 4 very pale green-white, rounded petals – often absent – much smaller than green sepals; borne on side shoots.

Lvs. Hairless, linear, with bristle-like point, in closely-spaced pairs.

Hab. Damp, gravelly ground, paths, lawns, walls & bare places. Widespread native perennial.

Fam. Pink/Caryophyllaceae.

☺ Mat-forming plant with central rosette & radiating shoots which root at intervals.

▶ Knotted Pearlwort (p. 34).

✿✿✿ Apr–Sep.

Sea Pearlwort
Sagina maritima
Mongán mara

Ht. 8 cm. **Fls.** 2–3mm, 4 pale green-white petals, frequently absent; sepals purple-green, larger than petals; on purplish, fleshy, branching stems.

Lvs. Dark green, fleshy, blunt.

Hab. Bare, rocky ground, shingle, mainly near the sea. Occasional coastal native annual.

Fam. Pink/Caryophyllaceae.

▶ Main difference between this species & Procumbent Pearlwort is lack of *bristle-like point* at end of leaf in *this* species.

✿✿ May–Sep.

Opposite-leaved Golden-saxifrage
Chrysosplenium oppositifolium
Glóiris

Ht. 15cm. **Fls.** 2–5mm, petals absent but 4 yellow-green sepals; in forked, umbel-like, flat-topped clusters; surrounded by large green-yellow bracts; on creeping, spreading, mat-forming stems which root at intervals.

Lvs. Opposite, oblong-rounded, blunt-toothed margin, slightly hairy, with stalk no longer than blade.

Hab. Damp river banks, woodland, wet rocks, mostly acid soil. Common native perennial.

Fam. Saxifrage/Saxifragaceae.

✿✿✿ Mar–Jul.

Sea Beet
Beta vulgaris ssp. *maritima*
Laíon na trá

Ht. 1m. **Fls.** Tiny, with 5 greenish sepals & 5 yellow stamens & styles; in clusters of 3 in dense, leafy spikes on erect or sprawling, often red-striped stems.

Lvs. Dark-green, glossy, leathery, untoothed, oval-lanceolate to triangular.

Hab. Coastal shingle, cliffs, beaches & sea walls. Native perennial, common on all coasts except NW.

Fam. Goosefoot/ Amaranthaceae.

✿✿✿ Jul–Sep.

Black-bindweed
Fallopia convolvulus
Glúineach dhubh

Ht. 1m. **Fls.** 2–3mm, 5 pale-green lobes which have pale pink borders; in loose clusters in leaf-axils; on angular, *clockwise-twining*, climbing or prostrate stems.

Lvs. Alternate, heart to arrow-shaped, untoothed, mealy below; short silvery sheaths where leaf-stalk is attached to stem.

Hab. Arable, cultivated & waste ground. Common native annual.

Fam. Knotweed/ Polygonaceae.

✿✿✿ Jul–Oct.

Atlantic Ivy
Hedera hibernica
Eidhneán

Ht. 20m. **Fls.** 8–10mm, greenish-yellow; 5 pointed petals, 5 triangular sepals, 5 prominent stamens with yellow anthers; in spherical umbels on woody, evergreen stems which cling to trees & walls by means of tiny stem roots.

Lvs. Alternate, leathery, glossy dark green; palmately lobed on non-flowering & juvenile stems; elliptical-heart-shaped on mature, flowering stems.

Hab. Trees, walls, woods. Widespread, native, woody, climbing perennial.

Fam. Ivy/Araliaceae.

☺ Not related to Ground-ivy (p. 244).

✿✿✿ Sep–Nov.

264

Lady's-mantle
Alchemilla vulgaris agg.
Dearna Mhuire

Ht. 30cm. **Fls.** 3–4mm, greenish-yellow, no petals, 4 sepals, 4–5 stamens; in branched, flat-topped clusters on hairy, spreading stems.

Lvs. Round, velvety, palmately lobed, pleated; small marginal teeth.

Hab. Grassy, rocky places, damp grassland, stream-sides. Native perennial, widespread in N, W & Midlands.

Fam. Rose/Rosaceae.

☺ Abbreviation 'agg.' (aggregate) means complex of micro-species, difficult to tell apart.

✿ May–Sep.

Salad Burnet
Poterium sanguisorba
Lus an uille

Ht. 40cm. **Fls.** 10–20mm globular heads of tiny, petalless, greenish flowers; lower flowers in heads are male, have many stamens & yellow anthers; upper flowers are female, with 2 red styles; on slender, red stems, branching towards top.

Lvs. Pinnately divided; rounded, deeply toothed leaflets with stipules at leaf bases.

Hab. Dry, calcareous soil, sandy places. Uncommon native perennial.

Fam. Rose/Rosaceae.

☺ Leaves smell of cucumber when crushed.

✿ May–Sep.

Giant-rhubarb
Gunnera tinctoria
Gunnaire

Ht. 2m. **Fls.** 1mm, stalkless, without petals but with tiny, reddish-brown sepals; in *densely-packed* inflorescences on up to 1m-long, cone-shaped panicles; on stout stems arising from rhizomes.

Lvs. 2m-wide, toothed & palmately-lobed; on stout stalks which have green bristles; very quick-growing in spring.

Hab. Damp places, river-banks, hillsides, coastal cliffs, derelict gardens. Perennial introduced from Chile, mainly found in the West.

Fam. Giant-rhubarb/Gunneraceae.

☺ Classed as potentially invasive.

✿✿ Jul–Aug. 🏃 ⚘

Brazilian Giant-rhubarb
Gunnera manicata
Gunnaire na mbláth mór

Ht. 2m. **Fls.** Tiny, 1mm long, green-brown, in inflorescences of loose narrow panicles on cone-shaped spikes up to 1m long.

Lvs. Extremely large, often more than 2m across, lobed & toothed; on stout, prickly stems often 1–2.5m high.

Hab. Damp ground, usually beside water. Perennial, introduced from Brazil, common in parts of W.

Fam. Giant-rhubarb/Gunneraceae.

☺ Current research indicates possibility of this hybridising with *G. tinctoria*.

✿ Jul–Aug. 🏃

Common Nettle
Urtica dioica ssp. *dioica*
Neantóg

Ht. 1m. **Fls.** Male &
female on separate plants;
males have 4 tiny, greenish
sepals, 4 stamens & are in
long, catkin-type clusters; females,
greyish-green, hairy; in short, dense heads
or clusters; on branched or unbranched
coarsely hairy, erect stems.

Lvs. Opposite, *heart-shaped*, coarsely toothed
& covered in stinging hairs.

Hab. Hedgerows, farms, especially on
enriched soils. Widespread native perennial.

Fam. Nettle/Urticaceae.

▶ Small nettle (p. 72).

✿✿✿ Jun–Oct.

Fen Nettle
Urtica dioica ssp. *galeopsifolia*
Neantóg eanaigh

Ht. 1.2m. **Fls.** Very similar to
Common Nettle but Fen Nettle's
flower clusters *begin* at a higher point
on the stem.

Lvs. Opposite, long-stalked,
coarsely-toothed, *long, narrow &
pointed*.

Hab. Damp, neutral soil such as
fens & riverbanks; not on waste
ground or disturbed habitats. Native
perennial found in SE only.

Fam. Nettle/Urticaceae.

☺ The dense hairs of this species
are *usually* non-stinging.

✿ Jul–Aug.

Sea Arrowgrass
Triglochin maritima
Barr an mhilltigh mara

Ht. 50cm. **Fls.** 3–4mm long, 6 tepals, green, purple-edged; 6 stamens with cream-white anthers; in dense, long, narrow spikes on stout, erect, unbranched, hairless stems.

Lvs. Fleshy, narrow, semicircular in section, *unfurrowed*.

Hab. Saltmarshes, brackish coastal sites. Common, native perennial frequent in given habitat.

Fam. Arrowgrass/Juncaginaceae.

☺ Fruits are egg-shaped with **6** segments.

 ✿✿ May–Sep.

Marsh Arrowgrass
Triglochin palustris
Barr an mhilltigh

Ht. 40cm. **Fls.** 2mm long, with 6 green, purple-edged tepals; in slender, erect spikes which elongate in fruit.

Lvs. Linear, rounded on lower side & *furrowed* on upper side.

Hab. Damp grassland, marshes, fens, meadows & freshwater habitats. Native perennial, common in given habitat.

Fam. Arrowgrass/ Juncaginaceae.

☺ Fruits are club-shaped with **3** segments.

✿✿ Jun–Aug.

268

Navelwort
Umbilicus rupestris
Cornán caisil

Ht. 40cm. **Fls.** 8–10mm
long, greenish-white, narrow,
tubular with 5 tiny teeth; flowers
drooping in long, tapering, spikes
on erect, hairless, unbranched,
pinkish stems.

Lvs. Fleshy, circular, mostly
basal; at centre is a small,
navel-like depression, behind
which is the leaf's stem.

Hab. Old stone walls, cliffs &
rocky places. Native perennial,
common except in centre of
Ireland.

Fam. Stonecrop/Crassulaceae.

✿✿✿ Jun–Aug.

Wood Sage
Teucrium scorodonia
Iúr sléibhe

Ht. 60cm. **Fls.** 8–9mm long, pale
greenish-white, with one 5-lobed
lip only; with 2 maroon-coloured,
protruding anthers; in opposite pairs
in bract axils; in spikes on erect,
hairy, branched stems, woody at
base.

Lvs. Opposite, oval-heart-shaped,
finely-toothed, stalked &
wrinkled.

Hab. Dry places, woodland,
hedgerows & heaths. Native
perennial, common except
in centre of Ireland.

Fam. Dead-nettle/
Lamiaceae.

☺ Leaves are aromatic.

✿✿✿ Jun–Sep.

Ribwort Plantain
Plantago lanceolata
Slánlus

Ht. 45cm. **Fls.** 4mm, greenish-brown, 4-lobed with prominent midribs; with long, white stamens; in oblong spike on *deeply ridged* stems, all arising from basal rosette.

Lvs. Long, tapering stalk, linear-lanceolate, untoothed or only slightly toothed margins; spreading or erect, with *parallel* veins.

Hab. Grassy places, fields, roadsides. Widespread native perennial.

Fam. Plantain/ Plantaginaceae.

✿✿✿ Apr–Oct.

*Members of **Plantain** family bear flowers in terminal spikes; flowers are tiny, 4-lobed with 4 long, prominent stamens. Leaves are usually in basal rosette.*

Greater Plantain
Plantago major
Cuach Phádraig

Ht. 20cm. **Fls.** 3mm, pale green-yellow; corolla lobes have *no midribs*; short stamens with anthers which start out lilac-purple, turning yellow-brown; in very slender spikes on *non-ridged* stems.

Lvs. Broadly ovate, with abrupt, round, base; 3–9 veined; in basal rosette.

Hab. Waste ground, roadsides, cultivated & disturbed arable land. Widespread native perennial.

Fam. Plantain/ Plantaginaceae.

✿✿✿ Jun–Oct.

Sea Plantain
Plantago maritima
Slánlus mara

Ht. 30cm. **Fls.** 3mm, corolla brownish with darker, broad midrib; stamens *yellow*; in slender spikes on *hairless*, erect, *unfurrowed* stems.

Lvs. Very narrow, untoothed or hardly toothed; *faintly* 3–5 veined & fleshy; in loose, basal rosette.

Hab. Saltmarshes, sea cliffs, occasionally inland on saline soil. Widespread native perennial.

Fam. Plantain/ Plantaginaceae.

✿✿✿ Jun–Aug.

Buck's-horn Plantain
Plantago coronopus
Adharca fia

Ht. 25cm. **Fls.** 2mm, brownish corolla, lobes without midrib; yellow stamens; in dense, slender, leafless spikes on *unridged* stems.

Lvs. Flat rosette of distinctive leaves; *downy*, long-stalked, linear-lanceolate, deeply cut side-lobes; 1-veined.

Hab. Rocky places, coastal walls, short grassland. Widespread native annual or perennial.

Fam. Plantain/ Plantaginaceae.

☺ Occasionally leaves are *unlobed*.

✿✿✿ May–Jul.

271

Lords-and-Ladies
Arum maculatum
Cluas chaoin

Ht. 40cm. **Fls.** Dense, fleshy, purply-brown, club-shaped spike (spadix); partly enveloped in large, pale-green, leaf-like bract with rolled basal section & pointed cowl-shaped tip (spathe); on erect hairless stems rising from underground tubers.

Lvs. Bright-green, arrow-shaped, untoothed, shiny, often purple-spotted.

Hab. Woodland, scrub, hedgerows. Native perennial, common throughout except for NW.

Fam. Arum/Araceae.

☺ Fruits are shiny, succulent, orange-red berries – *extremely poisonous.*

✿✿✿ Apr–May. ⚠

Bulrush
Typha latifolia
Coigeal na mban sí

Ht. 2m. **Fls.** Densely-packed, tiny flowers in long, cylindrical spike which has 2 *adjacent* parts; lower, stouter section comprised of brown female flowers; upper, terminal segment narrower, with yellowish male flowers; on robust, erect stems which grow from creeping rhizomes.

Lvs. Mainly basal, grey-green, strap-shaped.

Hab. River, pond, canal margins, lakes, loughs, wet meadows. Widespread, native perennial.

Fam. Bulrush/Typhaceae.

☺ AKA Reedmace.

☺ Seeds cottony & downy.

✿✿✿ Jun–Aug.

Bog Orchid
Hammarbya paludosa
Magairlín na móna

Ht. 12cm. **Fls.** 7mm long, honey-green, flattish profile; lip narrowly ovate, pointing *upward*; 2 lateral sepals & one *downward-pointing sepal*; *no spur*; in short spike-like racemes on erect, hairless stems arising from tiny bulb.

Lvs. Oval, concave, mainly basal; rounded tips of leaves are fringed with a row of *tiny* bulbils which will grow into new plants.

Hab. Bogs, sphagnum, wet acid ground. Rare native perennial.

Fam. Orchid/Orchidaceae.

✿ Jul–Sep. ✚

Frog Orchid
Coeloglossum viride
Magairlín an loscáin

Ht. 20cm. **Fls.** 8mm, greenish-purple; 5 upper tepals converge to form a hood & lower segment is a long, strap-shaped, yellow-brown petal with 3 small pointed lobes; behind each flower is a long, curved bract, lower bracts being *longer* than flowers; in short cylindrical spike on erect stem.

Lvs. Basal rosette of broad, oval, unspotted leaves, narrower stem leaves.

Hab. Dunes, calcareous grassland, limestone pavement, wet grassland & pastures. Uncommon native perennial.

Fam. Orchid/Orchidaceae.

✿ Jun–Aug.

273

Broad-leaved Helleborine
Epipactis helleborine
Ealabairín

Ht. 80cm. **Fls.** 15mm; 3 pale green-pink sepals surround 2 upper mauve-green petals & dark red lower lip; this lower lip is heart-shaped & curved below 2 brownish bosses or bumps; nodding in loose spikes on erect stems, 2–3 stems per plant.

Lvs. Strongly-veined, horizontally spreading, broadly ovate, spirally along stem.

Hab. Limestone, dune hollows, woodland, shady banks. Native perennial, occasional in N, W & SE.

Fam. Orchid/Orchidaceae.

✿✿ Jul–Sep.

Common Twayblade
Neottia ovata
Dédhuilleog

Ht. 50cm. **Fls.** 15–20mm long, yellowy-green; elliptical tepals form a distinct hood & a lower lip, forked halfway; in long, loose spikes on erect stems, small bract below each flower stalk; stems hairy in upper part only.

Lvs. One opposite pair of very *broad, ribbed*, ovate-elliptical leaves, *clasping stem* near to base.

Hab. Woodland, grassland, dune slacks, on calcareous or slightly acid soil. Widespread native perennial.

Fam. Orchid/ Orchidaceae.

▶ Lesser Twayblade (p. 207).

✿✿ May–Jul.

Fly Orchid
Ophrys insectifera
Magairlín na gcuileanna

Ht. 50cm. **Fls.** 8–10mm, 3 yellow-green sepals & long, divided, red-brown lower lip; across this is a shiny, silvery-white band, just below lip's 2 little lobes which resemble arms; 2 tiny little red-brown upper petals project like tiny horns; in a loose spike of 4–10 with long bracts curving upward behind each flower; on slender, upright stems.

Lvs. 3 shiny, oval basal leaves.

Hab. Calcareous meadows, limestone. Rare, native perennial, mainly in the Burren & Midland fenland.

Fam. Orchid/Orchidaceae.

☺ This is a rare plant which is worthy of our protection.

✿ May–Jun. ✚

Along with the ***Bee Orchid*** (p. 193), the ***Fly Orchid*** is one of the small group of Orchids which mimic insects in order to attract visitors. 'Pollination by pseudocopulation' is the scientific term for this pretence whereby a plant emits the scent & has the appearance of an insect. By this impersonation, an insect is drawn to the orchid & while trying to mate with the flower, pollen is gathered onto its body to be distributed onto the next orchid.

275

GLOSSARY OF BOTANICAL TERMS

Achene	Dry, one-seeded fruit that does not split.
Anther	Pollen-bearing tip of stamen ▶p. 3.
Appressed	Flattened against the stem – as in hairs.
Auricle	Lobe or pair of lobes at base of leaf, often clasping stem.
Axil	Angle between upper surface of leaf and stem
Basal	Appearing at bottom of plant at ground level ▶p. 3.
Beak	Elongated projection at tip of fruit.
Blade	Main part of an organ such as a leaf.
Bract	Scale-like modified leaf found where flower-stalk joins stem ▶p. 3.
Bracteole	Tiny leaf-like structure on a flower stalk.
Bulb	Underground structure from which next year's leaves and buds grow.
Bulbil	Bud-like organ at base of leaves that breaks off, forming new plant.
Calyx	Green, outer part of flower made up of sepals. (Pl. calyces) ▶p. 3.
Capitulum	Head of tiny flowers without individual stalks surrounded by involucre of bracts (as in Daisy family). ▶p. 4.
Capsule	Dry fruit that splits to allow seeds to be disseminated.
Carpel	Unit composed of female part of flower.
Clasping	Describing leaves with backward pointed lobes clasping the stem.
Clawed	(Of petal) having narrow, stalk-like base.
Cluster	Loose group of flowers.
Corolla	Collective term for the petals of a flower ▶p. 3.
Corymb	Inflorescence where all flowers are in a flat-topped cluster, stems arising from different points on flower stalk.
Cyme	Inflorescence, terminal flower opening first, lower flowers following ▶p. 4.
Deciduous	Plant whose leaves fall in autumn.
Dioecious	With male and female flowers on separate plants.
Disc floret	One of the inner florets (as in centre of a Daisy) ▶p. 68.
Drupe	Succulent fruit with seed inside encased in hard coat as in Blackberry.
Entire	Of a leaf – without teeth or lobes along margins.
Epicalyx	Extra circle of sepal-like bracts below true calyx.
Female	Without stamens – containing styles only.
Filament	Stalk part of stamen that bears anther at tip ▶p. 3.
Fruit	Seed of plant ▶p. 3.
Gland	Sticky structure at end of a hair.
Glaucous	Blue-grey.
Globose	Spherical.
Head	Crowded cluster of stalkless or near-stalkless flowers.
Hips	Brightly coloured false fruits.
Hoary	Greyish with short hairs.
Hybrid	Plant resulting from cross-fertilisation of 2 different species.
Inflorescence	The total flower, including bracts.
Involucre	Collar or whorl of bracts at base of a flower-head ▶p. 120.
Keel	(i) Two petals or sepals fused, boat-like ▶p. 114; (ii) flange or fold.
Labellum	Lip ▶pp. 77 & 208.
Latex	Fluid or sap within stem of plant.
Leaflet	Leaf-like part or lobe of leaf.
Lip	Lower part of flower with irregular petals as in Orchids ▶pp. 77 & 208.
Lobe	One of the divisions of a leaf.
Lobed	Divided but not into totally separate leaflets.
Male flower	Without styles – containing stamens only.

Mealy	With a whitish, floury texture.
Midrib	Central vein of leaf.
Monoecious	With male and female flowers separate but on same plant.
Nectar	Sugary substance secreted by many flowers, which attracts insects.
Nectary	Organ in a flower which produces nectar ▶p. 27.
Node	Point on stem where leaf or branches emerge ▶p. 3.
Ochrea	Tubular, silver or brown papery stipules or sheath in Knotweeds ▶pp. 9, 180.
Ovary	Swollen seed-producing part containing immature seeds or ovules ▶p. 3.
Panicle	Inflorescence which is branched ▶p. 4.
Pappus	Tuft or 'clock' of hairs for wind-dispersal of seeds as on Dandelion.
Perianth	Collective term for calyx and corolla.
Petals	Organs above sepals and surrounding reproductive organs of flower ▶p. 3.
Petiole	Stalk of a leaf ▶p. 3.
Pollen	Tiny grains containing male cells produced by flower's anthers.
Procumbent	Lying on the ground.
Prostrate	Growing very close to the ground.
Raceme	Long cluster of stalked flowers along central stem, oldest flowers at base, youngest at tip ▶p. 4.
Ray	One of the radiating stalks of an umbel ▶pp. 4, 57.
Ray floret	Flat outer strap-like flowers that surround central disc in a composite flower, as in white parts of a Daisy ▶p. 68.
Recurved	Curving or arching backwards.
Reflexed	Bent backwards sharply, downwards or outwards.
Rhizome	Underground stem such as in the Iris ▶p. 107.
Rosette	Circle of radiating leaves ▶p. 3.
Runner	Above-ground stem, horizontal, often rooting at nodes.
Scale	Small appendage, usually papery.
Seed pod	Simple pod with single row of seeds.
Sepal	One of the outer parts of flower immediately below petals ▶p. 3.
Sessile	Describing a leaf, flower or fruit without a stalk.
Spadix	Dense, fleshy, club-shaped spike, usually within a spathe ▶pp. 138, 272.
Spathe	Leaf-like bract with rolled basal section and pointed cowl-shaped tip ▶pp. 138, 272.
Spike	Long cluster of unstalked flowers along central stem ▶p. 4.
Spreading	Describing plant branching horizontally or hairs at right angles.
Spur	Hollow tubular extension of corolla.
Stamen	Male part of flower made up of anther and filament ▶p. 3.
Stigma	Surface of female part of the flower which receives pollen ▶p. 3.
Stipule	Leaf-like organ at base of leaf-stalk ▶p. 3.
Stolon	Creeping stem which roots at nodes, usually on the surface.
Style	Female part of flower between stigma and ovary ▶p. 3.
Succulent	Swollen and fleshy.
Tendril	Slender, twining tip of leaf or branch used for climbing.
Tepal	Meaning both sepals and petals, when they are similar in appearance.
Toothed	Leaf with saw tooth edge.
Truncate	Ending abruptly.
Tuber	Swollen part of stem or root (like a potato).
Umbel	Carrying flowers on upside-down umbrella-like structure ▶pp. 4, 57.
Whorl	Circle of leaves or petals ▶p. 4.
Wing	(i) Thin flange or membranous structure running down stem or leaf-stalk; (ii) lateral petal of Pea family flower ▶p. 114.

INDEX OF COMMON AND LATIN NAMES

INDEX OF IRISH NAMES

Plant family finder

Family name	Pages on which family occurs
Knotweed/Polygonaceae	8–9, 76, 180-1, 197, 258, 264
Mallow/Malvaceae	158–9
Meadow Saffron/Colchicaceae	173
Meadow–foam/Limnanthaceae	43
Mignonette/Resedaceae	137
Milkwort/Polygalaceae	210
Monkeyflower/Phrymaceae	104
Nettle/Urticaceae	9, 72, 255, 267
Nightshade/Solanaceae	36, 105, 228
Onion/Alliaceae	52, 54, 178
Orchid/Orchidaceae	77–81, 190–3, 207–9, 252–3, 273–5
Pea/Fabaceae	55, 114–7, 142–3, 171, 176–7, 194–5, 203, 250–1
Pennywort/Hydrocotylaceae	254
Periwinkle/Apocynaceae	220
Pink/Caryophyllaceae	23, 28–31, 34–5, 154–7, 262
Pipewort/Eriocaulaceae	67
Plantain/Plantaginaceae	270–1
Poppy/Papaveraceae	24, 82–3, 139, 181, 199, 211

Common Mallow
(Mallow Fam.)

Common Milkwort
(Milkwort Fam.)

Crow Garlic
(Onion Fam.)

White Campion
(Pink Fam.)

Cowslip
(Primrose Fam.)